01 14

HERE
WE GO

HERE WE GO

Lessons for Living
Fearlessly from Two
Traveling Nanas

ELEANOR HAMBY &
DR. SANDRA HAZELIP

with Elisa Petrini

VIKING

VIKING
An imprint of Penguin Random House LLC
1745 Broadway, New York, NY 10019
penguinrandomhouse.com

Designed by Cassandra Garruzzo Mueller

LIBRARY OF CONGRESS CATALOGING-IN-PUBLICATION DATA

Names: Hamby, Eleanor author | Hazelip, Sandra author
Title: Here we go : lessons for living fearlessly from two traveling nanas /
Eleanor Hamby & Sandra Hazelip ; with Elisa Petrini.
Description: New York : Viking, 2025. | Identifiers: LCCN 2025001913 |
ISBN 9780593832301 hardcover | ISBN 9780593832318 ebook
Subjects: LCSH: Older people—Travel | Hamby, Eleanor—Travel |
Hazelip, Sandra—Travel
Classification: LCC G151 .H358 2025 | DDC 910.4—dc23/eng/20250507
LC record available at https://lccn.loc.gov/2025001913

Printed in the United States of America
1st Printing

The authorized representative in the EU for product safety and compliance is
Penguin Random House Ireland, Morrison Chambers, 32 Nassau Street,
Dublin D02 YH68, Ireland, https://eu-contact.penguin.ie.

The authors will donate a portion of their proceeds from *Here We Go* to
the charitable organization Zambia Medical Mission.

To our late husbands, Kelly Hamby and Don Hazelip,
whose love empowered us and encouraged us to fulfill our dreams.
It was a privilege and a joy to share our Christian walk in this life
with two great men of faith.

Travel enables us to enrich our lives with new experiences, to enjoy and to be educated, to learn respect for foreign cultures, to establish friendships, and above all to contribute to international cooperation and peace throughout the world.

JULES VERNE

Contents

Prologue The Bali Swing   1

Part I
FINDING FRIENDSHIP

1 Gratitude Is the Heart of Reinvention   13

2 Lean Into the Unexpected   31

3 Just Say Yes—but Choose Who
   You're Saying Yes To   51

4 Attitude Is Everything, and
   Remember Okra   65

5 Honor Your Angels   85

6 Trust in God, but Tie Up Your Camel   95

Part II
ANYONE CAN BECOME
ADVENTUROUS

7 Embrace Your Potential to Live
   More Fully and Well   123

8 This Is What Grannies Look Like   143

Part III

CIRCUMNAVIGATING THE WORLD IN EIGHTY DAYS

9 Approach the World with Wonder   151

10 Age Won't Slow You Down If You Adapt,
    Stay Positive, and Dream Big   171

11 Home Fires Can Spark Renewal   201

12 Tolerance, Intervention, Innovation,
    and Ritual   213

13 Small Moments Can Lead to
    Monumental Shifts in Perspective   251

14 Make a Difference   265

Epilogue By the Grace of God   293

Acknowledgments   297

Historical Note   303

HERE
WE GO

PROLOGUE

The Bali Swing

If there's a single image that captures our lives in our eighties, it's this: The two of us, Ellie Hamby and Sandy Hazelip, legs outstretched, sneaker soles peeking from the hems of our flowing gowns, swinging off a cliff in Bali. We're hundreds of feet above a patchwork of green—lush, terraced rice fields and flowering slopes—scared to look down but shouting with joy and wonder.

As Sandy says, "We felt like butterflies."

That day we'd set out exploring with Ketut, our driver in Bali. When we travel together, we never stick to guidebooks but ask local people what to see. Maybe because we're grandmothers, everyone seems happy to help. Often, we strike up lasting friendships with guides, drivers, servers, and shopkeepers that are rewarding adventures in themselves.

When we asked Ketut where to go, he took us to Mount Batur, an active volcano sacred to Brahma, the Hindu fire god. Near its peak there's a beautiful lake in a caldera, or caved-in crater, that formed thousands of years ago. Along the narrow, two-lane mountain road were slopes on either side, planted with rice or else wild with tropical flora and giant ferns. There were few cars—mostly just workers in bamboo hats on foot or on bikes, with the occasional motor scooter zipping along. We were lulled by the beautiful scenery until Ellie called out, "Hey, what's that?"

She'd spotted a tiny sign, so Ketut turned back. The sign read: Happy Swing.

"We're all about happy," Ellie said. "Let's check it out."

At the end of a short path, we came upon an open-air stand serving Cokes and tea, and beyond that, at the cliff's edge, poised over a sheer 150-foot drop, wooden frames that held different swings. One was the old-fashioned kind, a board on two cables that would leave your legs dangling. Another was a double-seater that looked more like a porch swing but with a low, slatted back and a deep-as-a-bed padded seat.

Wow! We just looked at each other and said, "Let's do it!" We didn't have a moment's doubt.

"Hold on," the owner told us. "You have to pick out dresses."

"No, thank you," Sandy said. "It seems silly to dress up."

But he insisted. "Believe me, you'll want to. Really, you must."

He hauled out a giant suitcase, crammed full of dresses in all colors. They were ankle-length and huge enough for us to pull over our clothes. So, giggling a little, we both chose red ones, which fit us like muumuus, then stepped back to admire each other. To our surprise, we looked sort of queenly and didn't feel silly at all. We felt ceremonial.

Hitching our skirts up out of the dirt, we made our way to the double swing. Two workers pulled it back and steadied it as we settled on the padded seat, propped against the back with our legs out straight. There were no harnesses or seatbelts, just a couple of thin cords to circle our waists. We felt around nervously for a railing to clutch for dear life, but the workers said, "No, you don't need to hang on. Let your hands be free."

Deep breaths. Eyes wide, excited, we exchanged another we're-in-this-together grin. Then the workers gave a giant heave and released the swing.

We were soaring, reaching high into the cloudless blue sky, then falling back to glimpse the collage of color far below. The only sounds were the wind's slight *whoosh* and our own nervous *Whoa*s and excited gasps. Suspended in space, we were totally rapt. It was as if years fell away, and we were restored, magically, to the pure freedom of childhood.

We're dear friends whose thoughts often seem to meld, and we reveled in shared delight and fear-tinged excitement. But close as we are, we're very different people—Sandy is a charmer, and Ellie is a daredevil. So, we both knew that Ellie couldn't resist an even bigger thrill.

Sure enough, back on solid ground, Ellie beelined straight to the single swing. "Can I do this one?" she asked the workers, who looked shocked. Unfazed, she sat on the terrifying backless board and, gripping the cables, smiled as she was shoved off the cliff into thin air. It was heart-stopping for Sandy to see Ellie outlined against the sky, red skirt fluttering, so far above the ground. But Ellie seemed utterly fearless, exulting in the sensation, with her head thrown back, laughing.

"It was exhilarating," she said later. "Of course, if I slipped, I would have been a goner."

But our philosophy—within reason—is, what do we have to lose? Ellie says, "I'd rather die falling off a mountain than out of bed in a nursing home—assuming that I'm lucky enough to choose."

To us, life is more than a two-act play—youth and adulthood—followed only by shrinking horizons and decline. Our families are grown, and though we enjoy full-time work in rewarding careers serving others, we're busy staging and living an inspiring Act Three. The gift of age is freedom—and how better to enjoy it than by opening our hearts and minds to adventure and exploring our great big wonderful world?

> **The gift of age is freedom—and how better to enjoy it than by opening our hearts and minds to adventure and exploring our great big wonderful world?**

THE TRIP THAT GOT US TO THE HAPPY SWING IN BALI WAS SANDY'S idea. One night, as we sat at Ellie's kitchen table, drinking coffee and reminiscing about past adventures, Sandy said, "We have a milestone birthday coming up. Wouldn't it be fun to celebrate turning eighty by going around the world in eighty days?"

After a pause, Ellie leaned toward Sandy. "I love it."

Eighty days! That was a long stretch away from our lives, work, and families, relying only on each other. Circling the globe at such a pace might be grueling—or worse, might rush us too much to let us fully experience and enjoy other cultures.

But we both love a challenge and immediately did a search on Phileas Fogg, the fictional Jules Verne hero who made an infamous eighty-day trip to win a bet. Interestingly, the first real person to test his record was a woman, the intrepid newspaper reporter Nellie Bly. In 1889, traveling by steamship, train, and the occasional rickshaw, she covered twenty-five thousand miles in seventy-two days, beating Fogg's eighty-day deadline.

Of course, today the trip is easier, but we'd use similar modes of transport. For one thing, we're budget tourists who fly only when necessary (with airline miles, if possible); and for another, we both love trains. Bly stayed in grand hotels, but we seek out small local lodgings (under twenty-nine dollars each per night) that bring us inside the culture we're visiting, closer to the ordinary citizens, not the tourists. Budget travel offers greater exposure to real life in host countries and, we think, a greater chance for fun encounters. Sometimes we've been the fun encounters for guys who never dreamed they'd find octogenarians bunking below them in second-class sleeper cars.

We plotted an itinerary, inspired by Fogg's, that spanned all seven continents and featured ten wonders of the world.

1. Antarctica, traveling from Argentina by expedition ship through the infamous Drake Passage, where the waves can top forty feet

2. South America, seeing the world wonders on Easter Island and at Machu Picchu, with a backup plan to visit the majestic statue of Christ the Redeemer in Rio de Janeiro

3. Europe, including the world wonders of the northern lights in Lapland, Finland, and the Colosseum in Rome

4. Africa, focusing on the world wonders of Zambia's Victoria Falls and Egypt's Great Pyramids of Giza

5. Asia, including the world wonders of the Taj Mahal in India and Mount Everest in Nepal

6. Australia and its world wonder, the Great Barrier Reef

7. North America, with its world wonder the Grand Canyon, returning from there to our starting point, Dallas, Texas

We were set to leave on February 6, 2022, with a return date of April 27. We booked our flights and posted about our trip on social media, asking for suggested stops from anyone who wanted to share the fun. We chose a slogan for our journey: Around the World in Eighty Days at Eighty. Then COVID-19, still a global hazard, thwarted us.

The restrictions on foreign travelers proved hard to manage. Certain countries, like India, required long quarantines before they would admit us. Some places—notably Australia—flat-out barred tourists, even if vaccinated and testing negative. Worse, since the rules kept changing, we couldn't predict our reception at any given destination. Would we be welcomed at the border or turned away?

Finally, we had to concede that the snarl of regulations made our trip seem more of an obstacle course than an adventure. We weren't giving up—neither of us is the surrendering type—but decided to wait a year to reassess. Eighty was a milestone, but, after all, each new birthday is a chance to celebrate being alive.

> **Eighty was a milestone, but, after all, each new birthday is a chance to celebrate being alive.**

Soon we were able to seize that chance. When the world reopened to visitors, we started reconfiguring our journey to begin sometime in 2023. We'd no longer be eighty, so we had to think up a new slogan. We even got it printed on T-shirts: Eighty-One and Still on the Run.

We gave a presentation on our planned adventure at Wesley Court Senior Living, a retirement community in Abilene, Texas, where Dr. Sandy cares for patients. This is standard fare for us—volunteering to speak on various topics at community events. As it turned out, the *Abilene Reporter-News* and KTAB News, a CBS affiliate, were both present at our talk and featured us—in the daily paper and on TV. We were flattered and thought it was a hoot—another adventure!—and we figured that was that. Boy, were we wrong.

Before we knew it, surprisingly, media requests were flying in, especially once we embarked on our journey. Wherever we traveled, TV stations wanted to book us—and since our motto is Just Say Yes to everything (within reason), we leaned into the adventure of TV studios and greenroom snacks. Soon, people on the street from Easter Island to Tokyo to Sydney were asking, "Aren't you the traveling grannies?" Toward the end of our eighty-day adventure—on a lark, really—we began sharing our exploits on TikTok. Then, *Bam!* We had a new identity—the TikTok Traveling Grannies—and, suddenly, astonishingly, the whole world was watching us.

People asked to take selfies with us; they hailed us as celebrities, which struck us as hysterically funny. But we also kept hearing, over and over, from people wherever we went—*young and old!*—that we inspired them. That touched us, deeply. Knowing that we were providing real uplift for folks searching for positivity and that our example was motivating people gave us a new sense of purpose.

So, while this book celebrates adventure and recounts our most memorable moments, we intend it not as a travelogue but as an inspiration to seek joy. Part I, spanning the years from 2001 to 2018, describes how our friendship was forged through mission work in Zambia and deepened—thanks to our shared love of trains—as we traveled across Russia to China, from Singapore through Malaysia to Cambodia and Vietnam, and from Turkey to Syria and Jordan under the cloud of civil war. Part II looks at the life passages that helped embolden two timid Texas gals with thoughts that can empower any of us. Part III covers our recent eighty-day around-the-world journey, touching every continent on our planet, inspired by Phileas Fogg.

Traveling together—relying on each other in new thrilling and challenging situations, and sharing the intense pleasures of discovery, as well as the humdrum hassles of the journey—has cemented what was already a profound and sustaining friendship. Even more, it's given us each a new grasp of our personal strengths, crystallizing lessons and wisdom we've been accumulating all our lives. Chief among those strengths is the capacity to connect, to embrace the humanity of people of every language and culture. We hope that this book stands as a reminder that none of us is alone in the world, that we all are capable of far more than we imagine, and that we all can live fearlessly at any age.

Part I

FINDING
FRIENDSHIP

1

GRATITUDE IS THE
HEART OF REINVENTION

When God shuts a door, He opens a window." That saying could be the headline for our friendship. Twenty-three years before Bali and our around-the-world, eighty-day trip, we met at a medical mission conference in Dallas. It was six months after Sandy lost her beloved husband, Don Hazelip.

Widowhood is a barren landscape that seems impossible to navigate. The daily rituals that give life shape and texture fall away. Time blurs into a throbbing ache of absence. Grief can ease with time, but there's no ready fix for emptiness. Though work and loved ones offer comfort, learning to think and live for one instead of two can be a challenge. Six years later, Ellie would join Sandy in that desolate, lonely state of new widowhood.

How do you rebuild a life and recover a sense of wholeness? For both of us—for anyone—gratitude can be the heart of reinvention, seeing beyond the shock of loss to the blessings that remain. Our marriages gave us the foundation for choosing fulfilling lives, as well as a template for the sort of deep, enduring friendships that we'd need when we lost our partners.

> **For both of us—for anyone— gratitude can be the heart of reinvention, seeing beyond the shock of loss to the blessings that remain.**

As Sandy tells it: "I'm a doctor today because of Don's belief in me. When Larry, my middle child, was a toddler, he developed type 1 diabetes. To learn to care for him, I plunged into library research and, the more I read, the more drawn to medicine I became.

"But there was a major problem: I'd married at nineteen with a high school diploma. No one in my family had ever been to college. So, I felt timid about confessing, even to my husband, that I wanted to get an education. 'Sure, but why?' Don asked.

"'Well, Don, I want to become a doctor,' I declared.

"He didn't say, 'At your age?' or, 'That means years of full-time schooling!' In fact, he didn't even bat an eye. 'Well, honey, why didn't you say so?' was his answer.

"With Don's blessing and full support, I enrolled in college at age thirty-four and finally graduated from medical school at age forty-three. Through it all, he was a trouper!

"I opened a family medicine practice in Eastland, Texas, a small town between Fort Worth and Abilene. Being a CPA, Don had no trouble finding an accounting position there. By then, our three kids were grown, so it was just the two of us. Don was so warm and outgoing that we quickly made friends. A committed Christian, he was a pillar of our church and our community.

"We'd been in Eastland for ten years when Don was diagnosed with non-Hodgkin's lymphoma. Undaunted, he endured five rounds of chemotherapy and, after two years, was pronounced cancer-free.

"But our joy was short-lived. A year later, Eastland was gripped by an outbreak of hepatitis A. Seventy-nine people recovered, but one suffered acute renal failure and declined. That man was my husband.

"Over the next few weeks, he suffered overwhelming complications—intubation, a collapsed lung, emergency surgery, hemorrhaging, and finally stomach necrosis (tissue death). I gathered our children at his bedside, and with Don's blessing, told the doctors to remove all the tubes and machines. With us all beside him, singing hymns, he breathed his last on June 23, 1999.

"I was devastated, completely lost.

"But Don had a dream that he was never able to fulfill. He'd wanted us to take our grandchildren on mission trips during their summer vacations, but being a busy physician, I couldn't break away. When he was ill, Don mentioned the mission trips with the grandkids as a goal for his recovery. Now, for me, they were a signpost, pointing the way out of grief, and a way to honor his legacy.

"That's how I found myself aimlessly wandering the booths at the medical mission conference in Dallas. I knew nothing about this world and came to the conference to do research. When I saw a display with a vibrant picture of Africa, I turned away, intimidated. Then a rich, deep voice summoned me back. 'Hi, I'm Kelly Hamby. Who are you, and what's your interest in medical missions?'

"The man, Kelly, who looked kind and sincere, extended his hand. Beside him stood his wife, Ellie, beaming a radiant, welcoming smile. They explained that, every July, they took doctors, nurses, dentists, and Bible teachers to Zambia for a two-week trek deep into the bush to offer medical and spiritual help to remote villages.

"Africa was daunting to me, and I had no intention of going there. So, I told them, 'Don't waste your time telling me about your mission work because I'm looking for a safe place to bring my teenage grandsons.'

"'Oh, it's very safe,' they assured me. 'We take our grandchildren every year. In fact, we rely on young people for critical tasks, like pitching and moving our camp. They'd have lots to see and do.'

"That clinched it. It seemed like an unmistakable sign—one that led me not only to take a grandchild to Zambia shortly after the conference but, over the next twenty years, to bring different grandchildren on annual mission trips. We've been to Russia, China, Cambodia, and Romania, and every other year, we go back to Zambia. Kelly and Ellie's medical mission was the window God opened for me.

"Most importantly—and both of us feel certain of destiny's hand here—this is how Ellie and I first met. We would go on to travel together to exotic corners of the globe and to see extraordinary things, yet the essence of our journey is not the places we've been but the friendship that we've forged."

> The essence of our journey is not the places we've been but the friendship that we've forged.

"KELLY WAS A BRILLIANT TEACHER," ELLIE SAYS. "HE WAS A PROFESsor at Abilene Christian University, heading the graduate program for school administrators, when Dr. George Benson, former president of Harding University, asked him to recommend a headmaster for a small Christian boarding school in Zambia. Dr. Benson was visiting our home, so I called Kelly into the bedroom. I'd seen the fascination on my husband's face. 'You're going to take me to Africa,' I told him. 'I don't want to go!'

"Kelly had a determined look, with a slight grin, as if to say, 'Hang in there. It will all be okay.' That look told me where his heart was leading him.

"Sure enough, two months later we were in Zambia, filling in until the headmaster arrived. To my surprise, I fell in love with it all—the countryside, the people, the work. A couple years later, we moved to Zambia and worked full-time for the mission.

"With us were Moon and Roderick, two young men who lived with us in Abilene. Roderick returned to the States after a couple of years at the mission, but Moon stayed with us for our entire six years in Zambia. He loved Africa and was absolutely fearless. I cherish a photo of him proudly holding a dead black mamba, one of the world's most lethal snakes, that was longer than he was tall. Now a grown man, he remains a blessing in my life.

"In six years, under Kelly's leadership, that one small school became a full-blown educational complex encompassing grades one through college, with satellite schools in villages, and even a center for orphan care. All that was Kelly's genius. He was a world builder.

"When Dr. Benson, who had recruited Kelly, died, we had to return to Texas to take over his role handling fundraising and administration for the Zambia campus. Kelly resumed his ACU professorship but remained the Zambia school's stateside superintendent, and we returned for at least a month every July. Then, one day in 1994, at Jay's Superette gas station, Kelly ran into Dr. John Estes, an Abilene dentist. Dr. John wanted advice because his wife hoped to go birding in Africa. Kelly had another idea—to recruit him to do dentistry *in* Zambia—which Dr. John took a step further. He said, 'Let's create a medical mission in Zambia, with you and Ellie as the directors.'

"Of course, our expertise was education, not medicine, but the idea blossomed. The first year, we recruited a team of eleven health professionals, who treated five hundred patients. In 2026, the Zambia Medical Mission celebrates thirty years of service, with 225 American and African volunteers caring for more than thirteen thousand patients. Today it's acclaimed as one of the world's largest and most respected medical missions.

"If only Kelly could have lived to see that!

"But in August 2005, after our Zambia visit, Kelly developed an ear ailment. It affected his balance and, to his dismay, kept him from playing tennis. Finally, by November 11, he felt well enough to attempt a game. I came home that afternoon to find him with an icepack on his head. 'I stumbled and fell backward,' he told me. 'It's just a little bump.'

"By the next morning, however, he was suffering chest pain and shortness of breath. The emergency room doctors confirmed that he was having a heart attack. What followed was a tragic confluence. They gave him blood thinners to save his heart, which kicked off a massive hemorrhage in his brain as the 'little bump' exploded. He died the next morning, Saturday, November 12.

"I was just blown apart, the center no longer held. We'd been inseparable, working together for the entire forty-six years of our marriage. After the funeral, all I could do was lie in bed. The phone rang constantly, with friends and family members checking on me, but I ignored it. I didn't have the will or energy to answer. What eventually got me out of bed was Sandy. A phone call from Sandy, to be more precise. At that point, we were friends—not yet best friends, but friends. I'm sure she was determined to reach me because she heard that I wasn't doing well.

"Sandy can be persistent. That's actually an understatement. She's small, but once she's determined to do something, she's got the will of a thousand tornadoes. And she was ferociously smart about it, too. Like they say about true friends, sometimes they know us better than we know ourselves.

"When I picked up, Sandy didn't echo the usual heartfelt condolences, which was a relief because sympathy wasn't helping. I suspect

Sandy knew that commiseration wouldn't work, and she was right. Instead, she told me that she needed *my help*. She said, 'Hey, Ellie, I've got a deal for you. I've been recruited to start a geriatric clinic for Abilene Regional Hospital. So, I need a bed in Abilene a couple of nights a week. If you allow me to stay at your house, I'll take you out to eat as my room and board.'

"I just had a tiny spare room with a twin bed—I called it 'the closet'—and Sandy said, 'Great! I'll take it.'

"Our first dinner out was on a Taco Tuesday. I'll never forget that because it marked a huge shift in my mindset. Sometimes it takes a friend's steely strength and a clever ploy to force your heart back open. Not only had Sandy succeeded in getting me out of bed, but she'd put us both on a glidepath to change, not just in our friendship but, ultimately, in our lives. It goes to show that God, in His mercy, can open windows when you least expect them.

"The medical mission, along with my daughter, Sheryl, and my sons, Kel and Moon, greatly sustained me after Kelly passed away. Once Sandy pried me out of bed, my first big step was to go back to Zambia. According to Zambian tradition, the beloved is not truly laid to rest until a family member comes to tell the village about the death. Then, together, everyone openly mourns, wailing and falling to the ground. At the mission, I was brought into a big room where we circled and sang, standing for a long time as each person came to face me and cry in loving compassion for the loss and to share the pain. Their love was profoundly healing. Our experience, hand in hand, face-to-face, was cathartic. I'm sure that boosted my recovery.

"At the mission, I'd always been content in Kelly's shadow, playing a strong supportive role. Now, to honor his vision, I knew I'd have to become a leader. Luckily, my good friends KB Massingill and Ray Ferguson stepped up, too. I've continued to codirect the mission with each of them, at different times, ever since."

We healed, and our friendship deepened as Sandy took up part-time residence in Ellie's "closet." "My job in Abilene can be heartrending," Sandy says. "I'm a geriatrician, caring for patients in the October, November, and December of their lives. It's a powerful passage that I feel privileged both to witness and to offer comfort through. So, I work late, and when I get to Ellie's I'm tired but uplifted. We grab dinner, then sit together in her kitchen, where I review test results and write patients' notes while she handles mission business."

Over time, around Ellie's kitchen table, we not only shared meals and worked in companionable silence, but also talked late into the night and played tons of Scrabble and Farkle (we're both fiercely competitive!). Our friendship brought Ellie back to the land of the living, and even more, we began to dream of sharing adventures—a future, a big life with new chapters that neither of us had imagined.

During our late-night talks, we discussed our families, the state of the world, our hopes for the future—and, often, the joy of service. Helping others is instinctive for both of us. It gives us energy and purpose and is a cornerstone of our lives.

ELEANOR HAMBY & DR. SANDRA HAZELIP

> **Helping others is instinctive for both of us. It gives us energy and purpose and is a cornerstone of our lives.**

"Not 'helping,' as in, 'Let me, the grande dame, solve your problems,'" Ellie clarifies. "It's more like, 'Let me walk with you, side by side, so that we can raise each other up.' That's a major distinction I learned by example on my first trip to Zambia.

"Kelly and I arrived in Zambia in May 1980. During our initial year there, the nation's first president, Kenneth Kaunda, heard about the school we'd established at the mission and invited us to dinner to show his appreciation. From the time the country won independence in 1964, Kaunda had prioritized education. The dozen or so guests—Kelly and I, three mission workers, and Kaunda's staff—were served an elegant meal, with multiple courses and a fancy cut of beef. But, sitting next to Kaunda, I noticed that he was eating only a simple bowl of hominy.

"'Aren't you going to have some of this wonderful food that you're serving the guests?' I asked.

"'Oh no,' he said. 'When I became president, I vowed that I would never again touch animal flesh—no meat, chicken, or fish—until all of my countrymen no longer go hungry.'

"Then, after dinner, we all retired to the statehouse courtyard. Kaunda stood behind the tea trolley and personally served each of

22

us—filling our teacups, adding milk and sugar. Kaunda's words and actions taught me an indelible lesson: that humility is the essence of true, loving service to others."

> **Humility is the essence of true, loving service to others.**

IN JULY 2001, THE SUMMER AFTER THE MEDICAL CONFERENCE WHERE we met, we scooped up our respective grandkids—Sandy's grandson, Matthew, and Ellie's three, Ruth, Luke, and Caleb—and headed for the Zambia Medical Mission. Ellie describes Zambia as a jungle for the rainy half of the year, but in June and July it's just like West Texas, meaning dusty and dry. But any comparison to Texas ends with the climate. Outside the cities, most people live in mud huts with thatched roofs and travel by oxcart, donkey, and bicycle, or on foot. Women carry buckets for miles to get water for their households and walk back with the vessels balanced on their heads.

As mission volunteers, we head deep into the bush, where each of us is assigned a tent. There's no electricity, no running water, no plumbing. "Stalls" made of tall elephant grass enclose the "toilets" (holes in the ground) and "showers" (dippers and buckets). "It's not for the faint of heart," Ellie warns. "But Sandy braved it."

"'Braved it' is right," Sandy says. "Before I went to Zambia, I'd never been camping in my life! My husband's idea of roughing it was staying at the Holiday Inn instead of the Hilton. On top of that, I can't stand insects, never mind creatures like bats and snakes.

"Imagine how I felt when I learned that even nice homes in Zambia are infested with 'flatties,' or large wall spiders, the size of a hand. They come out at night and eat disease-bearing mosquitos. That makes them invaluable allies for humans—but, ugh! I'd never sleep knowing that marauding spiders were out there, creeping all around my bed.

"I didn't want my discomfort with creepy crawlers to keep me from fulfilling this dream, but I also didn't want to be miserable and a burden to others from the mission. So, I came up with a clever solution, one that still makes Ellie laugh. I sewed some heavy insect netting into the shape of a very large sack, with a Velcro opening that I could close from the inside. It was large enough that, using clothespins, I could clip the netting sack to the inner walls of my tent (or to the bedposts in people's homes) to create sort of an insect-proof bubble that could insulate me and my sleeping bag. In my sleeping bag, inside the protective bubble with the Velcro sealed tight, I was completely protected from insects. Even if they landed on the netting, they couldn't touch me. That let me sleep in peace.

"I told the other volunteers about my creation, thinking they'd laugh, but instead I was the envy of the camp! For my second trip to Zambia, my kids bought me a genius contraption called a 'cot tent.' When the cot unfolds, a compartment made of insect netting pops up on top of it. Over the past two decades, I've used it on all my trips to the Zambia Medical Mission.

"But from my first moment in Zambia, I could see that we were in very good hands. Back then, there were two hundred volunteers, half American and half Zambian, serving some three thousand patients a day. Those were mind-boggling numbers by an American doctor's standards, but Ellie had every single detail nailed to make things run smoothly. Five hours before clinic time, the advance team—the teenagers, including Ellie's grandkids and my grandson—headed into the bush to set up long rows of tents near the pit latrines and makeshift grass-walled bathing stations set up by local villagers. When the medical team reached the site, all we had to do was check the roster for the numbers of our assigned tents, which had our sleeping bags and backpacks already stowed inside.

"The system was perfect. We were all set to get to work. I was immediately struck by and somewhat in awe of Ellie's superpower, thinking, 'She's amazing—what a managerial wizard!'"

"What impressed me about Sandy from the very beginning was her genuine love of people," Ellie says. "As one of the medical mission's directors, I'm always checking on the staff and monitoring their interactions. With such a big operation, I have to be ever vigilant, spotting and resolving issues even before they manifest as problems. I keep an especially keen eye on all the first timers, medical staff new to these conditions.

"When it came to Sandy, I noticed that while communicating through a translator, she kept her eyes trained on the patient, smiling, touching the person reassuringly, conveying her concern with her whole being. I could see the patients respond to her immediately, opening up, feeling connected. All our volunteers are great, but Sandy was a standout, radiating a special warmth and caring."

That mutual admiration and respect for each other's special prowess drew us together. We instantly bonded. Then, once we started talking, we discovered such commonalities as a shared love of books that included all the same favorites—stories of adventurous women, like Amelia Earhart and Pearl S. Buck, along with a series of thrillers featuring our beloved Mrs. Pollifax, an older widow-turned-spy.

There are some notable similarities in our personal lives, too, not the least of which is that we're Texas-strong women. Beyond that, we both married young—at seventeen (Ellie) and nineteen (Sandy)—and welcomed our firstborn babies just nine months and a few days after our weddings. In fact, in a curious twist, two of our children, Barbara and Sheryl, share the same birthday, February 10, 1962.

It's fascinating to realize that, although we didn't know each other then, we'd been leading almost parallel lives.

Now, twenty-plus years later, the Zambia mission remains a mainstay of our shared experience. For thirty-odd years, Ellie has been organizing, then leading, the annual bush initiative, bringing medical care to remote villages. Her granddaughter Ruth, who started coming to the mission while still in diapers, considers Zambia a second home. Sandy has returned in alternate years since her initial trip—always with insect netting and often with a grandchild in tow—because, she says, "My heart tells me I must."

The needs of the mission's patients run the gamut from impacted teeth and cataracts to diseases like leprosy and AIDS, along with perils like snake and animal bites and accidents. Ellie recalls, "One memorable challenge was a young pregnant woman who'd walked with her husband for two days to give birth at our mobile clinic. But the baby couldn't wait and was born on the roadside. The woman bled so profusely that her husband, frightened, flagged down an oxcart transporting other patients. The cart with the mother and her newborn reached our site just as our caravan was pulling in.

"Nothing was unpacked, but the staff sprang into action, assembling a makeshift operating room. With the nearest hospital at least five hours away, no way could the mother survive the trip. Quickly, we determined that she had a second baby in her womb, blocked by her distended bladder from reaching the birth canal. So, while one doctor stemmed the hemorrhaging, another drained her bladder by inserting a catheter. All this was done by flashlight—we had no electricity—on the classroom desk serving as our operating table.

"Miraculously, the mother stabilized and delivered the child, a beautiful boy. Though exhausted, she managed to ask, 'Who's the male leader of this place?' That's how a Zambian baby boy got the name of my codirector, Ray.

"Recently, a woman came to the clinic bearing her husband on her back. Though being treated for leprosy, he couldn't afford to travel for more drugs, so his disease had come roaring back, consuming his feet and fingers. We gave him the needed medications and funds to cover trips for refills. But what would truly transform his life was restored mobility. The man's devoted wife had been carrying him on her back for the past six years.

"She'd done so while maintaining their home and raising their eight children. What a beautiful act of love!

"We keep a supply of locally built wheelchairs, designed for rough terrain. We presented one to the woman and her husband, who accepted it with tearful gratitude. The rest of us were just as choked up."

"Independence and mobility are profound gifts," Sandy says. "One of my own heartrending cases was an older patient who arrived lying on the floor of an oxcart. He looked frail and was unable to walk. When I examined him, he seemed disoriented but physically okay. 'What problems are you having?' I asked, through the translator. But I could see that the words didn't register.

"His caretaker sister explained that, since birth, he'd been blind and deaf. Those challenges, difficult anywhere, were extra tough in a bush village, where no one could imagine how to teach him to speak, if that were possible, or how best to manage his bodily functions. He got around by crawling, and thanks to his family's care, he had lived to a fairly advanced age.

"My heart went out to him and his sister. But I also began to panic. They'd come so far to get help, but what exactly could I offer? I feared that they were hoping for a miracle that even American medicine could never deliver.

"So, I asked the sister gently, 'What did you hope that we could do for your brother?'

"'I need some soap to wash his body, to help keep him clean,' she said.

"I almost cried at her modest request. For all his hardships, her brother could be uplifted by something as simple as a bar of soap. 'Wait right here,' I told her, and raced off to talk to Ellie.

"A short time later, Ellie and an assistant brought us body soap, lotion for the man's dry, cracked skin, laundry powder for his clothes, and some bags of 'mealie meal,' or corn meal, enough to feed him and his family for a while. Best of all, everything was piled in a wheelchair, which would spare him the misery of scrabbling in the dirt.

"When he sat in the wheelchair, his whole demeanor changed, from downcast and helpless to alert. All of us—his sister, the villagers with her, the staff, and Ellie and I—were fighting tears."

"These are happy stories," Ellie says, "but there are many tragic ones, of course, and I weep for the people we can't help. It can be hard not to feel overwhelmed.

"I remember making a last pit latrine trip one night in July, the depth of the harsh Zambian winter. Though bundled up in a warm coat and hat, I couldn't stop shivering. Arrayed before me, as far as I could see, were hundreds of points of light of little campfires. Then it struck me, hard, that around each fire, groups were huddled— thousands of people in all—stuck on the freezing ground, without tents, coats, or even blankets. Many were children, many were sick or injured.

"'How privileged am I?' my heart cried. "Why am I so blessed? How can I have a warm coat, a tent, and a comfortable home to return to when so many others—people who are suffering—have nothing?"

"A voice broke through my anguish—not the voice of God but the voice of my husband, Kelly. My mind heard him as clear as day, as if he were standing beside me. 'Just care for these people,' the Kelly voice said. 'Keep giving them what you can—the dignity that every human being deserves, even if only for one day.'

"It didn't say 'cure' or 'fix' them, which given the scale of the need was plainly impossible. Just—if only for a single day—uphold their dignity and affirm their humanity. I realized that I could, humbly and wholeheartedly, aspire to that."

LOVE OF ZAMBIA AND ITS PEOPLE HAS BECOME A DEFINING VALUE OF our friendship. The privilege of serving there is a gift, and so is the perspective it offers. Zambia is a reality check for those of us from affluent cultures, who tend to judge quality of life by what we have—a fancy degree, a big job, a nice car. But, as Ellie says, "While I've broken bread with kings and academic deans, the most profound idea I've ever heard was expressed by a student at the mission named Blessing. She came from a village in the bush, where she grew up in a hut with mud brick walls, sleeping on the floor and sharing a blanket with family members. One day Blessing raised her hand to ask the volunteer teacher, 'Is life as good in the United States as it is here?'

"She couldn't imagine that life elsewhere could be as fulfilling as her own. What Blessing had that so many of us lack—what made life good—was her community, and, importantly, she had the wisdom to know its worth. Her words struck me, then and now, as a mighty affirmation of what really matters."

2

LEAN INTO THE
UNEXPECTED

Z ambia's on the way to almost anywhere," Ellie says. "So, I've always promised my kids and grandkids that, on our way home from the medical mission, we could visit any country they wanted."

"You can see from all the stunning photos in Ellie's home just how extensively she's traveled," Sandy adds. "All seven continents and 120 countries, if you care to keep score. Those spectacular shots got me itching to see some of these wonders for myself. So, over coffee one night, I proposed our first adventure: Since Ellie loves trains as much I do, she embraced my longtime dream of riding the Trans-Siberian Railway."

The Trans-Siberian Railway, the longest train line in the world, stretches two continents and some 5,800 miles—from Moscow in western Russia, the part of the country located in Europe, to Vladivostok, in Asia, on Russia's Pacific Coast. Russia was off-limits to Americans during the Cold War and seemed too chaotic to visit in the 1990s, after the fall of the Soviet Union. But by 2008, conditions in Russia had calmed down enough that riding the Trans-Siberian Railway seemed possible.

One way to make the journey was to join a "luxury" train club, offering passage in private cabins, with elegant bar and dining cars, plus guided tours of cities along the way. Those tourist packages, lasting about ten days, cost fifteen to twenty thousand dollars. The alternative was a six-day journey by second-class train, sharing compartments in a communal sleeper car and grabbing meals from station vendors. The fare for each of us would be $302.

That choice was a no-brainer.

"Ellie and her husband were always budget travelers by choice," Sandy says. "They did it out of principle as much as fiscal prudence— to be immersed in local cultures, rather than isolated in first-class coaches and American-style hotels where you only meet other tourists. I loved that idea and wanted to try it. It sounded like so much fun."

Traveling with someone can be the ultimate test of a relationship. It's hard to know whether a friendship can withstand the stress of crowded flights, missed connections, dodgy hotels, competing interests, strange food, and all the rest. But having worked side by side in the Zambian bush, we had reason to think we'd mesh well and were game to try.

Everyone who interviews us about our travels asks about this— if we get on each other's nerves, if tempers ever flare—so we've had to consider the reasons why we're so travel-compatible. We even made a list:

- We both travel light, with just a backpack and a suitcase.

- We both eat anything and can easily get by on just one good meal a day (if necessary).

- We're both problem-solvers and are optimistic about finding answers. (Translation: Neither of us are fretters. We share the same capacity to lean into the unexpected and to remain upbeat about resolving problems when plans go awry. In fact, we take it on faith that any new outcome may well be better—or at least more interesting—than the planned one.)

- We accommodate each other's rhythms for waking and sleeping, pushing ahead and resting, daring and caution.

- We never fight. Ellie's daughter, Sheryl, calls us "conflict-avoidant," which may be true, but our style of peacekeeping can be a positive. We know how to let things go or just walk away.

- Most important, we're happy by nature and love to connect with people. Sandy is more open and friendly, always smiling, while Ellie is the perennially curious one. But the same drive spurs us: We both wake up in the morning eager to see just who will cross our path on any given day.

IT'S LUCKY WE GET ALONG SO WELL BECAUSE, RIGHT AWAY, UPON PLANning our first adventure as friends, we hit a snag. When we applied for visas to enter Russia, Sandy was blocked. "Why on earth?" Ellie asked. "This must be a mistake. Criminals get blocked, and that's not you. Who would block such a sweet, wholesome, play-by-the-rules grandmother?"

As it turned out, in Russia, Sandy did have a criminal record. "Wait, what?" Ellie said. "How is that possible? But more importantly, why didn't you mention this? We've been planning for months."

"I honestly didn't even remember," Sandy explains: "Really, it was nothing—a dumb technicality. I'd been to Russia twice on mission trips with my grandson. The second time, Putin was in power and had established new visitor protocols that even Russians didn't grasp. One was that we had to register in each city we visited. So, when we landed, I registered in Moscow and said, 'We're going to St. Petersburg. So, I register there, too, correct?'

"'No, don't worry about it,' I was told. 'As long as you're flying home from Moscow, it doesn't matter.'

"It turns out that it did matter, because when I got back to Moscow, I was challenged for skipping the St. Petersburg registration. That's how I came to find myself in a Russian jailhouse.

"The 'jailhouse' was a small police station with one barred holding cell and a husky, surly guard assigned to me. As I tried to explain my innocent mistake, he kept scolding me, saying, 'You broke our law.'

"'Please, I didn't mean to. I'm here to straighten things out.'

"Eventually he presented me with a handwritten page that was my 'confession.' It was written in Russian. I couldn't read a word of it. Then in broken English, he offered a loose translation, demanding that I sign the page.

"'Do you understand what it says?' he kept asking.

"'I understand what you're telling me it says,' I replied.

"That annoyed him, and he shot me a look that gave me chills.

'You have to sign it!' he insisted. So, I said, 'Yes, sir!' figuring it was my only way out.

"I also paid a fine, but as I turned to leave, I asked the guard if he'd mind snapping a picture of me in the jail cell. I don't know how I got the nerve, but I really wanted some visual proof to document this ridiculous story.

"At first he refused, but I smiled long and hard enough to get a yes. The guard took a picture of me inside the cell with his skinny sidekick, holding up my confession.

"Who knew that would be enough to get my name on a Russian watch list?"

To get a visa, Sandy would have to reapply and argue her case in person at the Russian consulate in Houston. Ellie loves this story because she's usually the one who gets in trouble. Knowing that Sandy could only remedy the situation by appearing at the consulate didn't faze Ellie a bit. "I had no doubt that Sandy would launch her charm offensive and win over the Russian envoys. And, of course, Sandy did."

WITH VISAS FINALLY IN HAND, WE BOOKED PASSAGE ON THE TRANS-Siberian Railway, departing in April 2008. We decided not to take it all the way to Vladivostok, but to peel off and transfer to the Trans-Mongolian branch, which terminates in Beijing. We'd each already seen many of the marvels of Beijing but would spend the night there with a friend of Sandy's before heading to Shanghai, our final destination. To reach Shanghai, we'd take another famous train—the world's fastest—the Jinghu High-Speed Railway.

Using air miles, we flew to Moscow and, cutting it tight, arrived three hours before train time. We were greeted at the airport by a Nigerian friend, Israel, who is a medical doctor/travel agent. Ellie, being tall, jumped in the front seat of his car, a Russian-made Lada, while Sandy, being small, squeezed into the back with all our luggage.

No sooner had we merged with traffic on the crowded freeway than the Lada began to sputter and jerked to a stop. Israel got out, raised the hood, and shook his head, looking hopeless. Every so often he'd return to the car, bow slightly in prayer, and whisper "Jesus," as if hoping for divine intervention.

But ultimately what saved us was Sandy's inspiration. "Maybe the radiator needs water?" she suggested. It worked, sort of. The Lada rallied enough to putt-putt to the station, and miraculously we made our train.

Our second-class train was a sturdy workhorse that looked capable of withstanding anything we might face in the Siberian forests. To us, it was utterly fairy-tale romantic.

Though it was April, we'd been advised to expect wintry conditions. Imagine our surprise, when we boarded in our boots and down jackets, to find the other passengers wearing flip-flops and shorts. The train's mighty engines cranked the heat as high as a steam bath.

We settled into a compartment in a sleeper car packed with families. Children started to approach us, little by little, curious. Sandy had lots of pictures on her computer to entertain them, as well as a storybook she'd written about a monster, which the kids just loved. She also showed them some slideshow images with Russian captions from her previous mission trips. Those, too, were a hit, and soon we found ourselves the belles of the ball, and not just with the children. We were the life of a four-day, nonstop party and loved every minute of it.

When it came to meals, we'd been told that there'd be little to eat on the train but that hot water was always available. So, we'd stockpiled instant oatmeal and ramen noodles, as well as peanut butter, energy bars, and other nonperishables. That way, we'd be covered in case the stations where we stopped didn't have food vendors.

. As it turned out, we needn't have bothered. Not only were there plenty of vendors, but their offerings were often delicious. At our very first stop, Ellie spotted a woman with a bag and said, "I smell bierox! I can't believe it." Growing up in western Oklahoma among people of Eastern European descent, she'd loved bierox, or hand pies filled with spiced meat, onions, and cabbage. "I hadn't had one since I was little," she says. "Now we were at the place where bierox originated. Of course, I bought a bunch. Like a kid in a candy store."

An accomplished photographer, Ellie hoped to shoot pictures from the train. She couldn't because the windows were too dirty. When she tried to open one, she drew the ire of a female conductor, who rightly pegged Ellie as a troublemaker. As soon as the conductor passed through the car, Ellie started tugging again at a window, only to have the woman—bent on catching her in the act—swoop down out of nowhere, like a large angry hawk, croaking "Nyet!" "But I was just as determined," Ellie says. "I locked myself in the bathroom and climbed on the toilet to open the window, then leaned out over the tracks to get my shots."

On the fourth day of our journey, we reached Irkutsk, Russia, where we disembarked to visit one of Siberia's natural wonders, Lake Baikal.

LAKE BAIKAL IS THE MOST ANCIENT, DEEPEST, AND LARGEST (BY VOL-ume) body of fresh water in the world. Some twenty-five million years old, it formed when a rift opened between the earth's tectonic plates—a rift that's still "young," geologically speaking, and expands by fractions of an inch each year. About 80 percent of its species of flora, fauna, and aquatic life—everything from its shrubbery to its seals, deer, and foxes, and its fish, sea worms, and exotic algae—are "endemic," found nowhere else on earth.

We stayed in a quaint lakeside village, Listvyanka, which is an assemblage of simple log homes. All the houses had beautifully stylized windows—shuttered, with ornately carved frames, pilasters, cornices, and corbels known as "wooden lace." It was like a storybook town with streets of charming gingerbread houses.

"For a photographer, that picturesque town was irresistible," Ellie says. "Today's digital cameras have streamlined the process, but back in 2008, I needed lots of equipment to capture the images I wanted, like tripods and heavy lenses. That's when I learned how patient and kind Sandy can be. Not only did she tolerate my constant stopping to shoot photos, but while I was shooting, she hung onto my gear, choreographing her movements to be in just the right spot at the right moment to let me hand off a piece of equipment or swap out a lens, like a golf caddy. I never even had to ask. She just slipped into that role with great generosity and good cheer and has maintained it throughout our travels. What a friend!"

"I didn't mind," Sandy says. "I like being part of Ellie's production crew. It's great to see her get so inspired and laser-focused."

There's a photo from Listvyanka that defines the spirit of our travels. We'd been trekking around the lake for five or six hours and had reached a very remote area, where tourists probably never go. That's when we came upon a group of teenage boys—five or six of them— some distance away but loping toward us. Listvyanka is a tiny community, and they certainly didn't recognize us as locals. But the second they spotted us, they lit up with excitement and began waving and smiling wildly. The gleeful warmth of their greeting—to two total strangers in a frozen Siberian woodland—ignited in us a boisterous joy. Waving and smiling madly, we beamed their exuberance right back at them. The encounter was a pure, exhilarating jolt of humanity, transcending huge gaps in age, language, and culture. That joy of human connection—often at the least expected times and in surprising circumstances—is what traveling (and life) is all about for us.

> **That joy of human connection— often at the least expected times and in surprising circumstances— is what traveling (and life) is all about for us.**

~~~~~~~~

FROM LAKE BAIKAL, WE HAD ANOTHER EIGHT-HOUR STRETCH ON THE Trans-Siberian before we'd connect with the Trans-Mongolian Railway. We were looking forward to meeting a lively new crop of partying Russian passengers. But to our surprise and disappointment, this time our entire car was deserted. We didn't see a soul for hours—not even a ticket taker or a conductor on patrol. It was weird. And creepy.

As we headed east, the landscape grew increasingly stark and snowy. By evening we arrived at Ulan-Ude, a desolate, frigid city near the Mongolian border. Finally, a person appeared—the first we'd seen since we'd boarded. It was the conductor, calling, "Passports." We handed ours over and then, to our surprise, again heard him call out "Passports," farther down the car. All this time, we thought we were alone. How could we have missed spotting a fellow passenger?

Heading out on a scouting mission, Ellie found a now-open door that had been shut the entire journey. Inside the compartment was a disheveled Russian man, dressed in what looked like his pajamas. "'Oh. I'm sorry to have disturbed you,' I said," Ellie recalls. "Then I quickly skittered away to describe 'Pajama Man' to Sandy."

Ellie was barely back in our compartment when we heard a commotion in the hall. We stuck our heads out the door to see what on earth was going on.

A small army of FSB, the new version of the KGB under Putin, in their distinctive uniforms and insignia, began tearing the car apart—throwing open doors, punching seat cushions, pulling down ceiling tiles. The white-hot center of the action was Pajama Man's compartment.

Horrified, we ducked back inside our own compartment and listened, in anxious silence, to the banging and thumping outside our door.

We'd already been in the station longer than the scheduled stop, but clearly, we wouldn't be leaving anytime soon. Worse yet, we realized that the conductor still had our passports. We joked nervously about being grilled by the FSB and then whisked off to a Siberian work camp to break rocks. Yes, we'd both seen too many Cold War spy movies. But the FSB was living up to its reputation for menace.

Through the windows we saw Pajama Man being led away with his hands behind his back.

Bang! Suddenly the FSB was at our door. We started to clear out, but agents pushed us back into the compartment, ordering us to stand off to one side. They swept through our compartment like a dirt devil and a twister joining forces. They tore open our luggage, flinging out folded clothes, running their hands over the lining, pawing through toiletries, turning pockets inside out. Anything wrapped got unwrapped, anything closed was yanked open—our belongings were strewn all over the seats.

They came up empty-handed but signaled for us to stay put. Agents remained stationed outside our cabin. Then, an official arrived, a large woman, who lumbered in wearing a big fur coat and a fur cap with ear flaps, in deference to the blizzard raging outside.

In broken English, she said, "You only witness to crime."

We said, "Crime!? What crime?"

There were heated exchanges between the woman and the agents that left us shaken. The little we could understand had to do with a bullet, maybe a gun, maybe something worse.

Had there been a murder on the Trans-Siberian Railway?

The one thing she made perfectly clear was, "You will testify!"

We protested. "But we saw nothing! We're two old women! We have no idea what you're talking about!"

With Pajama Man in custody, we hoped that the train would leave. But it didn't budge, and over the next few hours we were interrogated. Names, addresses, phone numbers, email. We handed over our cell phones. We sang like two little birdies—two American birds blown way off course.

At last, the agents left us, repeating, "You will come back to testify!"

"Okay," we said, unwilling to tangle further. The realization that we'd made it through the ordeal left us giddy as we repacked our things and waited for the train to leave.

We began sending jokey emails to our kids. "We've been detained on the Siberian-Mongolian border by the FSB. There may have been a murder on our train. If you don't hear from us in a few days, assume we're in a Siberian prison."

We didn't know at the time that, for two days after we sent those high-octane-jokey emails, any replies sent to us bounced back to their senders. During that period, no more of our emails got through either. Was that spy craft? Or some colossal temporary internet glitch in southern Siberia?

Sandy's son Larry grew alarmed by the silence that followed our joking missives. Already making inquiries, he was on the verge of calling Interpol when we finally resurfaced. To this day, we're not sure he has entirely forgiven us.

Finally, our conductor knocked on the door and returned our passports without a word of explanation. Then he jumped onto the platform, and we were off, soon to connect with the Trans-Mongolian Railway.

THE TRANS-SIBERIAN WAS A NO-FRILLS, CHUGGA-CHUGGA, IRON HORSE sort of train. But the Trans-Mongolian, though plain on the outside, was resplendent on the inside, like a faded relic of the Gilded Age. Even in second class, there were brass fittings and gorgeous wood paneling, and the dining car was subdivided by elaborate, carved screens. It served wonderful food, too.

Through our windows, the scenery grew bleaker as we entered the Gobi Desert. We luxuriated in the charm and the lore of our old-world rail line, comforted by its hypnotic lull—as if time itself had been suspended—reminding us anew how much we love traveling by train and why. Ellie has a book by Paul Theroux with a passage that perfectly sums up our feelings about rail travel: "If a train is large and comfortable you don't even need a destination. A corner seat is enough, and you can be one of those travelers who stay in motion, straddling the tracks, and never arrive or feel they ought to."

We passed occasional small villages, but the landscape was mostly an empty vastness of rocks and scrub grass, dotted only with occasional yurts and camels.

One of the most surprising sights we encountered was a nearly five-hundred-foot-tall geoglyph, or image made of painted rocks, on a desert mountainside. It depicted the face of a long-haired man. "How come there's a portrait of Jesus?" Sandy asked. "Isn't this a Buddhist country?"

"I burst out laughing," Ellie says. "I told her, 'That's not Jesus, Sandy. It's Genghis Khan, the great Mongolian emperor,' and Sandy chuckled."

Little by little the barren desert gave way to greenery and trees. It was a sign that we were approaching China and our train's final stop, Beijing.

DISEMBARKING FROM THE TRAIN IN BEIJING, WE GRABBED A CAB TO the home of Suen-Yae, whom Sandy had befriended on a previous mission trip. Suen-Yae, her daughter, Anna, and her husband (who was away on business) lived on the twenty-third floor of an ultra-modern high-rise in a ring of apartment buildings surrounding a lovely, gated park.

Suen-Yae welcomed us warmly though perhaps a little shyly, as if wondering how Americans might view Chinese life at home. But when we all went out to dinner, at one of the area's best restaurants, it was our turn to be shy—having to admit to our host that we had no idea how to eat what we'd been served.

The place specialized in hot pots. A pot of boiling broth was set on a burner in the big round table, and all around it were strewn plates of cut vegetables, mysterious condiments, and, most daunt-ing, strips of various raw fish. Suen-Yae patiently demonstrated how to grasp food with our chopsticks, then drop the pieces into the steaming broth to cook them. Combined with rice and daubed with condiments, the fish and vegetables were perfectly delicious. But we were equally charmed by the communal spirit of the dinner. With each of us choosing what to add to the pot, we were quite literally "sharing" the meal.

The next morning, we said goodbye to Suen-Yae and Anna and boarded the Jinghu High-Speed Railway, also known as the Bullet Train. Traveling at some two hundred miles an hour, it covers the eight-hundred-plus miles from Beijing to Shanghai, once a ten-hour trip, in four hours and eighteen minutes. The Bullet Train nickname refers not just to its speed but also to its appearance. It is a fully electrified, sleek and gleaming aluminum tube. We felt like we'd straddled three centuries on our train rides this trip: the nineteenth on the Trans-Mongolian, with its embellished interiors; the twentieth on the no-frills, gritty Trans-Siberian; and the twenty-first on the shiny, futuristic Bullet.

As usual, we struck up conversations with fellow passengers. Sandy, who is a magnet for people who speak English, met a couple traveling to a conference in Shanghai. The wife was a multilingual translator who'd worked with Placido Domingo, the famous opera singer, on his Chinese tour. She proudly showed us a newsclip of the two of them together.

In Shanghai, we grabbed a tuk-tuk (a motorized three-wheeler) to one of the most enchanting hotels we'd ever seen, let alone stayed at. Usually, our lodgings are comfortable but humble. We spend little time inside them, except to sleep, so we look for clean and functional (and budget!) in the heart of the places we want to explore. The glorious Astor House Hotel fit these criteria, but with an extra benefit—a grand dollop of character and historical significance.

Built in the 1850s and expanded over the years, it once advertised itself as "the Waldorf Astoria of the Orient." In its heyday, Charlie Chaplin and Albert Einstein stayed there. After surviving wars, unrest, and neglect, it hit bottom in the 1970s, when its lavish rooms were converted to dorms to create a backpacker hotel. But, lucky for us, by the time we visited, much of its fabled grandeur had been restored. We felt like royalty as we entered the marble-floored lobby with its vaulted ceiling, wood paneling, and stately white columns.

The hotel was located right on the Bund, the waterfront historic district of central Shanghai. It was like a mile-long plaza, in the midst of the city's most majestic buildings, where people jogged, practiced tai chi, and even flew kites. From there we could walk to most of the city's major sights.

Our favorite spot in the city, the Yuyuan Garden, was a short cab ride away. We seek out gardens wherever we go in our travels. Perhaps we love them so much because we're from West Texas, a climate exceedingly inhospitable to exuberant and exotic blooms. In Texas, Ellie has her own greenhouse and the green thumb to match. She is one of those people who can grow anything. In Zambia, too, she has a backyard orchard of tropical fruit trees—mango, guava, banana, orange, lime, papaya, and avocado—along with a bounty of flowering trees, including flamboyant jacaranda, frangipani, and even a large poinsettia.

Sandy is equally keen on gardens but lacks Ellie's hands-on experience, so our visits to formal ones always send her into a swoon of impractical longing.

Closing out our trip after six days riding the rails together, we planned a quick journey from Shanghai to Hangzhou, to see the area that Sandy's granddaughter Lily is from. The thirteenth-century explorer Marco Polo called Hangzhou "the greatest city in the world" because it was a hub of Silk Road commerce. We saw some remarkable temples and pagodas and enjoyed sampling the local brew, Dragon Well—or Longjing—tea, one of the most celebrated green teas in the world.

Boarding our bus to return to Shanghai was an abrupt return to earth. As Ellie explains, "We were happy to find seats as the bus was jam-packed. We were settling in as the bus pulled out, routine as could be, but things went sideways fast. Suddenly, the bus jerked to a halt. Outside, a woman, distracted on her phone, had stepped off the curb right in front of our bus! The driver's hard braking probably lessened the impact, but nonetheless, she was knocked to the ground.

"A huge crowd gathered as sirens wailed and police and emergency vehicles streamed onto the street. The woman, quickly attended to by medics, appeared to be conscious, thank goodness. There was a lot of arguing in Chinese, and then the police entered the bus, barking orders at all of us.

"'Everyone off the bus,' they announced.

"But none of us were free to leave. We were all 'witnesses.' 'Here we go again!' we thought.

"We always default to embracing and leaning into the unexpected—but not this time, not now. We'd seen this movie before and we had to make the last train out of Hangzhou to Shanghai in order to catch our flight back to the US in the morning!

"We approached the police officials about our predicament, with no luck. They were as short on patience as they were on English. We tried to smile, we tried to reason; we tried to plead, but we got absolutely nowhere. Still, we knew that for the squeaky-wheel approach to work we had to keep on squeaking.

"Eventually we found an official who had a good grasp of English. We explained our dilemma. If we didn't get to the train station in time, we'd miss our flight home. He said he would help us, and that he'd be right back.

"When he returned, there was a fresh blare of sirens and flashing lights as new police cars pulled up. We stared blankly, confused, but the nice official who'd promised to help whisked us toward the cars and told us to get inside one of them. And so, we did.

"That's how we came to have a full police escort, sirens ablaze, rushing us to the train station, where we did catch the train back to Shanghai and our flight home!"

DESPITE OCCASIONAL MISHAPS, SPEED BUMPS AND ALL, WE'D EXPERI-enced more than just a glorious trip. We'd quickly found such a compatible rhythm that often we didn't need to say things out loud to know what the other was thinking. We knew when to give the other space and, easily and instinctively, balanced our differences in schedules and preferences—like morning routines: Sandy wants to take her time to shower and coif her hair, whereas Ellie is up and out in a flash, at most giving her hair a quick tousle before sprinting out to catch the early light and shoot her first photographs of the new day. We were reassured to find that you don't need to be the same to be complementary—jigsaw puzzle pieces that fit. We'd each found our travel soulmate! So, the adventure wasn't ending; it was just getting started.

> **You don't need to be the same to be complementary—jigsaw puzzle pieces that fit.**

3

JUST SAY YES—
BUT CHOOSE WHO YOU'RE
SAYING YES TO

We loved China so much that, in 2010, we decided to push deeper into Southeast Asia, inspired by a description of the grand tourist train, the Eastern & Oriental Express. It was on this trip that Just Say Yes became our official mantra. The mantra means, "Don't hold back—even if we're tired, even if the activity doesn't sound thrilling, even if the details seem sketchy, even if we don't know where we're going . . ."

> **Just Say Yes became our official mantra. The mantra means, "Don't hold back—even if we're**

> tired, even if the activity doesn't
> sound thrilling, even if the details
> seem sketchy, even if we don't
> know where we're going . . ."

Of course, we do our best to avoid potentially risky situations. (We like to think that, at our age, we've developed good instincts and judgment.) But when we've said yes, as often as not, we've stumbled into grand experiences.

Our journey started in Singapore, an island that was a British colony until the 1960s and now is one of the world's richest nations. We landed in the middle of the night at its futuristic airport and grabbed a cab to the YMCA—we still chuckle at this choice. But it was one of the few affordable places in this ultraexpensive city, and it was perfect—very comfortable and well-located.

The cabbie who drove us there was a gem. We said, "We're only in Singapore for twenty-four hours. What should we do?" He had a great list of activities right on the tip of his tongue. In the morning, we set out to hit all of them.

Our first stop was the Singapore Botanic Gardens, renowned for its unique collection of exotic orchids. Usually, we see orchids confined to glass greenhouses, but here they were outdoors, in the wild—albeit in perfectly manicured gardens—growing free, in a riot of color. The lavish clusters and sheer profusion of otherworldly blossoms had us swooning.

The gardens lie at the end of Orchard Road, a super fancy shopping strip with designer stores like Chanel. Obviously, it was not exactly our scene, but since we travel to take in the culture, we happily window-shopped. What struck us more than the luxurious, upscale shops was how utterly pristine the Singapore streets were. "Almost cartoonishly clean," Sandy says. "You notice right away that Singapore feels different from an American city, but at first you can't quite figure out why. Then it strikes you that everything's spotless."

Our trusty cab driver/guide had urged us not to leave the city without visiting the legendary Raffles Hotel and trying its famous libation, the Singapore Sling. Though we aren't teetotalers, we rarely drink alcohol, but we were excited at the novel prospect. So, though it was only 10:30 a.m., we said yes!

Founded in the nineteenth century, the Raffles Hotel is a striking white, British-colonial-style edifice with multistory arched windows, open-air arcades with restaurants and luxury boutiques, and lush tropical gardens connecting its wings. A national monument, it has hosted countless celebrity guests, including authors like Rudyard Kipling, Noël Coward, and Somerset Maugham—honored in its handsome Writers Bar—and actors like Elizabeth Taylor and Ava Gardner. Turbaned doormen in gold-trimmed white morning coats stand by to greet the guests, prompting Sandy to joke, "Wow, this is not how I grew up!"

We made our way through the grand lobby to the two-story Long Bar, with mahogany fixtures and a coffered ceiling evoking a Malaysian plantation of the 1920s. It was empty at that hour, but when the bartender came over, we bravely announced, "We were told that we must try Singapore Slings."

"Of course," he replied, and filled us in on the history of the drink, which made us even more delighted to be upholding the tradition. Early in the twentieth century, respectable women didn't drink alcohol in public. But around 1915, a British woman asked a sympathetic bartender, Ngiam Tong Boon, to come up with a boozy drink that would fool disapproving husbands. The result was the gin-based Singapore Sling, which is rosy-pink enough to look like innocent fruit juice and to allow women to imbibe without rousing male suspicions.

The drink was such a hit that the original recipe was secured in a safe. Somehow, though, it was lost, and most Singapore Slings served today are not the real deal but wildly different approximations. Only Raffles still offers the authentic version, recreated from a visitor's notes dating back to the 1930s.

We loved the story and adored our Singapore Slings, so much so that we absorbed the sticker shock when we got the check. The price of two drinks exceeded the cost of our entire stay at the YMCA.

After checking off a couple of other sites on our list, and catching a few hours' sleep, we got up at 5 a.m., excited for the next stage of our journey—by train, of course, our budget version of the Eastern & Oriental Express.

The Eastern & Oriental Express debuted in the 1990s as a luxury cruise train linking Singapore and Bangkok, Thailand (and later, Bangkok and Vientiane, Laos). The beauty of the landscape— verdant rainforests and rice fields—is the heart of the train's appeal. At various points, tour buses meet it to take passengers on guided side trips for snorkeling, spa treatments, or sightseeing in cities like

Kuala Lumpur and Penang. Its carpeted, wood-paneled cabins range from the two-person Pullman, with huge windows, plush seating, bunks with crisp linens, and a private bathroom with shower to the suite-like Presidential, with two full rooms appointed with floor-level beds, caviar and fruit upon arrival, and free-flowing champagne. Naturally, all these perks come with a price: back then, around six thousand dollars for three nights.

Instead of biting that bullet, we booked passage on a second-class train following the route—even running on some of the same tracks—as the Eastern & Oriental Express. Rather than pile onto buses at preset tour stops, we planned our own sightseeing outings. We were delighted that our fare cost us one hundred dollars each, barely a sliver of the cost of the fancy tourist train for roughly the same experience. Emphasis on "roughly."

On the first leg of the trip, our seats were stuck in a peculiar half-reclining position that kept us perched on the edge, uncomfortably upright. When our included lunch arrived, it turned out to be a bottle of water and a roll in a cellophane bag. We consoled ourselves by remembering that, through our streaky and blurry windows, we were enjoying the same lush tropical greenery as the upscale tourists.

After five hours of travel, we reached Tampin, Malaysia, the stop for our first side trip, Melaka. Melaka dates back to the fifteenth century and is a multicultural living homage to the inclusivity of faiths and cultures—and a prime example of what inspired us to strike deeper into East Asia in the first place.

As the train slowed, we gathered our luggage. We were so filled with excitement and anticipation that we failed to be as observant of our surroundings as we normally are. What we failed to notice— for starters!—was that no one else from our very crowded train got off at the stop with us. Had we noticed, we wouldn't have gotten off the train at all. We would have assumed there was some *reason* no one was getting off. We would have stayed on board and asked some questions.

But step off the train we did, and right onto a concrete slab. With the train already pulling away, we soon realized that the concrete slab on which our feet and our bags were now planted was the only thing to be seen—for miles. There was no station. No shelter of any kind. "Oops!" we said to each other as we gradually began to take in the enormity of our mistake.

You hear people speak about being stuck in the middle of nowhere, but in those instances it is a figure of speech. We actually were in the middle of nowhere. This was before there were mapping apps. But in any case, our phones were out of charge. Not only had our train seats been stuck, but the train—at least in our car—had no charging ports.

Eventually we heard something. Like a mirage (we confirmed we both saw it), we could see off in the distance what appeared to be a car moving in our direction. The distant dot got bigger until eventually it was clear it was a car approaching. Relief and gratitude flooded us; we could have wept.

It hadn't even occurred to us that the car could be a new danger. When the beat-up vehicle arrived, the dodgy looking man who got out was not the savior we had pictured. For one thing, he seemed off, and also angry, screaming at someone on his phone. He barked something at us that we didn't understand. Nor did he understand our English. Then he said to us a word we all understood, "Taxi."

While he continued screaming into his phone, we whispered to each other: "Do you think he's actually a taxi driver? Or was this a ploy?" We'd been told that, in Malaysia, thieves lie in wait to prey on tourists. "Be careful," we'd been repeatedly warned. Also, Sandy reminded us of her safety rule: "When you need help, choose your helper, don't let the helper choose you."

> **When you need help, choose your helper, don't let the helper choose you.**

Yet we'd backed ourselves into such a tight corner, we didn't see any option but to get into the car of a screaming man that neither of us trusted.

We hoped his intent was merely to earn a fare. A wrinkle though: we didn't have a cent. Having been on the train when it crossed the Singapore-Malaysian border, we hadn't had a chance to get Malaysian currency. We'd intended to do that in the train station.

We said, "Melaka?" He nodded. He pointed to the car and opened the door. We said, "ATM" but he paid us no attention and continued his disagreement on the phone.

After riding for a while, with no sign of civilization, Ellie forcefully commanded the driver's attention by sternly saying, "ATM!" He nodded and we felt a sliver of hope. "We can jump out if we have to," Sandy whispered. Just then, Ellie spotted a signpost for Melaka, and we both exhaled.

He pulled up to an area with a few amenities, including an ATM. Ellie came back with the money, and soon all the harrowing possibilities of the day faded as we merged into the gloriously predictable bicycle and trishaw traffic of Melaka's colorful historic district.

Never has arriving at our destination been sweeter. And just like that, the world and our lives reverted to blessed normal. Melaka sure felt sacred to us.

IN MELAKA WE STAYED AT THE CENTURY-OLD HEEREN HOUSE, WHICH had just seven cozy guest rooms above a charming café. Ours looked out over the Melaka River, which we later enjoyed on one of a flotilla of sightseeing boats. The river's banks are lined with historic buildings of ornate design, stands of slender mangrove trees, and lots of brightly colored walls—Melaka is known for its street art. We could even see into people's waterfront backyards and catch glimpses of local life.

But our favorite way to see the city was by trishaw, a three-wheeled passenger cart propelled by a bicycle. Trishaw drivers personalize their vehicles with trimmings, giving them a festive air. We spent a day sightseeing in one with a peaked awning adorned with fringe, strings of beads, and sprays of artificial flowers. Our driver was very knowledgeable and proud of his city, and we could see why. After centuries as a trading center for China, India, the Middle East, and Europe, the city remains a melting pot of cultures and religions. One spot that he revered—and we'd been especially keen to see—was Jalan Tokong, the Street of Harmony, where for centuries three major houses of worship have peacefully coexisted: the Sri Poyyatha Vinayagar Moorthi Temple, the nation's oldest Hindi temple; the dramatic green-roofed Kampung Kling Mosque; and the Chinese Buddhist Cheng Hoon Teng Temple. Nearby are Christ Church, the oldest Protestant church in Malaysia, and the Roman Catholic Church of St. Francis Xavier.

We even learned from our driver why the train we thought would take us to Melaka stops in the middle of nowhere. During World War II, Japanese forces dismantled the tracks, leaving Melaka inaccessible by rail. At the time of our visit, the only mode of public transportation in or out of the city was the bus. Good to know! For the next leg of our journey, to reach Penang, we'd need to take the bus to Malaysia's capital, Kuala Lumpur.

DISEMBARKING AT THE KUALA LUMPUR BUS DEPOT, WE HAD TO FIND the train station to buy our tickets to Penang. We were looking for a taxi stand when a man dressed all in white approached us and asked if we needed a cab. We said yes, thinking he was an official who'd direct us to the cab dispatcher. "Follow me," he said, and picked up our luggage.

Here's where a cue card should have popped up, reading, "Beware!"

But we trailed after him—up a long flight of stairs, across an overpass above a bustling street, then back down to ground level in front of a small café. We started prickling with goosebumps when he entered it, heading straight into the kitchen, where the staff was hard at work—washing dishes, stirring pots, chopping bloody things with cleavers.

"That's when I got 'the look' from Sandy," Ellie says. "She gets this expression—eyebrows raised, stern gaze, lips turned down in a frown, and her face radiating disapproval, as if to say, 'What on earth are we doing?'

"All I could do was smile at her because, of course, I felt the same way. But I wasn't quite sure how we could extricate ourselves, and besides, he had our luggage."

Then he led us outside to the dirty, trash-filled alley. A guy waiting there addressed him in an unfamiliar language. Now we *really* felt like the quintessential naïve American tourists.

We were scoping out escape routes—ready to abandon the luggage—when the guy from the alley produced a taxi sign that he stuck on top of a parked car. "Get in," said the man in white.

So, he was legit, more or less? As we pulled out of the alley, Ellie shot photos out the back window in case there was ever a question of where we were last seen.

We don't want to encourage tourists to take chances because too many wind up in real trouble. In both of these cases, we got lucky. Adventuring off the beaten path, doing as we please, fearless, and independent, reaps a bounty of life-changing and soul-enriching experiences that we wouldn't give up for the world. But personal safety has to be part of the calculus. So we'd say to other travelers, be bold but vigilant. Don't count on luck. Count on common sense.

Our cab dropped us at the train station, where we got our tickets and connected with a Hop-On Hop-Off tour bus to make the most of our few hours in Kuala Lumpur. A highlight was visiting Kuala Lumpur Bird Park, the world's largest free-flight aviary, where we were immersed in a tropical paradise populated by more than three thousand spectacular birds. We also loved the city's landmark Twin Towers, modern spires that are not glass boxes but have a Far Eastern decorative flair. For a brief stretch from 1998 to 2004, they were officially recognized as the tallest buildings in the world.

Then we were off to Penang Island in the Strait of Melaka, the "food capital of Malaysia."

THOUGH WE'RE COMMITTED BUDGET TRAVELERS, WE'RE OPEN TO THE occasional splurge. The Blue Mansion in Penang, a glorious guesthouse with just sixteen rooms, was well worth pushing our limit. Built in the late nineteenth century by Cheong Fatt Tze, the so-called Rockefeller of China, it was Penang's most unusual and elegant home of the era, blending Chinese decorative styles from the three-thousand-year-old Su Chow dynasty with British aspects like art nouveau stained glass.

But, of course, the most distinctive element of the mansion was its color, inside and out—an intensely vivid sky blue. One of Ellie's most striking photos shows three antique black rickshaws, with stark white roofs, against its rich azure facade. While the meals we ate during our stay lived up to Penang's culinary reputation, what struck us was the presentation. Wherever we ate—even in tiny, hole-in-the-wall restaurants—the food was as much a feast for the eyes as it was for the palate.

After two nights on the island, we were headed to Bangkok, Thailand.

So far in our travels, the second-class sleeper cars on the trains we booked had been divided into separate compartments. But on the overnight train to Bangkok, we were stunned to find that the entire car was open, like a dorm full of double-decker bunks—an upper tier of berths above floor-level seats that opened into beds. All that shielded the bunks from the peeping eyes of anyone passing in the aisle were sets of thin blue curtains. Forget privacy!

It was our first experience of a communal sleeping car.

To avoid climbing, we got two lower berths across the aisle from each other. Our dinner was train food, delivered on a rolling cart, which consisted of rice and side dishes to spoon on top. Then, after some lively Scrabble games, we crawled into our bunks, curious to see what would happen in our open-dorm car during the night.

A smiling twenty-something woman climbed up above Sandy and drew her curtains. The bunk above Ellie stayed vacant as passengers jammed the aisle, talking, looking for bunk numbers, and getting situated. "Maybe I'll get lucky," Ellie said, "and can have the upper berth for my stuff." Then, just before departure, a young man threaded through the crowd. He stopped between our berths and pointed up. "Hello!" Ellie said. "Welcome." He didn't grasp the words but smiled at her tone, then heaved his bag and himself up onto the bunk.

Of course, we needed a photo of the arrangement. In it, Ellie grins slyly as she reclines in the lower berth, while the young man above her has a wide-eyed, startled look. He was probably shocked to find himself bunking above not just a Westerner but a grandmother.

We love to show off that picture to illustrate our Just Say Yes mantra and, importantly, its role in making memories. If we'd upgraded to first class to have our own compartment, we might have felt more comfortable, but we'd barely remember it now. As it is, we had a life-enhancing adventure—an experience that we'll always treasure.

4

ATTITUDE IS EVERYTHING,
AND REMEMBER OKRA

I n the morning we awoke in Bangkok. "It's the only city in the world where Ellie seemed uncomfortable," Sandy says. "I was surprised because she's so gung ho about every travel experience, eager to approach it with a huge smile and open arms."

But in Bangkok, Ellie wanted to stay just long enough to arrange passage to Cambodia, our next stop. "It's like Ellie had been body-snatched," Sandy says. "I told her, 'This is so out of character. You're a woman who copes with spitting cobras in your kitchen in Zambia. What could be so bad about Bangkok?'"

"Well, it's not that bad," Ellie said, laughing. "It's just that, when I was here with my husband, Kelly, the tuk-tuks drove us crazy."

Tuk-tuks, three-wheeled motorized rickshaws, are the chief way to get around the city. Ellie thought that they scammed tourists, taking them out of their way to jack up fares.

So, Ellie developed a plan. Before we ever got into a tuk-tuk, she laid down the law with the driver, settling on terms upfront, like a fixed fare and no extra stops. "It worked, mostly," Ellie says. "Though, probably no coincidence, we had some hair-raising rides—hurtling through traffic at high speeds, screeching around corners—from drivers expressing their annoyance at my insistence."

We did enjoy some memorable sights. One day, we took a ferry to Wat Arun, or the Temple of Dawn, on the western bank of the Chao Phraya River, which flows through the city. Its silhouette is striking—a tiered structure with a corncob-shaped prang, or tower, about 250 feet tall, topped by a seven-pronged trident, and surrounded by four smaller replica prangs. But even more impressive is its facade, which glitters in the sun because it's encrusted with ornate mosaics. The floral designs of the mosaics are made of shells, colored glass, and countless shards of glazed porcelain salvaged from ships, which used them as ballast.

A steep outdoor staircase stretches up the lower tiers of the temple. "Oooh, a stair challenge!" we said, laughing. We did our best to scale the steps, huffing and puffing, and made it about halfway. At least that's how high it looks like we climbed in the pictures—and who's counting?

"So, Bangkok did wind up being fun," Sandy says. "And we both learned a lesson from resolving the tuk-tuk issue—that if one of us feels unsettled, the other can step back and just let her work it out. We don't have to worry about fixing problems for each other."

> **If one of us feels unsettled, the other can step back and just let her work it out. We don't have to worry about fixing problems for each other.**

"Yes," Ellie says. "Our only real disappointment was that we had to fly to Cambodia. There was no train or reliable bus to get there, as we'd hoped."

OUR DESTINATION IN CAMBODIA WAS SIEM REAP, THE SITE OF WHAT many call the Eighth Wonder of the World, Angkor Wat.

"Now it was my turn to feel uncomfortable," Sandy says. "The hotel Ellie booked cost us each only twelve dollars a night. 'Ellie, I'm worried that it's too cheap!' I protested. 'It could be a dump—or maybe even dangerous!'"

"I had to admit that she had a point," Ellie says. "The online photos looked good but the price was almost too good to be true. I sure hoped I hadn't screwed up, for both our sakes, but especially Sandy's. I spent much of that flight trying to banish worst-case scenarios from my mind."

But, to our relief and delight, the Bopha Angkor was an absolute gem, a picturesque Khmer-style inn with gorgeous carved wood everywhere, guest rooms and cottages with private outdoor seating areas, lovely garden grounds, and a terrace overlooking the river. It even had a swimming pool and a restaurant good enough to attract outside visitors. "I apologized to Ellie for doubting her," Sandy says. "It was even perfectly located."

The location was critical because we'd have to leave before dawn so Ellie could photograph the sunrise at Angkor Wat. "Sunrise wherever you are in the world is always exciting," Ellie says. "You wait in the dark, and then you spot the first little rays. To see that moment and capture it is exhilarating."

When we checked in that afternoon, we had the hotel book a car to pick us up at the crack of dawn. Then Ellie suggested heading to Angkor Wat to try for some sunset pictures. That led us to a remarkable meeting, our favorite kind of adventure.

Angkor Wat is a complex of temples, constructed over several decades in the twelfth century, spanning some four hundred acres, making it the largest religious structure in the world. Its layout represents Mount Meru, the home of the Hindu gods, and its ornate sandstone buildings are renowned for their grandeur and for the thousands of feet of bas-reliefs, or carved images, that adorn their walls. Many of the bas-reliefs depict scenes from history or Hindu epics, as well as everyday life. Some of the Hindu images were replaced when, from the thirteenth century on, the temples became a center of Buddhist worship. Much of the complex is in ruins or in the process of restoration, but it remains a very magical, spiritual place.

When we got to the complex, we began to poke around the main temple. At one point we looked up and saw, two stories above us, a saffron-robed monk standing on a ledge. "I wonder what's on that level," Ellie said.

We then noticed a ladder, propped against the wall, stretching up to the monk's perch. "Should we climb up there and see?" Sandy asked. The ladder looked dauntingly tall.

But curiosity—and our Just Say Yes attitude—kicked in and, one at a time, we began to clamber up the rungs. We reached the top, breathless, and found ourselves in a small, dimly lit, inner chamber with a few benchlike depressions carved into its walls.

There we saw two monks, seemingly relaxing in the quiet—the one we'd spotted plus a taller companion. Both looked to be in their teens. All our guidebooks warned that tourists should not interact with monks, so we simply smiled and prepared to move along.

But, to our surprise, the shorter monk called out to us, in English: "Hello! How are you?" The monk introduced himself as Sen and his companion as Chhong.

As we chatted, Ellie ventured, "May I take your picture?" They agreed, excited, asking that we email them the images. The process of posing for photos seemed to build rapport, and they began to tell us about their lives.

"Families like mine, who can't afford to send their kids to school, will choose a son to enter the monastery," Sen explained. It was not a lifelong commitment, but a period of service caring for the temples that would also afford him an education. "That's how I learned English," he said. "After this, I want to get my own tuk-tuk and show visitors around the site."

For the next hour, he and Chhong practiced their tour guide

skills, as well as their English, by personally escorting us through the temple. What a privilege it was to see it with two of its dedicated guardians, who could bring its mysteries to life! We learned a lot about the lost world that the bas-reliefs depicted. But much as we prized that knowledge, we appreciated even more the time and caring that two young monks were willing to afford a couple of strangers.

No doubt our age had something to do with their solicitude. As older women travelers, we're often perceived as nonthreatening and as a novelty. Maybe we awaken warm feelings people have for their grandmothers. But, for travelers of any age, attitude is surely a factor. Even without a common language, people respond to smiles and genuine, respectful curiosity. That tug of human connection is irresistible to most of us.

> **As older women travelers, we're often perceived as nonthreatening and as a novelty. Maybe we awaken warm feelings people have for their grandmothers. But, for travelers of any age, attitude is surely a factor. Even without a common language, people respond to smiles and genuine,**

respectful curiosity. That tug of human connection is irresistible to most of us.

We returned to the temples a few more times during our stay, but we never again spotted *our* monks. Our chance meeting with them was a once-in-a-lifetime blessing, one that we'll always cherish.

Not far from Angkor Wat lie the Tonle Sap River and a vast lake of the same name. These bodies of water, part of the Lower Mekong River Basin, are so rich in fish that they provide 60 percent of the protein in the entire nation's diet. They are also the realm of incredible floating villages. Some eighty thousand people live right on the water, in houseboats that range from simple thatched-roofed rafts to brightly painted scrap-wood bungalows with tin roofs and front porches.

We spent a day on a boat touring the floating villages. We saw women bathing in sarongs, children swimming naked (or, even very young, paddling alone in metal washtubs), motorized fishing canoes heaped with nets, and vendor boats nosing up to the villages to hawk everything from dry goods to vegetables.

We were struck by the color of the river water—a muddy brown—that the houseboat dwellers used for drinking and cooking. "Plus, all the waste from the villages goes straight into that water," says Sandy, ever the health-conscious doctor. But houseboat life has persisted, no doubt for centuries, as a way to get by in a hardscrabble country.

Sandy had seen the river culture before, during her stints on the *Ship of Life* as a volunteer doctor. A floating clinic, the ship plies the waters of the Mekong River to bring medical and dental care to rural Cambodia. "The Khmer Rouge's persecution of the educated in the 1970s left a dearth of medical professionals," she says. "So, for decades—really, up until the past five years—the *Ship of Life* was a dire necessity."

The problems she encountered on the *Ship of Life* related less to dirty water than to the so-called diseases of affluence, like hypertension and diabetes. "Southeast Asia has huge problems because of the change in lifestyle," she says. "People now have cars and mopeds, so they don't need to walk. Like the rest of the world, they now have fast food joints on every corner, so the traditional diet of fish and homegrown vegetables is out the window.

"I once had a patient come aboard and ask to be tested for diabetes. 'Why do you want to get checked?' I asked.

"He said, 'Because, when I pee on the ground, all the flies are drawn to it.'

"The flies were right! Sure enough, his blood sugar was elevated! I gave him a regimen of pills and told him to return in a month, when the ship looped back around to his village.

"Diabetes, of course, is very close to my heart, since caring for my diabetic son led me to medical school. So, I was honored when, after my second or third volunteer stint, I was asked to give a three-day diabetes seminar on the ship for Cambodian doctors. They'd set up diabetes clinics around the country, but not one of them even had a glucometer (the device that measures sugar from a drop of blood). Instead of keeping their blood sugar steady by testing multiple times per day, patients could only be monitored in the hospital once every six months.

"Did this make treatment impossible? 'Not at all,' I was happy to assure them. I held up a picture of my son at thirteen months old, when he was diagnosed, beside a photo of him at forty, not just alive but thriving. I told them, 'For the first twenty years of his life, there were no home glucometers in America. We managed diabetes without them, with good survival rates, and so can you until enough glucometers reach your country.'

"I also counseled the doctors on the diabetes medications available in Cambodia and how the different classes of drugs should be mixed and matched. What a rewarding opportunity that was, contributing to the developing diabetes battle in a country beset by so many challenges.

"I returned to the *Ship of Life* for years, alternating with Zambia, as usual bringing along various grandchildren. One year, I taught fourteen-year-old James to take patients' vital signs. I was sitting in my office on the ship when he burst in, wide-eyed, to say, 'Nana! There's a gentleman I want you to see right away!'

"'What's wrong?' I asked.

"'His blood pressure is 160/100, and that's way out of range!'

"He was so serious and conscientious, stepping up like part of the medical team. I was so proud of his concern and, of course, charmed by his sweetness.

"There's a running joke Ellie and I have about the *Ship of Life*. I like to remind her, 'On the ship there are no pit latrines with scary wildlife. I have my own sparkling bathroom, en suite in my private bedroom, with crisp sheets on a real mattress—no sleeping bag and hand-sized bugs. And the food—it's just marvelous! I have every possible convenience.'

"'Sure, but you don't have me,' Ellie says. 'So, how much fun can you have?'

"'Friendship versus a clean hot shower?' I ask. 'Well, now, that's a toss-up!'"

We often joke that, except for our beloved trains, we never "sweat the small stuff" about public transportation. As long as there's a way to get from point A to point B, we take it on faith that we can figure it out. We'd flown from Bangkok to Siem Reap and missed seeing the countryside, so we were eager to travel by ground to our next destination, which was Saigon (the popular name), or more properly, Ho Chi Minh City.

The desk clerk at our hotel assured us that although the journey involved several steps, the process would be easy. "We'll take you to the station to catch the bus to Phnom Penh. From there you can buy a ticket to Saigon."

The Siem Reap bus station was just a desk in a dirt parking lot, manned by a lone agent. That was our first clue to expect a local shuttle rather than a comfy motor coach. The second clue was the cost of our tickets, just twelve dollars each for our trip, a journey of some thirteen hours, not counting our layover in Phnom Penh.

When we boarded the bus, we were greeted by squawking chickens. They weren't grouped together as if they were going to market. Instead, throughout the coach, people were juggling individual cages of birds amid other bundles of all shapes and sizes. We surmised that the passengers were going visiting and bringing chickens as hostess gifts. All over the world, chickens are the hospitality food—served to or brought by guests—maybe because they're a luxury but relatively inexpensive and convenient, easy to raise and to transport.

We had one scheduled stop en route to Phnom Penh, where we learned that the price of our ticket included lunch. The help-yourself meal was presented in large buckets, one containing steamed dumplings or buns and the other a mysterious brown mixture that we suspected incorporated crickets, popular in Southeast Asia. That was too much of an adventure for our West Texas palates.

Our driver flew down the road, swerving around oxcarts and cattle, while keeping a keen eye out for travelers along the way. When they waved him down, he'd screech to a stop. We felt lucky when we reached Phnom Penh in one piece.

CAMBODIA HAD ONE FINAL GIFT TO BESTOW ON US. AFTER BUYING OUR bus tickets to Ho Chi Minh City, we decided to see a bit of Phnom Penh. As we often do, we went out to the taxi stand to find an English-speaking driver. "We have three hours here," we told him. "Can we hire you to show us the city?"

We struck a deal, and we bonded as he drove us, pointing out the sights. Then, to our amazement, he invited us to his home.

It was one of a few small houses on the banks of a river. All stood on stilts a full story above the ground. "The water . . ." he explained, meaning that the river flooded.

He gestured for us to follow him up a sturdy ladder into the house. Inside was one big room, with a mattress on the floor and colorful cushions for seating. There was no kitchen (cooking was done under the house, on the ground), no electricity, no running water. But it didn't need amenities to feel comfortable and homey.

Welcoming us warmly, the driver's wife and children served tea, as we sat together, communicating with smiles and spotty English. The driver beamed with pride: pride in his handsome family; pride in his snug home, perched high above the water; maybe even pride at sharing the weird phenomenon—two older women traveling alone, from a far-off land—that he'd encountered on the job.

"Weren't you afraid to enter a stranger's home?" people ask us. We'd calculated the risks and decided, since we were in public and in daylight, that they were minimal. The driver, too, had taken a risk by inviting us over, Americans who might not respect—or might even disdain—his way of life.

People are so scared to step outside their comfort zones. We hear it so often, even from friends: "Oh, if only I could travel (or volunteer, or whatever) the way you do, but I just can't." If our comfort zones are that restrictive, it keeps our lives pinched and narrow. It's experience that makes us stretch and grow.

By the time we disembarked in Saigon from our thirteen-hour bus ride, crammed in among parcels and chickens, we were definitely up for some pampering. Luckily, we'd booked ourselves into the legendary Rex Hotel, whose reasonable pricing—fifty-five dollars per night, only a titch above our budget—pleased us, especially after we got a free upgrade to a suite. An imposing white, six-story landmark, it was an American armed forces center during the Vietnam War and used for daily press briefings, which were known as the Five O'Clock Follies. Its Rooftop Garden Bar was a famous hangout for military officials and international war correspondents.

We'd found a local travel agent online to help us make plans to tour the city. When we showed up at the agent's offices to get our itinerary that next day, they presented us with bikes—regular two-wheel pedal bicycles, the kind we rode as kids.

We stopped to think a moment and consider what we'd seen of Saigon so far. At any given moment, at least half the city's population of nine million people seems to be zipping through the streets on motor scooters. What people manage to bungee cord onto scooters is dazzling—multiple cartons the size of air conditioners, crates of produce, bales of hay, bolts of fabric; you name it. It's not unusual to see a huge bundle moving down the street, with only the wheels of the scooter visible below it. You often see an entire family on a single scooter—father, mother, and a child or two. For a pedestrian, crossing the street against the torrent of whizzing scooters is terrifying. "Sorry, no bikes for us," we had to say. We're usually game for anything, but biking in this whirlwind seemed crazy!

Still, we enjoyed walking the city. We loved the old market, featuring food, housewares, crafts, and more, just three blocks from the hotel. "We don't go to markets looking for food, but to experience the sight of food," as Ellie likes to say. For us, visiting markets is like peering through a window into local culture—the rhythms of public life, the color and spectacle of the displays.

We aren't souvenir hounds, exactly, but we pick up trinkets as keepsakes and gifts. For Ellie, the draw is handcrafted jewelry, usually unlike any we'd ever see in the States. "I like the big, bold, junky pieces," she says, "especially bracelets. But I've also scored some real finds, like genuine turquoise, at rock-bottom prices."

"I don't do jewelry," Sandy says, "because, for years, I assisted with surgeries. You can't wear rings and things under surgical gloves. So, I go for souvenirs like chopsticks in decorative cases, unusual placemats, and, sometimes, cookbooks. Back home, I pick recipes from them to cook for parties, which is really fun."

AFTER POKING AROUND SAIGON, WE TOOK A TWO-DAY DETOUR TO THE Mekong Delta. It's a fifteen-thousand-square-mile jumble of waterways, floodplains, and islands, where the Mekong River—one of Asia's longest, flowing through six countries—splits into branches and empties into the South China Sea. Some 22 million people inhabit the Mekong Delta, and their lives revolve around the water, with many villages accessible by rivers and canals instead of roads.

Our trip to the Delta began with a drive through rice fields that stretched to the horizon like a plush green carpet. The region is called the "rice bowl" of Vietnam because it yields more than half of the nation's staple food. At the river's edge, we boarded a boat for Binh Hoa Phuoc, a charming tropical island famed for its orchards. There, our guide steered us down a riverbank path alongside homes—

most on stilts—where people were going about daily life: cooking, fishing, tending vegetable gardens. Most stopped to smile and wave, and some even offered us fruit from their own trees. We were so touched by their welcome.

Then our guide asked, "Do you want to see how we make rice noodles?"

We sure did! He took us not to a shop or a factory but to an ordinary village home. The guide explained that since so many dishes—like pho, the famous soup—are based on noodles, lots of families dedicated a special place in the house to noodle production. We were fascinated by the process: forming a dough from rice flour, kneading it until elastic, cutting it into strands, then stretching loops of strands by hand until they grow thin and maybe ten feet long. Clearly, noodle-making takes real skill and plenty of practice.

Our next stop was what looked like a small house at the water's edge that was surrounded by a beautiful bonsai garden. It was actually a restaurant, and we were its only guests. As we sat overlooking the river, the proprietors brought out a foot-long elephant fish—whole, head and all—upright in a rack, as if it were swimming. For a moment we just sat there, thinking, "Oh no!" as each of us stared into one of its cloudy eyes.

When the servers returned with condiments and plates of cucumber, lettuce, and mint, they looked at us quizzically, as if to say, "Oh, aren't you going to eat?"

Smiling, we grabbed our chopsticks and screwed up our nerve—and were glad we did! Somehow, we grasped that we each should tackle our own side of the fish, rolling up the tender pieces with greens in rice paper wrappers, then dipping our rolls in the sauces. "This is just delicious," Sandy said. "And the bones stay behind in the rack. It's really the perfect way to eat fish."

Seeing our pleasure, our hosts beamed with pride. "It was a lesson," Ellie says. "When people see you relish the things they like, it makes them happy. It creates a bond. There are times when you just have to relax and engage with a new experience. This was one of those times.

> **When people see you relish the things they like, it makes them happy. It creates a bond.**

"Think about okra, which we love in the South. Some people think it's slimy and the idea of eating it freaks them out. But fried, it's just fantastic. You really miss out if you don't give it a chance."

After lunch, our guide suggested a rowboat ride. The job looked strenuous, so we were impressed to see some female rowers among the men. Naturally, we chose a woman's boat and set off down the river, all of us shielded from the sun in our conical hats.

We hadn't gone far when our rower, with smiles and gestures, indicated that it was our turn to take up paddling. "I was shooting pictures," Ellie says, "so it fell to Sandy to do the honors."

"Yes, that was a good excuse!" Sandy says.

Sandy took the long pole, with paddle-shaped ends, plunging each end into the water, as the rower had, on alternate sides of the boat. "Whoa," she said. "This is harder than it looks."

The nose of the boat veered wildly, heading into a spin. As Sandy tried to course correct, we wound up barreling straight for the shoreline's tangled vines.

"Look out!" Ellie shouted. "Don't run aground!" We were both helplessly cackling.

Sandy took some more bold swipes with the pole, sending the boat shooting out into the current. Luckily, there were no other boats nearby to crash into us.

Finally, the rower took back the pole, and we all relaxed, giggling with relief.

"Well, that was fun," Sandy said.

"Later I consoled her by showing her a photo," Ellie says, "and telling her, 'See how good you looked rowing.'"

As part of our package deal, we spent that night at the lovely Victoria Resort in Can Tho, the largest city in the Mekong Delta proper. In the morning, we awoke before dawn to see and photograph the sampans, or flat-bottom boats, many with fin-shaped sails, out on the river, silhouetted against the sunrise. "I was thrilled about this part of the trip," Ellie says. "We'd had a glimpse of life on the water on the Tonle Sap, but the floating world of the Mekong Delta is legendary. I'd always wanted to see and experience it."

We embarked on our own sampan and pushed out into the river. Though it was still early, hundreds of boats had already assembled

ELEANOR HAMBY & DR. SANDRA HAZELIP

in a riot of activity and color. For generations, boats large and small have gathered in these floating markets—there are many on the Delta—to hawk everything from fresh produce, seafood, and rice to fishing nets, housewares, machetes, building materials, and electronics. There were even boats zipping around peddling Vietnamese breakfasts (usually soup) and snacks to the sellers and shoppers.

Our boat plunged into the fray, weaving in and out of the vendors' sampans. Some had their wares displayed on poles. Others, hoping to entice us, held up products as we passed. One boat was manned by a child, surely no more than four or five, who offered us bunches of bananas and sodas in cans. It was a marvelous, vibrant scene of industry and high energy—and we enjoyed every minute of it.

The only flaw in our perfect day was the knowledge that we'd be heading home the next morning, leaving behind the warmth and color of Southeast Asia. Having grown up in the shadow of the Vietnam War, which embroiled Americans from the early 1960s to 1975, we were a little surprised at how enthusiastically we were welcomed in both Cambodia and Vietnam. Yet surely, many there still bear the cruel scars of that war, just as so many of our veteran friends do at home.

But our Southeast Asian hosts were willing to see us not as related to a decades-old enemy but as fellow human beings eager to experience and honor their culture. Engaging face-to-face, with openness and genuine esteem, can be a healing balm in our troubled world.

Once Ellie was asked, "How come you travel to all these places? Why, you can see the pyramids in Las Vegas!"

Of course, a replica can't begin to inspire the same awe as an ancient edifice. But as magnificent as these structures are—and how we marvel at the ingenuity of their builders—they don't stay top of mind when we get home. What sticks most with us from our travels are the personal encounters, the vivid moments of meaningful connection. Our memories of people are the ones we mentally replay and the ones that we cherish longest.

5

HONOR YOUR ANGELS

The idea for our 2011 trip took hold, as it often does for us, with the dream of a fabled train. The Hejaz Railway, envisaged as a crowning glory of the Ottoman Empire, was originally planned to stretch from Istanbul, Turkey, to Mecca, Saudi Arabia, Islam's most sacred city and the endpoint of the Hajj, the annual pilgrimage. Construction began in 1900, but by the outbreak of World War I in 1914, only the span from Damascus, Syria, to Medina, Saudi Arabia, had been completed.

Then, the railway became a target, attacked by everyone from Lawrence of Arabia to the bombers of Britain's Royal Air Force. Later conflicts, including World War II, wreaked more havoc. In the twenty-first century, what remained of the line was revived as a tourist train using the original Hejaz steam engine and hundred-year-old wooden passenger cars. A restored antique train was our kind of transport, even if the journey took fifteen hours (five times longer than the same distance by modern bus).

Sadly, though, the tracks in Syria were so damaged that the restored train was more a curiosity than a working rail line. But the research got us enthralled and eager to explore the Middle East as our next adventure.

We'd be halfway there anyway. Ellie would be leaving Zambia in late February 2011, just when Sandy would be en route to do mission work in Romania. So, after a brief detour to visit her grandson Caleb in Oxford, England, Ellie could easily join Sandy in Bucharest, Romania. From Bucharest we could begin our Middle Eastern trip by taking the Bosphorus Express train through Bulgaria to Istanbul. As usual, we booked a second-class sleeper and lucked out, getting a compartment designed for four entirely to ourselves. We both got to sleep on lower berths—no climbing—and could stash our luggage on the overhead bunks.

Around 2 a.m., the train stopped at the Bulgarian-Turkish border, where we had to disembark for passport control. The night was pitch-black, relieved only by a faint light emanating from the blocky station. At our train car door, there was no platform, no ladder, no stepstool—just a sheer drop to the tracks, which were shrouded in darkness.

"Oh dear," Sandy said. "How do we get down?"

Being tall, Ellie swung her legs out, landing with a light leap. But Sandy, short-legged, was stuck.

Just then, an older man materialized in the dimness. His head barely reached the level of the open door. He stretched out his arms and, with a few soothing words, egged Sandy into action. She jumped out—straight into his open arms!

"Sandy literally flew into the darkness," Ellie says. "I wish I'd snapped a picture."

"I had no choice," Sandy says. "He caught me under the arms, thank goodness, and set me gently on the ground."

That was our first brush with the sort of guardian angels who would guide us through the Middle East.

Daylight dawned as our train barreled toward Istanbul, the only city in the world that is spread across two continents. We entered on the European side but would depart from a station in the Asian sector for Syria, our first destination. So, we loaded our luggage onto a ferry across the fabled Bosphorus Strait. We planned to check our bags at the Asian station so we could spend the day touring Istanbul.

At the station, the only place to stow luggage was in lockers. We off-loaded our belongings, fed the coin slot, and got a retrieval ticket. Then we set out for Aya Sofya (the name means "Divine Wisdom"), a monument of the Byzantine Empire and an evolving symbol of Turkish history.

A cathedral consecrated by Emperor Justinian I in 537 AD, Aya Sofya (once Hagia Sophia) was the spiritual heart of Eastern Ortho-dox Christianity for nearly a thousand years. When the city (then called Constantinople) fell to an Ottoman invasion in 1453, the build-ing was converted to a mosque—its Christian mosaics plastered over and four minarets added to its campus. Then, when Turkey became a secular republic in 1928 with an amendment to its still-new constitu-tion, the mosque became a museum. It was a museum when we visited in 2011, but in 2020, it became a mosque once again.

We loved learning Aya Sofya's rich history and were awed by its magnificence. Its central dome rises 185 feet above the floor and rests on a base of forty arched windows. Many of the original mosaics and paintings were restored in this century, including images of six-winged angels guarding God's throne. The painstaking work has been a balancing act: to preserve iconic works of both Christian and Islamic art.

We were equally struck by the Blue Mosque, a marvel of Ottoman architecture. After visiting these sacred sites, we headed down Istiklal Avenue, considered the grandest street in Istanbul. On both sides, it's lined with historic buildings of every era from neoclassical and neo-Gothic to art nouveau and art deco. Lively street life and colorful historic trams add to its charm. Naturally, Ellie, the photographer, was enthralled.

Ellie was standing there shooting pictures when suddenly a man lunged at her, yanking her nearly off her feet. "Help!" Sandy cried out. Just then, the tram whooshed by. Ellie had planted herself, oblivious, smack in the middle of the tracks and had barely escaped being mowed down.

Breathless, we clutched at each other, shocked by the close call. Then the man who'd grabbed Ellie approached us to say, in English, "I just saved your life, so I think you should eat at my restaurant."

Laughing in relief, we agreed. We followed him to a nearby building and up the stairs to a roof garden café, where we enjoyed a delicious Turkish meal. Another guardian angel—and one who cooked. Who could ask for more?

It was now late—time to head to the station to make our train. At the luggage locker, we inserted our ticket, only to get the message that more money was owed. Frustrated, we pushed more coins into the slot, but the door remained locked.

"Can you help us?" we asked a young man who was unloading luggage from his own locker. Seemingly, he had the touch. He took our ticket and tried to insert it, banging on the door as it kept spitting the ticket back out. Finally, he shrugged and had to give up. Handing us back the ticket, he dashed off to catch his train.

We again tried to insert the ticket, but this time, it didn't register at all. We realized then, with horror, that we were holding his used ticket. Ours was gone, forever, in the hand of our would-be helper.

We were stuck, out of luck. No one we stopped could understand us. "Let's not panic," Sandy said. "We'll board the train, and then in Syria, we can just . . . replace all our stuff. It's no great loss."

We travel light, but we were demoralized by the thought of going on with nothing.

Then Ellie spotted a little café and said, "Maybe someone there can help us."

At the door, Sandy called out, "Does anyone here speak English?"

A distinguished gentleman in a suit and tie—another guardian angel!—stood up.

He accompanied us out into the station, where he explained our predicament to an attendant. While the attendant made phone calls, our angel introduced himself, telling us about his son, who lived in the States. Mercifully, our train was delayed, so we returned with him to the café—"Please, let me treat you to some snacks," he insisted—while awaiting word from the locker company.

"I want you to meet my wife," the man said. He actually called her to join us, saying, "Come out and see my two new American friends, who are so nice."

She begged off, claiming that her hair was a mess and that she had nothing suitable to wear to meet us. If only she could have seen how sloppy and frazzled we looked! But his wish to introduce us touched our hearts.

Finally, the attendant summoned us to return to the lockers. There we stood until we heard a *ding, ding!* and the door popped open! At last!

Collecting our luggage, we bade a heartfelt goodbye to our guardian angel—our third rescuer in a brief span of time. Normally, when we picture our guardian angels, we don't see robes, halos, and wings but the images of our beloved husbands watching over us. Though we're eternal optimists, confident that we can muddle through any chancy situation, feeling that our watchers are on high alert has been a comfort.

But in the Middle East, more than in other places we've traveled, we were blessed with the help of real, flesh-and-blood guardian angels whenever we hit a brick wall (or even faced real peril). Sandy's "catcher" in Bulgaria, Ellie's savior in Istanbul, and the man at the locker were just the beginning—there were more to come. Sometimes we had no idea that unseen hands—or whose benevolent hands—were pulling strings for us.

The generosity of spirit and guidance we experienced felt like ingrained kindliness, reflecting a Muslim parallel to our Christian commandment "Love Thy Neighbor": "Do good—to parents, kinsfolk, orphans, those in need, neighbors who are near, neighbors who are strangers, the companion by your side, the wayfarer (ye meet)" (The Holy Qur'an, al-Nisaa 4:36).

WE'D HOPED TO TAKE THE TRAIN FROM ISTANBUL TO ALEPPO, SYRIA, but the tracks didn't stretch that far. As usual, we didn't "sweat the small stuff." Knowing that we couldn't be the only people who wanted to travel this route, we assumed that, at the end of the line in Adana, Turkey, we'd be able to find whatever means of transportation was available.

We were booked into the Hotel Bosnali, a charming nineteenth-century mansion-turned-guesthouse, with airy wood-paneled and -ceilinged rooms, precious antiques in the common areas, and a rooftop offering stunning views of the Seyhan River and the city. One of the most dramatic sights was the Sabanci Mosque, with a lofty dome and six minarets that were lit up at night. The same view from the nearby Hilton cost $250 per night. Our room was a fifth of the price!

We asked our hosts at the hotel about traveling to Aleppo. "No problem," they assured us. "You can take the bus."

But they cautioned us that it wouldn't be easy. "You can't get to Aleppo in one day," we were told. "The bus reaches Antakya"—the connection point—"too late to transfer, so you'll have to spend the night."

"Shoot!" Ellie said softly. Though we loved Turkey, we hated to postpone our eagerly awaited trip to Syria and Jordan another day. But we thanked them and smiled sweetly, half resigned and half scheming how to beat the delay. (Would a taxi in Antakya take us to Aleppo? Could we save both a hotel bill and time?)

The next morning, we caught the bus, determined to enjoy whatever happened. We were the only tourists, but this time, none of the other passengers brought chickens. We managed to get our favorite seats, right up front.

The bus driver's cell phone rang, and he began chatting in Turkish. Then he turned around and called out, "Sandy?"

Sandy raised her hand and anxiously squeaked, "Yes?"

The driver reached back and handed her his phone. A male voice on the line asked, "Do you want to go to Aleppo, Syria?"

"I couldn't speak till Ellie poked me, nodding," Sandy says. "Then—a little too loudly—I told him, 'Yes.'"

"Twelve o'clock," the mystery man intoned. And—*click!*—he hung up.

"Sandy looked so flummoxed on the phone that I snapped her photo," Ellie says. "Then I asked her, 'Who was that?'"

We spent the rest of the trip wondering what on earth would transpire at noon, when the bus arrived at the Antakya station. As we pulled in, we saw a man waiting there, wearing an official-looking badge.

"Sandy and Ellie?" he hollered when the doors opened. Collecting our luggage, he led us to a nearby bus, with its motor idling, and hefted our bags into its belly. Then he motioned for us to board. Only two seats were empty. We had no tickets, no reservations, but the bus to Syria had delayed its departure—we later learned—just to wait for us.

Why?

Had the staff at the Hotel Bosnali picked up on our disappointment? We'd barely expressed it out loud. Did they have the power to change a bus schedule? Had the bus station clerk, who'd seemed merely businesslike, decided to "do good" for two grandmotherly American travelers? And who had called us on the driver's phone?

To this day, we don't know. We never will. We could only attribute our good fortune to guardian angels.

We expressed heartfelt gratitude to everyone in sight—the man with the badge, the bus driver, and especially our fellow passengers, who to our amazement seemed completely unruffled by the holdup.

"No way this could happen back home," Ellie whispered. "The passengers would go nuts."

During the trip, we got to know some of those passengers, most of whom were all young men. One was a young Iranian, who was eager for our take on his language skills. "I've never spoken to an American," he said. "How's my English? Is it any good?"

"More than good—it's excellent!" we were pleased to tell him. He'd been in Istanbul studying for his PhD in architecture. He offered us a fascinating global perspective on Americans. "Americans view the people of a country and its government as one," he said. "You don't like the people if you don't like the government. But the rest of the world sees the people and the government as two. We don't like your government, but we love Americans."

That not only struck us as generous and wise, it comported closely with our own travel philosophy. We've come to believe that conversation can heal the world, as an affirmation of what we share as human beings.

> **We've come to believe that conversation can heal the world, as an affirmation of what we share as human beings.**

6

TRUST IN GOD, BUT
TIE UP YOUR CAMEL

At the Syrian border, all of us were ordered to disembark. We followed the other passengers to the customs office. *Thwack, thwack*—the papers of those ahead of us were quickly stamped, but because of our American passports, we were pulled out of line. Since we'd gotten our visas back home, we knew they were valid. So, what was the problem? No one could explain, though an official who spoke a little English counseled us, "One must always smile when entering Syria."

Funny—Keep Smiling was one of our mottoes. So, with huge grins on our faces, we did our best to follow directions as, with barked Arabic commands, we were waved from window to window.

That's when our Iranian friend sprang into action. Collecting our documents, he literally walked us through the process, talking to clerks, checking the masses of photocopies thrust upon us, helping us field endless questions. "I doubt that we could have run that gauntlet without him," Ellie says. It took two or three hours for us to get our stamped passports and be on our way.

Of course, we wanted to reward our heroic friend, but he waved us off, like our locker angel in Turkey who'd declined to let us share the café check. We were learning that, in this part of the world, helping strangers is a reflex.

We returned to the bus, sheepish and apologetic for yet again delaying its departure. Again, to our surprise, our companions hadn't been fuming but were patiently waiting. When we boarded, they burst into applause!

Soon, though, we'd be leaving these kind passengers behind. Our current bus was headed to Damascus, so we'd have to transfer to reach Aleppo. As the driver pulled off the road, we wondered if this was another mysterious, unseen-hands connection. But, no, our previous driver had arranged the meet up—and there was our next bus, a fancy Mercedes forty-seater waiting just for us.

Literally just for us—we were the only passengers aboard. We felt like queens of the desert.

But it didn't take long for our crowns to slip. We heard grating mechanical sounds, and the bus wheezed to a stop. We all got out, and the driver set off into a field. "What's he up to?" Sandy wondered.

After years in Zambia, we could guess—and were proven right when he returned brandishing a length of baling wire. Around the world, baling wire and duct tape seem to be the cure for engine trouble. Sure enough, while we enjoyed the coffee and cookies he kindly shared, he worked some magic with the wire and got the motor running. Though the bus would suffer a few more breakdowns, we managed to limp into Aleppo by late afternoon.

Our mechanic/driver dropped us off smack in the middle of the city. "Now what?" Ellie said, as we searched for a taxi. Then Sandy spotted some men passing by wearing Sheraton Hotel badges. "They'll be able to help us," she said; and indeed, they spoke perfect English and easily hailed us a cab.

OUR DESTINATION WAS THE ANCIENT AL-MADINA SOUQ, THE LARGEST historic covered market in the world. Its oldest section was built in the fifteenth century, and from there it mushroomed into an assemblage of mini-markets—we'll mention some estimates of its specialized vendors to illustrate the Souq's scale—offering shoes (eighty-four vendors); traditional handicrafts; fur (seventy-seven vendors); silk (forty-three vendors), wool, cotton, and other textiles (more than a hundred vendors), as well as tailoring (fifty-nine workshops); leather (forty-eight vendors); jewelry (ninety-nine vendors in two separate alleys); foodstuff and herbs; metalwork—and much more. There was a special women's market with stalls full of bridal gear and one dedicated to the famous Aleppo soap, which is said to be the world's oldest, made of olive and laurel oils.

At various times, trading partners like Venice and Belgium had embassies within the Souq's walls. The British consulate was housed there until the early twentieth century. The Souq's layout is a vast maze of narrow streets and branching alleyways that stretches approximately eight miles.

Somewhere in that labyrinth lay our goal, the Dar Halabia Hotel.

Standing at one of the Souq's timeworn gates, we had no idea which way to go. The stalls were shutting down for the day, so shoppers were scarce. Luckily, an older man pushing a dolly came to our aid. After we showed him the hotel's name written in Arabic, he urged us, in sign language, to drop our luggage on his dolly, and off we went.

Twisting and turning through the stone-walled passages, we finally came to a dead end, where a wooden double door, with decorative inlays, marked our hotel. Inside was an open, two-story courtyard hung with ornate metal lanterns, ringed by sixteen guest rooms. We loved it.

The next morning, we enjoyed a buffet breakfast in the courtyard, featuring figs and other fruits, olives, hummus, cheese, and pita bread. Before going out, we draped our hair with long scarves, in deference to the conservative culture of Aleppo. Most women there wear traditional abayas, or long, often lavishly embroidered robes, with hijabs or veils that leave only the face showing, or even niqabs, which conceal all but the wearer's eyes.

We were told we didn't have to cover up—that Syrians were used to bareheaded Westerners—but it was a small gesture, costing us nothing, that we hoped might mean a lot to those we met. Honoring the culture of others is a prerequisite for friendship. To bridge the gap between people, you need that respect.

> **Honoring the culture of others is a prerequisite for friendship. To bridge the gap between people, you need that respect.**

Then we plunged again into the Souq. The night before, we'd been too anxious to pay close attention, but now we marveled at the beauty of its construction. It was like a rough-hewn cathedral, with a high, vaulted ceiling of small rocks mortared together, surely by hand. Beneath our feet was a floor of brick-sized paving stones worn smooth by centuries of walkers. We could almost feel their spirits echoing in our footsteps.

The stalls erupted with sensory delights—the pungent aromas of spices and teas, the air sugared by sticky sweets on our lips, the constant chatter of evaluation and haggling, the silky feel of fabrics we ran through our fingers. Sandy couldn't resist buying a glorious floor-length black dress shot through with threads of gold and scarlet. "It wasn't exactly everyday Texas attire," she says. "But it was gorgeous. I wore it to play Queen Esther at a church pageant."

Ellie loved the jewelry. "I got a beautiful ring, with some semi-precious stones," she says. "Or maybe they were colored glass—who knows? It was only about twenty-five dollars, but when I wear it, people ooh and ahh."

One thing that shocked us was the lingerie, sold not just in the women's market but throughout the Souq. In a country so modest that women don't even reveal their arms, it was jarring to see lacy pushup bras, thongs, and other seductive underthings so openly displayed. "It's not that we were shocked that women wore them," Sandy says. "It's just that, considering the restrictions on women's dress, we'd have expected the sellers to keep them under wraps."

Ellie agrees. "A few years later, I got a closer look at that contradiction when visiting my daughter, Sheryl, who was teaching in Saudi

Arabia. We went out on a boat to snorkel with about thirty-five other people, mostly Saudis. All of us women were in abayas. We'd been cruising for an hour when one of the deckhands announced, 'We are now in international waters. Women, you may remove your abayas.'

"We flung them off. Some of the women were in burkinis— either full-length dresses or tunics and leggings—complete with little turbans to replace their hijabs. Others, who'd looked just as pious, went bareheaded in bikinis as skimpy as any you'd see on an American beach.

"We snorkeled, we frolicked in the water, and then, when we were back on the boat, the warning came: 'Women, we are back in Saudi Arabia.' Everyone scrambled to put on their abayas and hijabs, as if they'd never undressed.

"The way women in the Middle East juggle freedom and constraint is too complex and culturally encoded for Westerners to readily understand, never mind judge."

We could have spent days in the Souq, just poking through all the markets, but we wanted to see more of the ancient city of Aleppo. Our next stop was the Citadel, one of the world's oldest castles, which dates back almost five thousand years, to the third millennium BC.

Occupying a limestone ridge rising a hundred feet above the city, the Citadel was expanded, over time, into an oval-shaped fortress by each new ruler of Aleppo—Hittites, Assyrians, Arabs, Mongols, Mamelukes, and Ottomans. On the outside, it's a blocky medieval behemoth with crenellated walls. Inside, the architecture of the different royal residences, bathhouses, and mosques—as well as the stone carvings on its gates and walls—forms a living time-line of its history. From the top of the Citadel, we could see Aleppo sprawled out below us.

While we were touring the Citadel, an older Arab gentleman approached us, dressed traditionally in a black thobe, or robe, with a white headscarf secured by a black band. "Hello," he said in En-glish. "Do you like our city?"

"Oh yes," we told him, mentioning our time in the Souq. But as we talked, he began to focus ever more intently on Sandy—as if he was developing a little crush.

Suddenly, he blurted out, "Will you marry me?"

Sandy was startled but quickly recovered. Smiling sweetly, she told him, "Thank you for asking, but no thanks."

Sandy's suitor accepted her refusal with a good-natured laugh.

Even in our short time in Aleppo, we'd come to love it—not just because of its magical Souq but because of its old soul, its mystical, visible history stretching to biblical times and beyond. In retro-spect, we feel deeply grateful to have stopped there because, unbe-knownst to us, the clouds of war were gathering—an uprising against repression, then a brutal civil war—and many of Aleppo's manifes-tations of the fabled past would be destroyed.

THE NEXT DAY WE ARRIVED AT THE BUS STATION TO TRAVEL TO OUR next destination, Damascus. To our consternation, every sign was written in Arabic. Leave it to Ellie to come up with a solution:

"Let's stand in the middle of the station," she said. "I'll yell 'Damascus'—I have the loudest voice in the world—and we'll see what happens."

Within moments, a man came running up to us and asked, "Now?"

"Yes!" we replied, and he led us to a bus that was ready to pull out.

It was a journey of four-plus hours, through all kinds of terrain, from fertile farmland to stark desert with snow-capped mountains in the distance. We saw shepherds grazing flocks of fat, fluffy sheep. The cost for each of us was only four dollars.

In Damascus we had another language glitch, this one our fault. We had the name of our hotel written in English, not Arabic. Our taxi driver couldn't read it, so we all stood in the street trying to find an English speaker to help. A woman emerged from a nearby cab dressed in a tailored business suit. She was the first Syrian woman we'd seen traveling alone—not with a husband or male relative, as required in more religious areas—and wearing Western dress without even a hijab.

The woman, who spoke excellent English, quickly solved our problem, and we were on our way to the Orient Palace Hotel.

We'd chosen it because it overlooked the grand old Hejaz train station, the starting point of the historic rail line that inspired our trip. Though no longer operational, the station was still a marvel, with a palatial exterior and, inside, a soaring, decorated ceiling, a floor of diamond-shaped tiles, and huge stained-glass windows to let in light.

There was no internet service at our hotel, so after checking in, we headed down the block to an internet café. Even to send a simple email we had to follow stringent rules—we had to apply to use the internet, via a complicated form, and once approved, surrender our passports to the person working at the café. It was our first brush with the authoritarian Bashar al-Assad regime.

While we were writing to our families, some men burst into the café, talking loudly in Arabic. Sandy, being a doctor, thought that there might be an emergency outside. "Is there a problem?" she said. "Can I help?"

Instantly the men fell silent. They studied us for a moment, then looked at one another. Finally, one of them, in the best English he could muster, told us, "No, no, there is no problem. Everything is just fine."

In retrospect, their hesitation is telling, but in the moment we smiled and assumed the best. The clouds of war were gathering thick and fast . . .

By the time we reclaimed our passports, darkness had fallen, so stores were closing, but we spotted one lighted doorway. It was a bookstore, with a charming proprietor, who invited us in for a cup of tea. Tea is the foundation of Middle Eastern hospitality, and we've learned that to refuse it is to reject a proffered relationship. Our high-pressure, twenty-first-century Western society could learn a lot from a culture so attuned to connection that it prizes welcome over efficient transactions and saving time.

Of course, we accepted the invitation.

Over tea, we chatted with the proprietor about books and life in our respective countries. We scanned the shelves, which were lined with books in Arabic. "Do you have any in English?" we asked.

At first, he said no, but then he rose and pulled out some volumes.

Hidden behind them were two English titles, *The Citadel of Aleppo* and *Damascus Arts and Reigns.* Delighted by his find, we bought them both and cherish them to this day.

Back at the hotel, we booked a cab for the next morning so we could catch a bus to Palmyra, the preserved ruins of a desert city dating to the second millennium BC. We'd deliberately planned our departure to avoid being stuck in Damascus on a Friday, when everything would be closed for Muslim weekly prayers.

But en route to the bus station we wanted the taxi to drive us down Straight Street. In the New Testament, it's named as the site where Saul of Tarsus embraced Christianity and became Paul the Apostle, the author of the Epistles.

How thrilling that we could actually see such a major biblical setting! But the hotel clerk didn't share our excitement. "I'll arrange it with the taxi," he said, "as long as you go early." Looking back, it's obvious that he knew conflict was brewing.

On Friday morning, all the shops on Straight Street were closed for prayer. But the streets were full of men, milling around, talking in groups. And there was a tension there so thick we could almost feel our skin prickling. Ellie whipped out her camera and snapped a photo as we passed. We later learned that a Western tourist who'd taken a similar shot that afternoon was arrested and imprisoned in Syria for several months.

In the bus station, being foreigners, we had to jump through hoops—registering in a separate building and awaiting permission before going to the window to buy a ticket. Behind Sandy in the ticket line was a Bedouin man in a colorful checkered headdress.

Drawn by his garb and striking features, Ellie lifted her camera and shot a picture. Suddenly, the whole room snapped to attention. All eyes were on us as a furious man demanded, "Why did you take that photo?"

Ellie was shocked. Fumbling with the camera, she showed the man the image of the Bedouin with Sandy standing, slightly blurred, in the foreground. "I was just taking a picture of my friend," she said.

Luckily, he believed her. By now we could tell that trouble was in the air. But, unable to speak the language, having internet access only in cafés, and being assured by locals reluctant to scare off tourists that everything was "just fine," we couldn't imagine what was up.

With a deep sense of foreboding, we boarded our bus to Palmyra. "About an hour out of Damascus," Ellie says, "I started brooding. I'd been photographing people, peering at their faces. Fear and anxiety were etched on every one. That—combined with the mood in the internet café, the tension on Straight Street, and the harsh reaction when I snapped the photo in the station—made me wonder if getting on this bus was a mistake. Were we heading into danger that we didn't understand?

"I glanced at Sandy, who was staring out the window at a road sign, reading 'Palmyra' and 'Baghdad,' with arrows pointing straight ahead. I could sense that she shared my trepidation."

Were we that close to Baghdad—the capital of Iraq, where American troops were still on the ground, at war? We looked at each other, thinking, "Are we out of our minds? What on earth are we doing here?" But there was no way out in this desolate land-scape. All we could do was keep going.

MERCIFULLY, OUR FEARS EASED SOMEWHAT WHEN WE REACHED PAL-myra. As soon as we disembarked, some men standing in a cluster of parked cars came running over to greet us. "Hello! Where are you from?"

When we told them, they raised their wide-open arms, in an air embrace. "Americans, Americans!" they said. "You are welcome in our country!"

We've never been so well received anywhere—not even in Texas!

"Where are you going?" they asked.

We showed them the name, Al-Nakheel—written in Arabic this time—and one said, "That's where I work. Come with me."

We'd discovered the place through pure serendipity. Reading about Palmyra, Ellie had come across a small notice, reading (roughly): "In Palmyra, if you want to stay in a Bedouin tent, non-touristy, contact Mohammed," with an email address. She'd written him with our dates and gotten the answer: "No problem. Plus, I have a small hotel where you can stay."

The Al-Nakheel had just fourteen rooms and was decorated, Bedouin style, with colorful carpets and tasseled hangings on every wall. Before we could even drop our bags in our cozy room, our host, Mohammed, invited us to have tea. "It's tradition," he said. "We have to get to know each other."

Again, we were charmed by the civility of the gesture. Besides, since we were slated to spend that first night in a desert tent, we wanted to get an idea of what to expect.

We spent the next hour in the lobby with Mohammed sipping tea and talking about our lives. A good-looking man with a red-and-white-checked scarf tied around his head like a cap, he told us about his family and his Scandinavian girlfriend. Then he took us to the shelter where some camels were tethered. They would be our mode of transportation in the desert.

After dumping our luggage, we were—more or less—ready for our camel ride. The tent where we'd spend the night was about three hours away.

Sandy, who'd never been on a camel, eyed them nervously. Long-legged Ellie, an experienced horsewoman, climbed up easily, but short Sandy had to be lifted by Mohammed and Abdul, his cousin, into the small saddle, perched over blankets, on the camel's hump. Asim, a teenage boy, would be our guide, leading our camels out to the desert camp.

Asim, who spoke no English, delivered the perfect valediction: "Goodbye, Palmyra. Hello, Bedouin."

Then we were off. Before long, Sandy began calling out, "Hello? Hello?" Turning around, Ellie saw her face twisted in a grimace. She looked terrified.

Clearly, she was having trouble sitting on the camel without stirrups or a saddle horn to clutch. "I was up so high above the ground, and that bumpy gait," Sandy says. "I was struggling hard not to slip off."

Pointing to herself and then to the ground, she made Asim

understand that she wanted to get down. He had the camel kneel and then helped Sandy slide to the ground. "I'll just walk," she announced. "That'll be easier." Mercifully, it was not dangerously scorching, but it was hot.

Sandy's camel, now tethered to Ellie's, seemed peeved by the rejection. He kept nipping at Ellie's legs and saddle blankets as if trying to dislodge her. On foot, Sandy trailed the two camels on a travelers' path worn in the sand.

We passed small tents that housed entire Bedouin families and shepherds tending flocks of goats and sheep. At one point, Sandy got entangled in a swirl of large sheep and had to be rescued again by Asim. Ellie shot photo after photo from her camelback perch.

Finally, we reached the small, patched tent of our host family. The mother and three young children were sitting outside. Behind their tent was a larger, newer one, meant for us, with plush carpets on the floor, cushions to sit and sleep on, some decorative pots and pitchers, and a small wood-burning stove. Though more comfortable than the family's tent, which slept five, it was, as Mohammed's ad had promised, definitely "not touristy." The "bathroom" was an outhouse a little farther out in the desert, and, of course, there was no running water.

After Asim left to take the camels back to the hotel, the father of our host family, trailed by the others, came to our tent with a pot of tea. Since none of them spoke English, we all just sipped and smiled until Sandy thought of a way to break the ice. She started singing "Itsy Bitsy Spider," doing the hand gestures—climbing up the spout, rain washing the spider out, the sun coming up, and so on.

Needless to say, the children were enthralled. The father brought out a drum, which Sandy played, keeping time with her vocals. Soon, everyone was laughing and trying to carry the tune. What fun!

Night was coming, and our stomachs had just begun to rumble when Abdul, Mohammed's cousin, appeared with a sumptuous spread his mother had prepared. Our hosts had gone back to their tent. The three of us sat on the tent floor and dug into the platter of chicken with rice and vegetables, hummus, and homemade pita bread, eating the Bedouin way, with our hands.

Abdul, who spoke English well, told us about his family. "My parents had a wonderful marriage," he said. "At first, they had only girls, so everyone told my father he should take a new wife, who could give him a son. 'Why would I do that?' my father said. 'She's a beautiful woman and I love her.' Then they went on to have more children, all sons. Now I myself can't get married because my older brother is still single. I have to wait my turn."

"The life of a Bedouin must be very difficult," Sandy said, thinking of our host family, all five of them crammed into the neighboring small tent.

"Oh no," Abdul told us. "It's the most beautiful life in the world. You aren't stuck in one place but get to move around. You make your home in nature. Even my family, who live in Palmyra now, have to come out into the desert every day. It's in their blood. We aren't camping in tents—that's where we live."

When Abdul said he would spend the night with us in the tent, we were relieved. Even after our enthusiastic welcome, we still felt shaken by our experience in Damascus. Then, too, though we definitely wanted a non-tourist experience, the desert darkness and vastness seemed a little daunting. It was hard not to feel vulnerable, with no cell phone service or transportation, miles from town, in a place where we couldn't communicate in case of trouble. Having Abdul, an English speaker, with us in the tent would be a comfort.

While Abdul went to fetch his bedroll, the man of our host family brought a bale of twigs to light our stove and bring us some welcome warmth. The night had grown frigid as the full moon rose. Sandy likes to say that a full moon in a clear sky augurs cold because the clouds are God's blankets. It was true that night. And we saw a million dazzling stars.

Naturally, Ellie was up before dawn to shoot the sunrise over the desert vastness. Then, Abdul announced that he and another man would drive us back to town. No more nipping camels or three-hour walks across the desert!

IN THE CAR, THE PREVIOUS NIGHT'S CAMARADERIE VANISHED AS THE other man immediately launched into an intense discussion with Abdul. Since they were speaking Arabic, we couldn't understand the words, but their tone was clear, flooding us with unease. Something had happened. When we reached Palmyra, we rushed to an internet café to check in with our families and get the news.

The country was in revolt! We'd entered Syria on March 16, 2011, not knowing that March 15 had been a so-called Day of Rage, when pro-democracy demonstrators had marched in Aleppo and Damascus, demanding the overthrow of Bashar al-Assad. In Damascus alone, more than thirty-five protestors were arrested. That's why the men in the internet café and the bus station were so agitated.

March 18, when we left for Palmyra, had been proclaimed a "Friday of Dignity," marked by mass protests in Damascus and other cities. In the ensuing pushback, six protestors were killed. In fact, shots were fired on Straight Street just hours after we left.

These were some early salvos in the Syrian Revolution, part of the wider Arab Spring uprising against dictators in the Middle East. By July 2012, the Assad government would brutally quash it, at the cost of an estimated sixty thousand civilian lives. But the conflict didn't end. Instead, it escalated into a decade-long civil war, one of the deadliest of the twenty-first century.

At that point, we didn't know what to make of the Damascus news—whether the demonstrations were a flare-up of tensions or the start of something bigger. We decided to keep to our plans and visit the rose-gold, sandstone ruins of Palmyra.

One of the most impressive structures was the Temple of Bel, a Mesopotamian god, which was once completely ringed by colonnaded porticos. Some of the rows of massive, carved columns were still standing, along with stretches of the fortified walls protecting the temple grounds and pieces of its massive gateways. The grandeur even of those remains filled us with awe.

There were other striking structures, in varying stages of decay—a Roman amphitheater; the doorway of Baths of Diocletian, with columns four feet in diameter and forty-one feet high; other temples; a Valley of Tombs. The stones still held the glow of a lost, great civilization.

As we wandered, we saw few other visitors—so few that we felt bad for the curio sellers, who were out in force. They were obviously desperate, offering deep discounts, so we bought what we could—things like scarves and knickknacks that would be easy to carry. In the evening, we checked the news at the internet café, but what little we could find was hard to interpret.

On our second day of exploring, we connected with a knowledgeable guide. He was so welcoming and kind that, at one point, Sandy pulled him aside. "Some people say that war has broken out in Damascus. Is that true?" she asked.

His answer was troubling. "Yes, we have heard that. We don't want this war. We make our living from tourists. Without them, we can't survive."

At that point, we decided that it might be time to leave Syria—that whatever was happening was growing dire. But amid the unrest, how would we get to Jordan? Surely, we couldn't expect to catch a bus.

Over tea, we presented the question to Mohammed, our host. As always, he said, "No problem." We'd learned that, whatever came up, Mohammed could solve it. We'd come to trust him—and we had no choice.

"What will it cost?" we asked. "And, of course, we'll settle our bill. Where can we find an ATM?"

"There are no ATMs in Palmyra," he said.

"Well, can we give you a credit card?"

"We don't use credit cards in Palmyra," he told us.

Now we had a problem. Since we were leaving, we'd spent the dregs of our Syrian money on curios, and we were clean out of American dollars.

Mohammed was characteristically unfazed. The nearest ATM was hours away in the old quarter of Damascus—the site of arrests

and killings just days before. But this, he insisted, was "no problem." He had a plan.

At four the next morning, his driver—also named Mohammed—
would take us to Damascus, so we'd arrive early, before any skir-
mishes were underway. We'd give Mohammed's payment to the
driver, Mohammed II, who'd connect us with a friend who could
drive us to Jordan. The border crossing was near the city of Daraa,
where we'd learned the revolt had been triggered on March 6 by
the arrest and torture of fifteen students for writing anti-government
graffiti.

From the internet café, we wrote our families about fleeing
Syria. Ellie's daughter, Sheryl, replied, in effect, "Well, at least you
look too old to be spies. If you act like two old ladies, I bet no one
will bother you."

"Thanks a lot!" Ellie wrote back, huffy at being called old.

THAT NIGHT, MOHAMMED'S MOTHER PREPARED AND BROUGHT A FABU-
lous meal to our hotel—a lamb dish, hummus and olives, and some
delicious fried pastries. We napped and then, at four in the morning,
got into Mohammed II's car. At that hour the road was deserted
until we passed the turnoff to Baghdad, where big trucks were
rumbling ominously to and from Iraq.

A bathroom stop at the famous Bagdad Cafe 66—the only sign
of habitation in the desert vastness—lulled our anxiety. It was a
lovely old stone building with arched, paned windows, where we
loaded up on snacks. Then, it was on to Damascus!

The streets were spooky-silent at that early hour. But the

plaza in the old city, where the ATM was located, was bustling with life—military life. Soldiers armed with AK-47s lined the perimeter, and we could see pairs of guards inside the plaza patrolling the buildings.

"Stay in the car," Mohammed II told us. He got out and went over to talk to the soldiers. We watched, breathless, scrutinizing their faces for a reaction. They looked serious, guns at attention, as Mohammed II explained our situation.

Finally, one soldier broke into a smile. For the first time, he looked directly at us, then lay down his weapon. He gestured, with a wave of his arm, "Come."

The two of us jumped out of the car and sprinted toward the soldiers, with our ATM cards aloft. Would they work? We plugged in our cards, and to our great relief—we practically sobbed— money came out.

At that moment, in Eastland, Texas, halfway around the world, a banker got a ping. Someone in Damascus was trying to extract cash from a machine. Was it fraud? He knew Sandy so he tried to reach her, then phoned her daughter Dawn. "Yep, that sounds about right," Dawn told him. "That's my mother."

We gave Mohammed II the cash we owed, and more. Then, driving us to a different part of the city, Mohammed II said, "Watch for an unmarked white vehicle, parked, with its door open. That's the car that will take you to Jordan."

We soon spotted it—a white, mini-SUV—with a well-dressed man standing beside it in the street. Entering a mysterious car on the street of an embattled city, full of soldiers armed with AK-47s, was frightening, but what were our options? Clearly, we had to leave Syria, which was a tinderbox. So, after bidding farewell, with heartfelt thanks, to Mohammed II, we got in the car.

Since our driver spoke little English, he couldn't fill us in on the deepening crisis. Had we grasped the enormity of it, we would've been even more terrified. But, speeding to the border, some sixty miles away, we felt more heartsick than fearful and panicked. We could escape, but the people we'd befriended, in a country we'd come to love, were stuck there, with their livelihoods and even their very lives under threat.

We also felt grateful to be together. We each had perfect confidence in the other's steadiness and calm.

> **We each had perfect confidence in the other's steadiness and calm.**
>
> . . .
>
> **Neither of us was likely to collapse under pressure. Our shared capacity for problem-solving is a pillar of our friendship. And a great comfort.**

Sandy had done years of emergency room rotations, coping with high-stakes situations of life and death. Ellie, in her time in

Zambia, had dealt with everything from deadly reptiles to lethal contagion to arrest and robbery at gunpoint. Neither of us was likely to collapse under pressure. Our shared capacity for problem-solving is a pillar of our friendship. And a great comfort.

As we passed Daraa, we shared a solemn look. Thick, gray smoke billowed from the skyline. The city was burning—from angry insurgents? From government bombs? We didn't know.

Then we reached the border. The driver took our passports, signaling for us to stay put. We watched as he approached the officials and entered the customs station, acutely—and anxiously—aware that we had no visas to enter Jordan.

Twenty minutes passed. "What do you think is happening?" Sandy asked. She was just filling time; we had no way of knowing. Thirty minutes, then forty—would we be sent back into Syria?

Finally, after an hour, the driver emerged from the building. When we saw him smiling, we both exhaled. Back at the car, he showed us our passports, stamped with a permit to exit Syria and another to enter Jordan. Mohammed's brilliant plan had worked.

The driver delivered us to our hotel in Petra, for which we showered him with thanks and a handsome fee. But after our hair-raising flight from Syria, our arrival felt almost too anticlimactic to celebrate.

BY THE NEXT DAY, WE'D RECOVERED ENOUGH TO THINK ABOUT OUR surroundings. Petra is known as the Rose-Red City because, like Palmyra, it's fashioned out of richly colored sandstone. But while Palmyra's buildings are freestanding, many of Petra's feature elaborate facades, built or carved, fronting interiors cut directly into the mountains.

Thought to be inhabited as early as 7000 BC, Petra gained prominence as a trading hub around the first century AD, when much of the city was constructed. Its settlers, the Arabic Nabataeans, created a complex system of cisterns, channels, and dams to collect water to support a population of some twenty thousand people. According to tradition, one source of Petra's water was the spring that arose when Moses struck the rock with his staff, while leading the Israelites on their Exodus from Egypt.

As usual, Ellie planned to shoot sunrise photos of Petra. Before dawn, we headed to the Siq, the passageway through the cliffs into the city, to meet the tour guide we'd booked to help us. There we found a different guide, waiting for his partner, who was about to lead a group tour of Petra on horseback. The darkness was ebbing, with no sign of our escort.

Ellie had begun to fret about missing the sunrise when a man came up, bedecked with cameras. He was a Lufthansa pilot, as it turned out, with the same love of shooting at dawn. "Sandy, would you mind if I went with him to get some pictures?" Ellie asked. "When the guide comes, you can meet us inside."

Sandy said, "Of course not." She waited, chatting with the horseback tour guide. When his partner appeared, he told him, "Go ahead and start the tour. I'm not going to leave this lady here all by herself."

By daybreak, it was clear that our guide wasn't coming. Sandy's new friend asked, "Would you like to ride a horse into Petra like Indiana Jones?"

Sandy agreed, laughing.

Meanwhile, Ellie, having captured spectacular photos, was waiting at the other end of the Siq for Sandy to emerge. "Imagine my surprise at seeing Sandy on horseback," she says. "Even more, that she wasn't quaking in fear but seemed to be having fun! When she spotted me, she actually waved and shouted, 'Yahoo!' I'll never forget that moment!"

WHEN IT CAME TO TRANSPORTATION IN THE MIDDLE EAST, WE'D BEEN dependent on the kindness of strangers. The last leg that remained was traveling from Petra to Amman, where we'd catch our flight back to the United States. Given our hasty exit from Syria, we'd had no chance to plan, a fact we confessed to Sandy's new friend, the horseback tour guide.

"Don't worry," he said. "My uncle can drive you in his pickup."

It was uncanny—more angels, right on the eve of our departure. What luck!

The next day, the uncle collected us in his comfortable four-door truck. We threw our luggage into the bed and climbed into the backseat to head home.

AFTER WE ARRIVED BACK IN TEXAS, WE MONITORED THE CATA-strophic developments in Syria. Ellie's photos—likely among some of the last visitor images taken there—bear mournful witness to the glories that have been lost. Her shot of thriving Aleppo, a fascinating fusion of ancient and modern, stands in harsh contrast to a

2012 news photo of bombed-out rubble. Her image of the Souq, vibrant with life and color, is an indictment of the 2012 wire service shot of its charred remains.

Ellie's shots of Palmyra are even more moving. In 2015, ISIS invaded the city expressly to crush the historic relics of its "heathen" civilization. The Temple of Bel, a remarkably intact structure in Ellie's rendering, was blown up, leaving only its grand gateway listing against the sky. Its precious artifacts—carvings and statues created by ancestors in past millennia—were smashed to bits with sledgehammers by hooded raiders.

These grievous losses, of course, pale in comparison to the human calamity. Amid so much displacement and death, what could have become of our Bedouin hosts; of young Asim, who led our camels; of Abdul; of our two angel Mohammeds; and all the others who welcomed us with open arms and generous warmth? Our hearts—and heartfelt prayers—remain with them and all the other victims of our century's conflicts. Our most fervent wish is peace for our troubled Earth.

Part II

ANYONE CAN BECOME
ADVENTUROUS

7

EMBRACE YOUR POTENTIAL TO
LIVE MORE FULLY AND WELL

People often think that, because the two of us love adventure, we have some inborn inclination, like an explorer gene. Or they assume that, growing up, we traveled with our families or were encouraged to become unusually independent. Nothing could be further from the truth.

In fact, we both grew up with little exposure to outside influences. Church, school, and family formed the contours of our lives. We were middle children—Ellie one of three, Sandy the second of four. Both of us, when we were young, were timid and painfully shy.

Obviously, that changed! What moves the needle in someone's life? We were both blessed with husbands who actively encouraged us to grow, and Zambia—for each of us, at different times, in different ways—awakened our commitment to the world beyond ourselves. Certainly, our friendship plays a role in our readiness to push life's limits.

Of course, great relationships and immersion in a new culture are not required elements for change. Whatever our circumstances, we all have the potential to live more fully and well. What it takes is curiosity, being open to others, and the willingness to brave—even in small doses, to start—uncertainty and discomfort. The payoff—joy—is well worth it.

> **Whatever our circumstances, we all have the potential to live more fully and well. What it takes is curiosity, being open to others, and the willingness to brave—even in small doses, to start—uncertainty and discomfort. The payoff—joy—is well worth it.**

NOTHING IN OUR BACKGROUNDS WOULD SUGGEST THAT WE'D EVER BE-come travelers, or, as we like to think of it, students of the world.

Ellie says of her childhood, "I grew up on a wheat and cattle farm in rural Oklahoma near the town of Arnett (population five hundred). My father ran a bulk dairy route, supplying milk to processing plants, while my mother single-handedly managed the farm. She was larger-than-life, a real character, who'd dropped out of school by the eighth grade to help her family. Her experience left her super-competent: a fine farmer; a skilled sportswoman, who loved hunting and fishing; and a hands-on mother, who handled all the child-rearing, cooking, and housework. She even made our clothes and cleaned the church.

"Temperamentally, she could not have been more different from my father. He was an introvert, the quietest man in the world. My mother was fun: unfailingly high energy and upbeat. The only negative words she ever uttered were to the cows. They'd try to slip their stanchions or kick during milking, and she'd let loose with a blast of profanity that shook the rafters. We kids would shriek, hearing that language.

"My older brother, Clifford, also had a big personality and my younger sister, Marilyn, whom we lost about twenty years ago, was serious and sweet. As the middle child, I was a dreamer, who loved sitting in the field and envisioning faraway places or reading about famous women like Amelia Earhart or Pearl S. Buck, who made a difference in the world. Being a swimmer—then and now—I idolized Esther Williams and Gertrude Ederle, who swam the English Channel. But I was too insecure ever to imagine myself in their place. I much more resembled my subdued father than my vibrant mother."

Sandy says, "Unlike Ellie, I was born in the city—Fort Worth, Texas, to be exact. My brother Kenneth, three years older, grew up to be a disk jockey, anchoring major stations in Texas and Oklahoma. He passed away about fifteen years ago. When I was four years old, my younger siblings—the twins, Ronnie and Connie—were born. My father came home from the hospital and said, 'Kenneth, you wanted a baby brother, and Sandy, you wanted a baby sister. So, your mother surprised us with one of each!'

"My mother, like Ellie's, had an eighth-grade education. Born during the Great Depression, she was one of six children in a share-cropper family. They kept moving from farm to farm, tending the fields. She met my father when her family got work in Oklahoma, on his parents' land. When she was sixteen and he was eighteen, they got married.

"They settled in Fort Worth, where my father worked as an ice man, delivering frozen blocks for ice boxes, the forerunners of refrig-erators, that people used to chill food back then. Then he got a job in a foundry, shoveling sand. But my father, who had a very high IQ, began to study the equipment, learning how the furnaces ran, how the molds were made, how the metals were mixed together. Soon, he'd mastered all the foundry processes so fully that they made him foreman. While still young, he was in charge of a huge crew of men.

"Sadly, my father had a demon—alcohol. By his early thirties, he was fully in its grip. Lucky for us, drunk or sober, he was never abusive. He could be funny and full of joy. But his alcoholic sprees spilled over into gambling and chasing women, leaving our house-hold in chaos, always stormy and, usually, impoverished.

"When I was in second grade, my mother contracted polio. For the entire year she was hospitalized and undergoing therapy, all four of us kids were sent to live with relatives. I stayed with my grandmother and attended a different school in her neighborhood.

"Finally, my mother, weakened, but fortunately not paralyzed, could care for us. We all came home, back into the commotion. As my parents continued to argue, I grew increasingly withdrawn and insecure, abashed by the secret of the turmoil in my home."

~~~~~~~~~

IN HIGH SCHOOL, WE BOTH BLOSSOMED, A LITTLE. BORN FOUR MONTHS apart in 1941, we came of age in the 1950s—the era of rock 'n' roll and, especially, Elvis Presley, whom we both loved. Ellie watched Elvis's legendary TV debut on *The Ed Sullivan Show.* "What a thrill," she says. "And once I got to appear on Dick Clark's *American Bandstand.* I did a mean jitterbug back then."

"That was brave," Sandy says. "Back then I was so skinny and shy that I always had to dance alone. My mother and aunts were tall, with jet black hair, and curvaceous, like Marilyn Monroe. So, I expected to look like that when I grew up. I kept waiting to be transformed, but it never happened. Eventually I did fill out—not to Marilyn Monroe proportions, but enough that I was asked to try out for the Miss Midland Pageant. Though I didn't win, it sure gave me a lift!"

High school also brought Ellie a boost of confidence. "A big event for teenagers was the Fat Stock Show," she says, "where we'd each show an animal to compete for prizes like 'Best Sheep' or 'Cleanest Pen.' Since winning would've meant the world to my sister, Marilyn, my parents would always make sure that her animal was superior to mine.

"But then I'd step up, dressed in my cute cowgirl clothes, smile at the judges, and I'd always win! My parents would shake their heads, laughing. 'Would you look at that, Ellie getting another prize . . .'

"It must have been maddening. Especially since, by then, Marilyn—

true to her selfless love for animals—would be tidying up the pen while I'd be off drinking Cokes with my friends.

"At the Fat Stock Show, the kids were buzzing about a new guy in school. That was headline news in a town of five hundred! We didn't see many new faces. So, on Monday, I raced into study hall to check him out.

"I took my seat in the back, as always, with the cool crew. Then Kelly Hamby strolled in and plopped down in the front row. He wasn't wearing boots and jeans, as I expected, but khakis and penny loafers. 'Oh no,' I thought. 'What a nerd!' Or whatever word we used back then. He was very good looking, so too bad!

"Smart enough to pick up on social cues, Kelly soon showed up in the perfect jeans, the best cowboy boots—red, white, and blue, with an American eagle—and a cowboy belt with a giant buckle. In short, he looked cool. He was also a great athlete, which impressed me.

"So, when he asked me out, I accepted. But we didn't click.

"Six months later, four male basketball stars (one of them Kelly) invited four top women's basketball players (one being me) on a mildly mutinous outing. Our coach had imposed a strict nine o'clock curfew and would actually track us down to ensure compliance. To flout the curfew, we all piled into one car (with me on top of Kelly) and headed to the next town for a movie. Afterward, we took our transistor radios to a nearby hilltop and danced.

"Somehow, the coach found out and benched us. But that fun, mischievous night—rare because neither of us was at all rebellious—brought Kelly and me together. From then on, we were a couple.

"Kelly left for college and, near the end of his first year, proposed marriage. I was seventeen, still in high school. When I told my mother, she burst out laughing. 'You've got to be kidding,' she said. Not because of my age but because Kelly's family was poor, in her opinion. While we were far from rich, we owned land, our farm. Kelly's father worked for the county, and his mother cooked for the school. Besides, Kelly didn't hunt or fish or fix things. My mother considered him 'only good for book-learning.'

"Being underage, I couldn't get married without permission. That's when my quiet father piped up. 'Pretty soon, she'll be eighteen and can do what she wants,' he said. 'If you try to stop her now, there will be hard feelings. So, let's just sign the papers and get it over with.'

"Right after my high school graduation, Kelly and I married, on May 31, 1959."

"My high school was much bigger than Ellie's," Sandy says. "There were more than four hundred kids in my graduating class. So, it was easy for me, being shy, to stay under the radar.

"Unlike Ellie, I was no good at sports. Even today, I can't swim. High school for me was mostly a blur of effort—homework and my weekend job at a local dress shop. I didn't have many friends or participate much in school activities.

"For one thing, there was the secret of my father's drinking, and for another, I felt embarrassed by being poorer than my classmates. The one place I felt comfortable was our little country church, where, like us, other people wore hand-me-downs.

"The minister and his wife there became my mentors. I think they knew that my home life was challenging. When I was fourteen or fifteen, they enrolled me in Bible-teacher training, driving me back and forth to the six-week class. At week four, the preacher's wife told me, 'When you finish the course, you'll run the toddlers' Bible class at church.'

"So, of course, I ran it. I never thought to question it. That's who I was in high school. I did what people told me.

"When I graduated, one of my aunts reached out. She and her geologist husband—the only person in my extended family to attend college—invited me to live with them in Midland, Texas, which was booming and had lots of jobs. So, I moved there, brushed up on my clerical skills, and got a great secretarial position with an independent oil company. I joined a lively church full of young professionals. Finally, I was coming into my own.

"I began dating a young lawyer. After a few months, he brought up marriage—but with a catch. His mother would never accept his marrying a mere high school graduate. So, he proposed that I attend Abilene Christian College, his alma mater, returning to Midland to work at his law firm on summer breaks. Then, once I graduated, we could marry.

"Being still on the timid side, I agreed. My kindly bosses knew the owner of the Sands Hotel in Abilene and asked if he'd give me a part-time job. Back then, hotels connected guest calls through switchboards, so I was brought on to train as a switchboard operator. After a week learning the ropes, I'd work Friday through Sunday nights so I could enroll in daytime classes.

"My first night of work was a Friday. Half an hour before eleven, when my shift ended, the night auditor, Donald Hazelip, popped in to meet the new girl. He worked overnights on weekends because he, too, attended Abilene Christian, with a year and a half till graduation.

"I thought he was cute and nice. I was charmed when, the next night, Don came by at eight-thirty and kept me company till eleven. I learned that he was a preacher's son, with values like mine. On Sunday, he offered to drive me back to my brother Ken's, where I was staying until the semester began. Then I saw Don Monday, Tuesday, Wednesday . . . On the seventh night, he asked me to marry him.

"I said yes. It was the boldest thing I'd ever done. Here I was, half engaged to a lawyer and about to enroll in college to please his mother. But with Don, there were no strings. He loved me as I was. That struck me, at nineteen, as a good enough reason to share his life.

"When I told my grandmother I was engaged, she asked, 'What color are his eyes?' 'Black,' I said. 'Oh, that will never work,' she told me.

"Happily, she was wrong. Though my parents were shocked at my swift engagement, they accepted Don, especially my father. Don appreciated my father's happy-go-lucky streak, viewed his lapses with compassion, and loved him dearly all his life.

"So, after seven dates and a four-month engagement, I married Don Hazelip on April 22, 1961. I was one week shy of my twentieth birthday. My father, though a little looped, managed to walk me down the aisle."

NEITHER OF OUR MARRIAGES SHOULD HAVE WORKED. WE WERE SO young—teenagers in love—without a clue of what to look for in a husband. Luckily we wound up with very similar men—strong leaders with deeply held ideals and a gift for empowering others.

"In a way, I married my mother," Ellie says. "A big personality, who would tell me what to do, as she did. Of course, once I realized that Kelly valued my opinion, I got a whole lot better about expressing it."

"I refused to marry a drinker," Sandy says, "That was my top requirement. Then, when my first child was born, I held her in my arms and pledged, 'You will never hear your parents fight like mine did.' So, we never raised our voices."

College wasn't in the cards for either of us. Ellie entered Northwestern Oklahoma State University at Alva just as Kelly was beginning his sophomore year. But soon after school started, she developed a persistent "flu." "Actually, I was pregnant," she says. "That was a shock. My son Kel was born exactly nine months and three days after my wedding, followed two years later by my daughter, Sheryl."

With children in the picture, two tuitions were a stretch. Ellie left school to care for the kids while Kelly finished up his bachelor's. Then he won a National Science Foundation Fellowship to study at the University of Texas at Austin, where he completed a master's degree in mathematics and a PhD in education administration.

Sandy never enrolled in Abilene Christian but worked so Don could finish his bachelor's and CPA degrees. Nine months and three weeks after her wedding, she gave birth to her daughter Barbara, followed in three years by Larry and, two years later, by Dawn.

So, we were both home with children. "Let's not forget what an adventure parenthood can be," Sandy says. "It takes courage, kindness, empathy, strength, and more to do right by the little people who depend on you."

Ellie cared for not just her two but also a series of foster kids—"anyone who needed help and somewhere to stay," she says.

"Helping those in need, especially kids, opens your mind. It bursts the bubble of your comfortable world, exposing you to a side of life that, otherwise, you might never be pushed to try to understand. You never know what other people face until you walk alongside them."

One child in particular that Ellie and Kelly helped raise, Moon, remained part of the Hamby family. Finishing college, he told Ellie, "When I get my diploma, I want to lay it on Kelly's grave because I could never have achieved it without him."

"I just burst into tears," Ellie says.

WE TWO TIMID GIRLS WERE FINALLY EMERGING FROM OUR SHELLS, thanks in part to our husbands. "I was so blessed to have married Kelly," Ellie says, "It's like I had an inner being who would never have emerged had I married a different person."

Kelly had strong convictions but also a deep respect for other viewpoints. "He was an atheist when we met," Ellie says. "He promised to accompany me to church once we had children, which he did. That didn't alter his thinking on religion, and I wasn't strong enough to debate him. Then, one day, he came home troubled from one of his PhD classes. He felt that the professor—with whom he fully agreed—was disparaging the faith of the Christian students. He said, 'It's wrong for him to use his position to twist their minds to his beliefs.'

"He felt honor-bound to defend the students but didn't know enough about Christianity to argue. So, he began to read the Bible, just to stick up for beliefs he didn't share. In time, his Bible study took hold, and—to my surprise and delight—he decided to be baptized. Kelly's religious awakening, as it turned out, would define our lives, leading to his professorship at Abilene Christian University and, of course, to our mission work in Zambia.

"But the whole process, starting with the impulse to defend the students, was pure Kelly. He lived to champion underdogs. As a professor, he'd seek out students who were learning-challenged or disadvantaged, making it his mission to mentor them and help them rise. He'd connect with people on their own level, never as some high-and-mighty authority.

"The people Kelly met on their own level included me. He never pushed me to finish college or to get a job. To him, that was my decision. But he welcomed my involvement in his work—drafting his speeches, writing business letters—confident that I'd handle it well. And I did, because of his faith in me.

"Little by little, I took over family functions that didn't interest Kelly, like our finances. We switched roles, from Kelly running the show to me being in charge. The same was true of our work in Zambia, where I took on the administration—planning, organizing, and supervising the volunteers, you name it—freeing Kelly to focus on his university job. I handled all those logistics from behind the scenes, which was how I liked it. I didn't need the limelight.

"One day Kelly announced, 'You're not the same girl that I married.'

"He didn't say it reproachfully. He was simply—even gratefully—acknowledging my evolution from a shy teenager, wracked with self-doubt and needing guidance, to an essential partner, the skilled manager of our work and home lives. Sometimes the way he relied on me was funny, like the time he called to ask me how to make a

TV dinner. I had to laugh, thinking, 'You're the one with the PhD! Just read the directions!' But I didn't say it out loud.

"Still, he wasn't like some husbands, expecting lots of coddling. He even urged me not to push myself so hard. 'Ellie, you've really got to stop and smell the roses,' he'd tell me.

"One realm in which I still lacked confidence was my photography. My daughter, Sheryl, who loves the arts, was visiting a local gallery and happened to mention my work to the manager. 'Have her submit a portfolio,' he said. When she told me, all excited, my thoughts were: (1) What's a portfolio? and (2) No way! Rejection would be too humiliating.

"But Sheryl kept pushing and enlisted Kelly. Pressured by the two of them, I stuffed ten shots of people—uncropped prints, all different sizes—in a manila envelope and went down to the gallery. The owner spread out my photos on the table and called his partner, 'Hey, come look at these.'

"The partner said, 'These are magazine covers!' I must have looked puzzled because he laughed and said, 'We want to show your work! We'll walk you through the process of preparing an exhibition.'

"I was shocked and worried. How could I ever afford to produce big, framed prints . . .

"'Don't panic,' they said. 'There's no rush. Getting you on our calendar will take a few years.'

"It took three years to mount my show of thirty prints. The night of the opening, I was shaking with embarrassment, thinking, 'How can I expose myself to ridicule?' But I was standing near a man who said, 'These photos are amazing!' People bought prints. I got a rave review in the newspaper. It was unbelievable—and utterly thrilling!

"Even now, I get choked up thinking about how Sheryl made it happen. What a gift that was, giving me my first big chance. Kelly was overjoyed at my success, and I have to credit him, too. After all, Sheryl opened the door, but it was Kelly who—by his example, his love, and his years of cheering me on—gave me the courage to walk through it.

"The most powerful lesson I've learned is that fear is a cloud, not a physical trap. It can be dispelled by mere words—whether from others or conjured up in your own mind.

> **Fear is a cloud, not a physical trap. It can be dispelled by mere words—whether from others or conjured up in your own mind.**

"After Kelly's death, some people assumed that the Zambia Medical Mission would collapse, but that didn't happen at all. The reason is that, under Kelly's leadership, the Zambian staff was already running it. Kelly was not a controlling boss but a dreamer, a visionary who inspired people, spurring them to take action and assume responsibility. That's one of the reasons that he was so well loved.

"People knew that, as Kelly's helpmeet, I worked for the mission, even if they didn't quite realize how much. So, it was easy for me to begin leading the medical mission as a codirector. All I had to do was step out of the shadows. With Kelly's blessing, I'd been doing the work all along."

"Donald and I underwent a similar role reversal," Sandy says. "While I was painfully shy and withdrawn, he was the most outgoing person in the whole wide world. Curious by nature, he talked to everyone. He never met a stranger. Everybody loved Don Hazelip.

"Today most people find me friendly and even seem drawn to me, which is a huge change. I think that some reasons are, first, that Don's infectious good nature rubbed off on me; and second— more seriously—that he taught me to look outward. Being naturally shy, I was prone to looking inward and hyperconscious of my own deficiencies. Being prodded to shift my focus to others freed me from such thoughts and helped me grow more gentle and generous, both with myself and those around me.

"Don helped me shift focus by example but also by consciously drawing me out. He'd constantly ask me, 'What do you think?' or 'What should we do?' You can't hide from that loving attentiveness.

"He also—deliberately or not—counteracted the heartache of my childhood. Knowing my fear of conflict, he was quick to repair fractures in our relationship. Once, he made some harsh but true remarks about a member of my family. The next morning, I got up the nerve to say, 'You were right, but you hurt my feelings.' That night he came home from work with a beautifully wrapped gift for me. It was a lovely watch, which he delivered with an apology, saying, 'Please know that hurting you is the last thing I ever want to do.'

"Early in our marriage, he eased the anxieties born of my father's womanizing. Don was still in college, working at the Sands, when a very attractive guest propositioned him. He turned her down, then came home and told me all about it, with the assurance, 'I did not—and I will never—break my wedding vows to you.'

"I thought, 'Who even knew a man could be like that?' and, of course, 'How did I get so lucky?'

"Despite his personal morality, Don loved and accepted my father, for which I was grateful. Don had an inborn generosity, even when we were young and struggling. On the rare occasions when we ate out, he'd leave big tips, saying, 'You know, our server isn't waiting tables for pleasure. Let's be a blessing for her today.'

"Later in life, when Don became the county auditor in Eastland, he was shocked to discover that funds for the indigent were rarely used. With his scrupulous honesty and care for the needy, he changed the system so that full disbursements were made promptly. I was so proud when, after his death, people called me to say, 'My family could eat [or pay rent or get medicine], thanks to your husband.'

"Don was cut from clerical cloth—not just his father but also his three uncles were preachers. During the 1960s and 1970s, one uncle was renowned throughout the South and even traveled the world giving sermons. Though he was an accountant, Don, too, had the gift and taught Bible classes wherever we worshipped. When we lived for a time in Durango, Colorado, his classes were such a hit that the congregation begged him to come on as their full-time minister. He wasn't trained or ordained—he was just that good.

"Don was torn. I told him, 'Sweetheart, I think you want this. You may not ever be at peace with yourself unless you do it.'

"But having grown up a preacher's son, he knew the drawbacks. A big one was living in a fishbowl, under constant scrutiny by church members. He said, 'Sandy, I would never do that to my family.'

"He put us first, ahead of the opportunity. Of course, when the time came for me to follow my dream, he was all for it.

"Don helped found the Fort Worth chapter of the American Diabetes Association. It met monthly, with guest speakers, and at Don's urging, I became one of them. The talks I gave there to pediatricians and other parents of diabetic children helped fuel my ambition to go to college and become a doctor.

"In college, I majored in biology and minored in chemistry. I graduated near the top of my class, with a grade point average of almost 3.9. When I aced the MCAT, the admission test for medical school, Don was proud.

"Despite my grades and test score, I faced hurdles. I couldn't apply all over the country with a family at home. The nearest major medical school was the University of Texas Southwestern, in Dallas. So, I met with the admissions director to discuss my application.

"He said, 'I'll tell you right now, I won't back your acceptance. It costs the state of Texas a lot of money to train a physician. At your age, you won't have that many working years to give back. Besides, you won't make it. The program is rigorous. I doubt that you'll have the energy to get through internship and residency.

"'What nonsense,' I thought.

"Undeterred, I entered the Texas College of Osteopathic Medicine in Fort Worth. The training differed slightly, but we had all the same requirements. The medical board exams I passed were exactly the same. There is no difference between my medical license and that of any doctor from a conventional medical school anywhere in the States. And since I lived in Fort Worth, it was more convenient.

"Today, the youngsters who were admitted to UT Southwestern instead of me have mostly retired, while I'm still working full-time in my eighties. What's more, when I established my clinic in Eastland, students entering their three-month rotation in family medicine were warned, 'Watch out for that practice. The old lady will run you ragged. You'll never be able to keep up with her!'

"So, I got the last laugh, thank you very much.

"Through it all, Don stood by me. When our kids were young, he did audits all over the US and Canada. Often, he traveled Monday through Friday and was home only on weekends. It was a little challenging, with three children, but we were happy.

"When I started my clinic, working eighty hours a week, the kids were grown. One night, I came home late, and Don turned off the TV to say, 'Sandy, please know that I don't mean to complain. For so many years, I was on the road, while you were at home. Now it's your time—but, honey, I just miss you when you're gone!'

"Ellie and I grew up in an era when women ran the home. Housekeeping was our responsibility, even if we had jobs. So, I was stunned when, one day, Don called to ask me how to work the washing machine. Then he said, 'I've seen you sort the clothes— what's that all about?'

"I explained, and from then on, Don was the laundry king! Until the day he died, he insisted that no one washed clothes as well as he did.

"Soon afterward, he asked me how to plan the grocery shopping. He took on that task, too, just to give me relief. I was so blessed! Few men our age would ever dream of sharing the burden that way. As it was, plenty of our friends thought that I was a nut and that Don was a saint.

"And, for me, he was!"

MANY DIVORCED AND WIDOWED WOMEN WE KNOW DEDICATE THEIR lives to finding a man. They're lonely—we can empathize. We've been down that sad and rocky road.

The priorities are different for us. We're lucky, we know, to have had phenomenal marriages and great kids. As Sandy says, "I've already had the best husband in the world. I don't want second best."

It's not just that we're independent—it's that we live with purpose, which we were fortunate enough to find, explore, and develop within our marriages. That purpose is serving others—working to improve other lives besides our own. If you don't contribute to the greater good, even in some small way, you're not really pulling your weight in the world.

And we can't resist sharing this key piece of advice: Find a friend. "When we first met," Ellie says, "Sandy and I had no idea that we had so much in common. Being a true friend involves more than just feeling good with somebody. It takes a little sacrifice to connect with someone, to accommodate their needs. But even more, it takes the capacity to revel in their joys. You live more fully when you share, experiencing the world through someone else's eyes."

> **Being a true friend involves more than just feeling good with somebody. It takes a little sacrifice to connect with someone, to accommodate their needs. But even more, it takes the capacity to revel in their joys. You live more fully when you share, experiencing the world through someone else's eyes.**

Life is a jigsaw puzzle of strengths and weaknesses, sorrows and joys, experiences and missed opportunities, the satisfaction of achievement, the awe of discovery, and more. It's up to each of us how we fit all those pieces together.

8

THIS IS WHAT
GRANNIES LOOK LIKE

January 11, 2023, would mark the beginning of our most ambitious adventure yet—a trip to all seven continents, including ten world wonders—reprising the travels of Phileas Fogg and Nelly Bly. Phileas Fogg, of course, was fictional, and Nellie Bly was twenty-five when she made her journey—less than a third of our age, but that only heightened our commitment. At the outset, we had no idea that embarking on the journey in our eighties would make us a media sensation.

We'd originally settled on a departure date of February 2022, but COVID scuttled our plans. Then, one by one, countries lifted their restrictions, and we were able to start booking again. We were determined to uphold our new slogan, Eighty-One and Still on the Run, by completing our eighty-day sprint before Sandy turned eighty-two, a few months ahead of Ellie, in late April 2023.

It was Sandy's idea that we should get matching T-shirts for the trip. At first Ellie was appalled. "T-shirts?" she said. "I hardly ever wear them, and matchy-match is not my style." Our daughters Barbara and Sheryl took Ellie's side, finding the notion of wearing matching T-shirts "goofy."

But Sandy persisted, claiming, "We'll only wear them on the plane," and Ellie eventually gave in. "It seemed like a small enough compromise," she says.

When choosing a logo for our shirts, we were dismayed to find nothing but hackneyed depictions of older women. The designer pulled up a website of cartoonish images of hunched-over crones pushing walkers or tottering on canes, with Mr. Magoo glasses and hair swept into scraggly buns. "Talk about the wrong message!" we said to each other. "This is definitely not us!"

One day, we may need mobility aids—and more power to those who use them—but circumnavigating the earth was certainly the antithesis of stooped, enfeebled old ladyhood.

Then, one night, a college student visited Ellie. After hearing about our trip, she said, "Stand behind the globe, so I can snap y'all's picture."

"That's it!" Ellie exclaimed when she saw the image. "That's as perfect a logo as we'll ever get!"

So, we each got a set of shirts with our globe photo on the front, encircled by the words "Around the World in Eighty Days," and our slogan on the back. Now that we've become known as the Tik-Tok Traveling Grannies, we've added those words, too, if only to skewer people's assumptions. We're living proof of the pluck and vigor of grandmothers and octogenarians!

> ## We're living proof of the pluck and vigor of grandmothers and octogenarians!

"I now admit that those T-shirts were a great idea," Ellie says. "Everywhere we went, our shirts encouraged people to talk to us. And I don't mean senior citizens—a lot of the people who approached us were younger, saying, 'I wish my parents had the nerve to emulate you.'"

OUR PREVIOUS TRIPS HAD LASTED ABOUT TWO AND HALF WEEKS, LIMited by Sandy's vacation time from her job. Even on the road, she'd check in often to keep tabs on patients. But now we'd be traveling for two and half months, too long to stay effectively involved in cases. "For the first time in forty-five years, I was going off the grid," Sandy says. "No emails from nurses and other doctors, no questions from family members. I'd be totally unplugged. What a strange feeling!

"By now I was the medical director of Hospice of the Big Country, serving Abilene and outlying areas within about an eighty-mile radius. I could reassign those duties, but I still had patients, whom I loved. Other doctors would care for them, but leaving was wrenching, since people in hospice, by definition, are in the twilight of their lives."

In the course of saying her goodbyes, Sandy visited a patient at the Wesley Court Retirement Center. There she bumped into the activities director, who'd often engaged her to speak on health topics; the two of us had also given talks on our travels. She asked, "What happened with that eighty-day trip you were taking last year?"

When Sandy said that we were leaving soon, she got excited. "Residents have been wondering about it," she said. "Would you give us a presentation on your plans?"

That's how we wound up addressing an enthusiastic Wesley Court crowd. We had no idea that, among them, were people from KTAB-TV and the *Abilene Reporter-News.*

Afterward, the reporters asked us to stick around for interviews. Then Noah McKinney of KTAB said, "I want to rush this back to the studio. Will you send me some photos we can use on air—as many and as quickly as you can?"

That night KTAB News made us the lead feature. "We want to follow you on your trip," the reporter told us. "Please send us updates." Then he added words that proved to be prophetic: "This is a great story. You never know, but I bet it gets picked up."

FINALLY, JANUARY 11, OUR DEPARTURE DATE, DAWNED. WE'D CHOSEN it to take advantage of the limited window when tourists can visit Antarctica, the first continent on our list. It would be summer there, since the Southern Hemisphere has seasons the opposite of ours—though, of course, the Antarctic summer bears no resemblance to our Texas scorchers.

To get there, we drove to Dallas to catch a flight to Buenos Aires, where we'd connect with a plane to Ushuaia, Argentina, the city at the bottom of the world.

We reached the Dallas airport hours ahead of our flight, as usual. We were checking in at the counter when Ellie's phone rang. "This is NBC 5 Dallas-Fort Worth," a voice said. "Where are you?"

They must have seen our KTAB broadcast, which mentioned our departure date but not the time.

"At the airport," Ellie replied. "We just got our boarding passes. We're starting a trip around the world."

"Well, we want to talk to you. We have a reporter on the way. Can you wait?"

"Sure!" we said.

Ten minutes later, a reporter/cameraman found us. He was charmed to find us decked out in matching T-shirts.

The reporter interviewed us at length about our trip—who we were, our destinations, what inspired and excited us, etc. Then, with the camera rolling, he put us though a lot of staged actions: dropping our luggage on the belt, checking the departures board, walking by souvenir stores, joining the security line, and so on. All this, he explained to us, was B-roll.

Being a photographer, Ellie was familiar with the term, but this was our first performance as B-roll stars. B-roll is background action video, shot horizontally to match the shape of a TV screen. It's often recorded soundless so they can dub narration over it. It's like visual filler, adding variety to otherwise static interviews, leading into and out of segments, and plugging gaps in a story. Once you start looking for it, you'll see B-roll everywhere, especially in television newscasts.

We didn't see ourselves that night, leading the NBC 5 Dallas-Fort Worth News, because, of course, we were in the air. But that segment, in a major media market, inflamed the press. When we touched down in Buenos Aires, there was an email on Ellie's phone: "I'm a producer at CBS News. We just heard about your story, and we want it. Can we talk? In the meantime, please don't take calls from ABC, NBC, CNN, or Fox."

"Oh boy," Sandy said. "Here we go!"

We set up a call for the next day, when we'd land in Ushuaia. After some back and forth by email and phone, CBS decided to film us in London, some weeks into our trip.

"I bet they want to make sure we're legit," Ellie said.

Sandy agreed. "Yes, that we won't give up and go right home!"

Not a chance!

One more thing: CBS wanted B-roll. "Shoot it everywhere you can," they told us. "Don't think about a script; don't bother to stage it. Just pick a background that tells a story and film yourselves doing something in front of it: walking, eating, interacting . . ."

It was going to be hard to film ourselves in action without a selfie stick. So, we made do by asking every Tom, Dick, and Mary we saw to shoot our B-roll.

Still, the experience proved rewarding. "Old people thought we were crazy," Sandy says, "or they got intimidated. But the young people loved doing it."

Afterward, they'd want to pose for photos with us. We'd laugh and chat and take selfies. We wound up with scores of photos of ourselves and young people, beaming with pride at their video artistry.

"It was such fun," Sandy says. "We made lots of new pals."

What better way to meet people—our favorite part of traveling—than to say, "We're going on TV. Would you shoot our B-roll?"

We still joke that we didn't just travel, we B-rolled the world.

Part III

CIRCUMNAVIGATING THE WORLD IN EIGHTY DAYS

9

APPROACH THE
WORLD WITH WONDER

Antarctica

Of the world's seven continents, Antarctica is the most mysterious and demanding, the least changed by human habitation—and perhaps also the most harmonious, untroubled by clashing cultures or jockeying rulers. It's governed by a council of several dozen nations, parties to a 1959 treaty banning military activity, mining, and nuclear detonations and waste disposal and promoting scientific research, fishing, and tourism.

Antarctica is the last great wilderness. It is the driest continent on earth, a polar desert; the coldest, with the world's lowest recorded temperature (about -129 degrees Fahrenheit), and the windiest. It has the highest elevation, formed of mountains kicked up by clashing tectonic plates, and is covered by a nearly unbroken ice sheet that is, on average, more than a mile thick.

To see it, we figured, would be to experience nature's power at its rawest, purest, and most majestic.

To reach Antarctica, we would leave Ushuaia, Argentina, aboard a sturdy expedition ship, the *Ocean Nova*. Hardened against iceberg collisions and the pummeling of fifty-foot waves, it would carry us—we hoped!—through the Drake Passage, the most treacherous waterway on the planet.

Stretching from Chile to Antarctica, the Drake Passage is the vortex where the Atlantic and Pacific oceans collide, at the bottom of the world, in a ferocious display of power. Its fury has claimed at least eight hundred ships over the years, along with as many as twenty thousand lives. Right before we left, a modern cruise ship, the *Viking Polaris*, was struck by a rogue wave, killing one passenger, an American, and injuring four others. Facts like these we keep secret from our children.

But for us, the time-honored voyage through tempestuous seas was integral to the adventure. We were awed by the explorers of history who traversed the Drake in fragile vessels, including Ernest Shackleton, on the aptly named HMS *Endurance*, and Charles Darwin on the HMS *Beagle*, in his quest to understand life on earth. Ironically, Sir Francis Drake, the passage's namesake, never made it through but just glimpsed it after he was blown off course.

> **For us, the time-honored voyage through tempestuous seas was integral to the adventure.**

From the moment we stepped aboard the *Ocean Nova*, we could feel the weight of history and, looking out over the leaden gray sea, the presence of ghosts.

Crossing the six-hundred-mile passage could take up to two days, depending on the weather. We spent our first morning hearing fascinating talks by the naturalist staff on the history of the passage, sea life and birds, and what we'd see in Antarctica.

By afternoon, the wind was up, and the weather forecast unambiguous. We would not be among the lucky few who got the "Drake Lake," an easy passage. Instead, we were in for turbulence, the so-called Drake Shake. That meant waves—big ones—some cresting as high as twenty to thirty feet.

Already the ship was pitching and yawing. Gripping the handrails in the corridors, we made our way back to our cabin, with its twin beds bolted to the floor and walls. There, we flung ourselves into our bunks and held on for dear life. With our feet pointed toward the porthole, we could see huge waves peaking outside.

With scopolamine patches and motion-relief wristbands, we hoped to fend off seasickness. Sandy managed to escape it, but Ellie succumbed. That meant braving the bathroom—clinging to the railing by the door, fighting to stay erect while yanking it open, and then, after lurching inside, wrestling the heaving door to keep it from slamming onto loose limbs.

Our ship was known for its good food, so when we boarded, we were excited about dinner. After a stomach-churning afternoon, we were less thrilled but still game to try it. Picking our way out to the dining room, we found all sixty of our fellow passengers there, looking as queasy as we did but milling around the buffet tables.

The continental spread was impressive enough to whet even shaky appetites. The rough part was loading our plates on the rocking ship and walking to our tables. All of us tried to perfect the Drake waddle, inching along with feet wide apart for balance, one hand holding a plate while the other clutched at chair backs and shoulders. The air was full of *Oops*es and *Sorry*s and sheepish chuckles.

The long tables were flanked by swivel chairs bolted to the floor. We chose seats by the window—a rookie mistake, in retrospect.

We'd finished our entrees, and waiters were circulating with desserts when terror struck. A massive wave caught us broadside on the other side of the ship, tipping up the floor by what felt like 45 degrees. There was no jolt of impact, just a sudden mighty roll, leaving us staring down into the roiling water. We grabbed the table to keep from being flung onto the window, praying that our dining companions were also holding tight enough not to pile on top of us.

No one screamed. A hush of shock gripped the room.

The ship's tilt launched a cascade, on every table, of plates, forks, spoons, saltshakers, and half-full glasses and coffee cups. Crockery, cutlery, drinks, and food came surging our way, crashing into the window and spilling onto our laps. But seated diners like us were lucky. People who'd been standing were knocked down, bruised and battered.

Then, slowly the ship righted. We'd heard that a head-on hit was much less dangerous than a sidelong blow, which could flip it. Fortunately, the *Ocean Nova* had stayed erect. The crew, solicitous and steady, knew the choreography to this dance. They moved through the dining room, helping the fallen to their feet, brushing off people covered in debris, dabbing at our hair and clothes with towels. "This happens all the time," they assured us. "That was just a typical swell on the Drake Passage." Nevertheless, for our safety, they asked us to return to our cabins.

"What will we do there?" Sandy asked. "Can we sleep?"

"I guess we should try," Ellie said.

Toddling, clinging to the walls, we managed to scuttle back to our bolted-down bunks. But the way the ship was pitching, we couldn't sit up without sliding. Lying down was a little more stable but still dicey. We'd start with our heads toward the door, feet toward the porthole, then slip down into a heap at the foot of the bed. There were no railings on the beds to clutch and remain stationary.

Eventually, we drifted off but woke repeatedly. Sandy found herself balled up in the middle of the bed, turned sideways. Ellie wound up reversed, with her head by the window. All night long, we did the Drake rock and roll, a-slipping and a-sliding till the break of dawn.

The ship's captain later told us that we'd endured the full Drake Shake, lasting nearly twenty-four hours.

Finally, we were through the chute. The thrill ride was over, replaced by an eerie calm. Putting our feet on the floor the next morning, we found it solid and unmoving. We could stand without effort. We could walk! With a new confidence, we strode, heads held high, to the dining room.

"I want to pop outdoors for a minute," Ellie said.

"Go ahead," Sandy told her. "I want coffee."

"On the deck, the air was freezing cold," Ellie says. "It hit my face like a slap. Suddenly I heard an unexpected sound—the cries of birds—and saw gulls and petrels wheeling overhead. I thought, 'We're nearing land!'

"I climbed to the prow of the ship, with the great sea arrayed before me. Like Rose in the movie *Titanic*, I was flying. With my eyes closed and my arms stretched wide, I could almost hear Celine Dion singing, 'My heart will go on and on . . .' It was a moment of overcoming, of triumphing over fear—and of wild, unbridled joy.

"I whipped out my binoculars and caught sight of a giant tail fin—a blue whale diving too fast for me to photograph. In the distance, I could make out tiny black dots on a white background, which I later learned were seals on an ice cap.

"Then I lowered the binoculars and let the frigid, stark beauty envelop me: the sensation of the boat slicing through the waves—now dark blue rather than leaden gray; the sight of blue-white icebergs, sculptural and huge but somehow graceful, gliding by in an unruly parade; the hum of the engines and the thrum of the wind in my ears; the clean salt air on my lips and stinging my eyes, making me blink hot tears; and most dazzling of all, the sheer vastness of the sea and sky.

"Never had I experienced such a pure expression of nature's power, a sense of being in God's dominion, a cathedral of the air. The word 'awe' is almost too tame to describe the feeling of being a tiny speck in the flow of creation, yet sharing in its exhilarating, wild energy.

> **The word "awe" is almost too tame to describe the feeling of being a tiny speck in the flow of**

> creation, yet sharing in its
> exhilarating, wild energy.

"Breathless with cold and emotion, I went back inside. Sandy was at a table far from the window (lesson learned!). When I sat down with my food, she looked at me, curious. I must have had a faraway expression on my face.

"'What's it like out there?' she asked. 'What did you see?'

"'I saw Oz,' I told her. It was that magical."

THE NEXT MORNING, WE REACHED HALF MOON ISLAND, THE FIRST stop on many Antarctic cruises. A barrier island off the coast of Antarctica proper, it's a crescent-shaped rocky mass just over a mile long. Half Moon Island is an important breeding ground for many Antarctic birds, including terns, skuas, gulls, petrels, shags, and our favorite, the comical chinstrap penguins.

Our ship dropped anchor a short distance from the shore. There was no port or dock where it could land. The only way to get from the ship to the island was on a Zodiac, a rubbery boat that Sandy describes as "an overgrown inner tube with a floor."

We'd been given a list of clothes to bring—down jackets, insulated underwear, caps and gloves, sunglasses because of the brutal glare off the snow, and for this leg of the trip, waterproof pants. We pulled them on over our regular pants, then stepped into the provided heavy-duty, knee-high boots. Our last bit of gear was life vests, which would afford only minimal protection. We were warned that anyone falling into the icy water would die in minutes of hypothermia.

In fact, just months before, two passengers had perished in the sea after tumbling out of a Zodiac. "So, hold on tight," we were told.

That was hard. In a Zodiac, you put your feet on the floor and perch on the rounded top of the innertube, which is slippery. A heavy rope encircling the edge behind you is all you can clutch to hold yourself steady.

Launched from the ship, our Zodiac, with eight of us ringing its edges, plunged into the waves. Gaining speed, it kicked up a freezing, drenching spray. By the time we reached Half Moon Island, fifteen minutes later, we were dripping. Then, after the Zodiac nosed into shore, we had to climb out into the water—hence the heavy-duty boots—and wade onto the rocky beach.

But once there, we all stood speechless. "I could see that everyone was experiencing the epiphany that I'd had on the prow," Ellie says. "We were filled with reverence at the silence, broken only by bird calls; the drama of the rugged, icy landscape; and the unearthly serenity of the place."

We had trekking poles to help us navigate the slick, cobblestone-like shoreline. In the near distance lay a snowy cliff that looked like a great observation and photo site. A few passengers headed toward it, and Sandy said, "Ellie, go on with them. I'll catch up."

But as Ellie scrambled up the craggy path, wet with melting snow, the wind gained strength. "The higher I climbed, the less there was to obstruct it," she says. "I had to bend nearly in half, clutching at rocks, to withstand the buffeting. I realized then that Sandy could never make it."

"I saw Ellie gingerly climbing back down," Sandy says. "Then, she called, 'Wait, stay where you are.' When she reached me, she said, 'You're too light to fight the wind. You'll be blown right off the cliff!'"

At the shoreline, where the winds were calmer, we continued exploring. We came across the hull of a nineteenth-century whaling ship lying on the rocks, mostly intact, its wooden face scoured by a hundred-plus winters and bleached by sun. It looked so frail and tiny. "How did they ever make it here?" Sandy said.

Ellie photographed the weathered wreck against the backdrop of our large, fortified expedition ship, anchored offshore. What a contrast!

We also encountered a few huddles, as groups are called, of chinstrap penguins, hopping from rock to rock, flapping their wings at one another. Standing about thirty inches tall, they looked like a bunch of lively children, gamboling on the beach like it was their playground. As they called to each other, their neckbands made them look like they were laughing. Despite their cheery demeanor, they're supposedly the most aggressive and cantankerous of the penguin species.

Seals draped on the rocks seemed to have smirking expressions on their faces. We were acutely conscious that we were mere guests in their domain, a realm where few humans would ever trespass.

After several hours, we were summoned back to the Zodiac for another soaking. When we reached the *Ocean Nova*, we faced the wet, slippery challenge of climbing a narrow gangplank to get back on board. It was rough, with the waves smacking the lightweight Zodiac against the hull.

We wished we had weeks, not days, to spend exploring Antarctica. But, with our jam-packed eighty-day itinerary, this phase was ending. The next day, we'd catch a charter flight from King George, one of the South Shetland Islands, to Punta Arenas, Chile, to resume our journey.

The winds were severe the next morning, so it was a wait-and-see game as to whether our flight could safely depart. Finally, the *Ocean Nova*'s captain got the go-ahead, and we piled into the Zodiac with our luggage to head for King George Island.

What passed for an airport was a small building beside a dirt landing strip that ran between the Russian and Argentine research stations. In the distance, we could see the spire of Trinity Church, a tiny Russian Orthodox chapel that is one of only eight houses of worship on the entire continent.

When our plane touched down, we were a little surprised by how small it was—not that we expected a 747. Inside, there was limited seating, as if it was also used to transport cargo. But all of us who were waiting managed to cram in, and we took off.

SITTING SIDE BY SIDE ON THE PLANE, WE CELEBRATED THE MOMENT, SAYing, "We did it! One continent down, six to go!" But beyond reaching our first milestone, we felt grateful to have seen Antarctica first—to have launched our journey in the place closest to the Creator's original design. Over all the millennia that we humans have inhabited the earth, we've recast much of it in our own image. But not Antarctica.

It seemed eminently fitting to begin a trip around our great big world in a state of awe.

Awe and gratitude are also fitting sentiments for the friendship our trip affirmed. In the twenty-three years since we met at the medical mission conference, we'd covered so much ground together—in miles logged, yes, but also in healing, self-discovery, and cultivating "big" purposeful, adventurous lives. Our eighty-day journey was a capstone and celebration of that shared effort. The later decades of our lives have been a series of doors, and, grabbing hands, we continue to burst through them together.

> **The later decades of our lives have been a series of doors, and, grabbing hands, we continue to burst through them together.**

Easter Island

After the fierce cold of Antarctica, it was a shock to find ourselves in the springlike weather of Punta Arenas, Chile. Our expedition company had booked us into a nice hotel. Ellie had showered and was drying her hair when a call came from the front desk. "Are you okay?" the clerk asked.

"Oh yes," Sandy said. "Everything's fine."

Sandy had just headed downstairs when Ellie heard pounding on the door and a frantic voice demanding: "What's burning in there?"

Evidently, steam rising from Ellie's hair dryer had set off the bathroom smoke detector, triggering the alarm system. Who knew? Now the entire hotel was in an uproar over the blaring fire siren.

Funnily, that scenario would be reenacted in other hotels, in other cities, until Ellie tried drying her hair near an open window.

From Punta Arenas, we flew to Santiago, Chile's capital, established by a Spanish conquistador in the sixteenth century. It's a charming, bustling metropolis famous for offering skiing in the Andes a mere forty-five minutes from the sunny city beaches closer to sea level. We enjoyed visiting its historic main square, the Plaza de Armas, lined with colonial-era buildings and full of small tables hosting pairs of intense, dedicated chess players. Each table was thronged with spectators, cheering on their favorites, all too engrossed in the games to notice two American observers.

From the square, we caught the funicular, a narrow-gauge cable car, up San Cristóbal Hill. At the top we enjoyed a meal and magnificent views of the city and its sheltering mountains.

In Santiago, we reverted to our favorite sightseeing strategy, hiring a taxi driver to show us around. So, we were delighted when Ricardo, who'd picked us up at the airport, agreed to be our tour guide for a day. We were even happier when he suggested that we collect his wife and visit nearby Valparaíso.

Valparaíso, a Pacific seaport, is the cultural capital of Chile, home to such famous figures as Pablo Neruda, the Nobel Prize–winning poet. It's bowl-shaped, with brightly painted houses perched on its

steep hillsides, accessed through a network of funiculars and eleva-
tors, some dating back to the nineteenth century.

Ricardo and his wife seemed to take great pleasure in driving us
up the narrow, winding streets, where buildings, retaining walls,
and even public staircases were adorned with brilliantly colored
murals. Some were political, depicting suffering under the Pinochet
regime, when many dissidents were "disappeared"; others were
cityscapes showing life on streets sloping down to the harbor, ren-
dered in perfect perspective; still others were playful, like the image
of a six-legged dog and one that looked just like the American cowboy Roy Rogers; others were simply decorative and beautiful. Ellie
shot photo after photo. "I could have spent days there just looking
at them," she says.

Our hosts also showed us a picturesque vineyard nestled on a hillside; the busy harbor, where fishing boats mingled with container
ships; the beautiful white-sand beach overhung by a boardwalk; and
other charms of the city, including a working clock made of flowers.
We stopped to eat at a little, nondescript hole-in-the-wall, where we
two Texas gals stared helplessly at the Spanish menu. Smiling at our
awkwardness, Ricardo and his wife ordered us a selection of delicious
dishes.

Talking with them, bonding, we felt that we were back in our
element as travelers. Antarctica had been stupendous and inspiring,
but seeing Valparaíso under the guidance of Ricardo and his wife
was deeply gratifying.

It was the second great kickoff to our trip, adding the joy of
human connection to our wonderment at the beauty of Creation.
We couldn't wait to keep going!

~~~~~~~~~~

SANTIAGO WAS THE TRANSFER POINT FOR OUR TRUE DESTINATION—
Easter Island, one of the most isolated places of human habitation
on the planet. Located in the southeastern Pacific at the tip of the
Polynesian Triangle in Oceania, it is a "special province" of Chile,
more than two thousand miles away from the mainland.

Easter Island was settled, probably by Polynesian explorers,
sometime between 800 and 1200 AD. Its people, known as the
Rapa Nui, nearly vanished in the nineteenth century through ab-
duction by Peruvian slave traders and the influx of European diseases like tuberculosis and smallpox. At its nadir in the 1870s, the
Rapa Nui population stood at 111, only 36 of whom had children.
All the roughly 4,000 indigenous Rapa Nui people on the island
today are descended from those 36 survivors. Many have intermar-
ried with Chileans, who make up most of the balance of its population of some 7,700 citizens.

What Easter Island is known for is a great mystery of human
ingenuity: the enormous monolithic statues, or moai, constructed
by its early settlers. Carved from tufa (solidified volcanic ash), they
are thought to be representations of powerful ancestors that form a
sacred bridge, in the words of Jo Anne Van Tilburg, who studied them
for decades, "between sky and earth, people and chiefs, and chiefs
and gods."

Most of the moai are oversized heads, with broad noses and chins,
strong brows, oblong ears, and eye slits or sockets once filled with
coral irises and stone pupils, standing atop blocky torsos. They're
huge, with an average height of around thirteen feet and a weight of

some fourteen tons. But some are much bigger, notably the aptly nicknamed El Gigante, unfinished at 72 feet long and 165 tons, and Paro, the tallest complete statue, standing almost 33 feet high and weighing 82 tons.

Of the nine-hundred-plus moai that exist, about 45 percent remain, complete or half-crafted, in the Rano Raraku Quarry where they were formed; others lie on the ground, seemingly dropped in transit; and 288 were placed, erect, on ahu, or stone platforms. Seven identical moai, placed at Ahu Akivi, a sacred inland site, face out to sea, possibly to bless ships or guide them to the island. The rest stand along a stretch of the fifteen-by-eight-mile island's perimeter, with their backs to the ocean, watching over the populace.

But how did they get there? Mythology holds that the gods commanded them to walk. Modern researchers, including Van Tilburg, have hatched and even tested various theories, such as being rolled on logs, pulled on sledges, or encircled with ropes and inched, from side to side, into position. So far no one has come up with a truly credible explanation for how a civilization equipped with only primitive tools could possibly have accomplished such a feat of engineering (forget the fanciful, who claim that aliens dropped them from outer space).

We both had longed to see the moai, captivated by the mystery and their magnificence in photos. For our five-day stay, we'd booked ourselves into a cabana near the beach in a quiet, residential setting. The proprietor, Miguel, met us at the airport in his sputtering, rusty van, excited, with gorgeous leis that he strung around our necks. We could tell right away that we'd become good friends.

The first thing he asked was, "Are you hungry?" We were, after the long flight. "We'll go to the cabana afterward," he said. "But now, you must have tuna steaks!"

We'd heard of tuna steaks but had never tried them. In Texas, tuna comes smushed up in cans. Still, we said, "Great!"

Driving along the island's main drag, we saw a string of little open-air cafés. Miguel kept pulling up to yell out the window, "Fresh tuna steaks?"

When he got a no, we'd move on. Finally, someone gave him a thumbs up. "This is it!" he told us.

The tuna, a large, freshly caught pink slab, looked gorgeous. It came to our table perfectly grilled, like the best cut of prime beef we ever ate. "It was so delicious," Sandy says. "After that, we ate it whenever we got the chance."

"And the juices," Ellie adds. "All made with tropical fruits like mangos. We enjoyed them so much. What a welcome!"

Our comfortable cabana was one of a cluster that Miguel owned. Two or three were rented to tourists, with the rest occupied by his family. He and his wife lived in a somewhat nicer house nearby, close enough that Miguel and the van—which we dubbed "the little engine that could"—were at our service for transportation.

Ellie's top priority was photography, and Sandy, primed by assisting in surgery, was long accustomed to being her deputy. "We had our rhythm down," Sandy says. "Waking in darkness and getting perfectly positioned for sunrise, it was always worth it to see those dramatic moments when the first rays of light peeked out on the horizon, in shades ranging from yellow to coral. I could well understand why Ellie loved it."

During the day, we'd often scout for spots where Ellie could best capture the sun going down on the moai. "Photographers speak of the 'magic hour,'" Ellie says, "that time around sunset when there's a very special, evocative quality of light."

The moai themselves, huge and hulking, had a somber nobility that made us feel dwarfed, not just in size but in our ephemeral humanity. "When you're gone, we'll still be here, standing guard," they seemed to say. In their shadow, we could sense the dignity and power of the ancestors they depicted. They were wreathed in an air of the supernatural.

> **The moai themselves, huge and hulking, had a somber nobility that made us feel dwarfed, not just in size but in our ephemeral humanity. "When you're gone, we'll still be here, standing guard," they seemed to say.**

Peering into the quarry, where hundreds of moai lay buried, broken, or half-fashioned, we could hardly imagine the tiny craftsmen clambering over them with toki, or handheld chisels made of rock. It seemed inconceivable that such simple implements in human hands could create such grandeur. We were dazzled by the immensity of their effort—and, as in Antarctica, overcome by a profound humility.

A surprising counterpoint to the moai's colossal gravity was the energy of wild horses, which were everywhere on the island—racing in small herds along the beach, leaping in the surf, and grazing in the hills. Evidently, they were imported, perhaps by European or South American landowners, and then grew feral. We heard several times that there were more horses on Easter Island than people.

We were blown away by the warmth of the (non-equestrian) Easter Islanders we met. Miguel seemed to know—or was, in fact, related to—everyone and was generous with introductions. That interrelatedness that seemed so special to us could also be a problem, as one waiter we chatted with confided, telling us, "I'm still single because, being Rapa Nui, I never meet anyone who isn't a family member."

Miguel, who was Rapa Nui, had stepped outside his family circle and married a Chilean. She was a lovely woman, who embraced us with open-hearted joy. The manager of a small curio shop, she kindly gifted us with "good-luck" necklaces that were strings of small moai, some wooden, some stone, to bless our trip.

One day, Miguel suggested that we hike up Mount Terevaka, the youngest of the three major volcanos, all extinct, on Easter Island. It is also the tallest, at roughly 1,700 feet, and a moderate climb on a popular, gradually sloping trail. When we reached the summit, we were glad to relax on a bench beside the crater lake and enjoy panoramic views of the sparkling blue Pacific.

But there was a smaller, steeper hill with a better view of the moai, Miguel told us. "Let's give it a try!" we said. Once there, Ellie struck out ahead, in search of photos, but Sandy struggled to keep her footing on the uneven path. "One of my hips was acting up," she says. "I've since had it replaced. Still, since the pain wasn't that bad and the view promised to be amazing, I didn't want to turn back."

Miguel, seeing Sandy falter, gallantly offered her his arm. The two of them, in lockstep, trailed Ellie up the hillside. "With that little extra support, I could make it," Sandy says. "Even better, I had Miguel's encouragement. The whole way, he was kind enough to point out rough patches and to praise my perseverance."

Finally, the three of us reunited near the top. The glorious view of the island spread out below us, with the stately moai dark against the sky, was worth the climb. Then, suddenly, Miguel got down on one knee in front of Sandy. Taking her hand, he declared, "I crown you Queen of Easter Island!"

Ellie quickly snapped a photo to send to Sandy's kids with the caption "Did she say yes?" Imagine their surprise at the image of a seeming marriage proposal—and their relief at learning that it depicted merely a coronation, not the moment when they gained a new dad!

"Sandy's charm is a true gift," Ellie says. "It's so much fun to travel with her because she's constantly collecting fans like Miguel. Of course, he liked me, too, but that couldn't compare to his fondness for Sandy."

Not long before we left, Sandy acquired yet another admirer. "I was off shooting pictures when she began talking to a young man from England. We weren't even wearing our shirts—the usual icebreaker—when they struck up a conversation."

When we ran into him later, he made a point of telling us, "I've been emailing my family about you—all about your trip and how remarkable you are. I wanted them to get the message, loud and clear, 'Just because you're getting older, you can't stop living.'"

> ## Just because you're getting older, you can't stop living.

That could be our motto, but, of course, it has never occurred to us that, being older, we should "stop living." Between us, we have four artificial knees, one revamped rotator cuff, arthritis, and now a new hip. None of those impediments have slowed us down. And at that point, a few weeks into our trip, we were nowhere near stopping. We were just beginning!

10

AGE WON'T SLOW YOU DOWN
IF YOU ADAPT, STAY POSITIVE,
AND DREAM BIG

Argentina

After seeing the magnificent, enigmatic moai, we were eager to visit another site of historical mystery, Machu Picchu, the "Lost City of the Incas." Nestled in a mountain saddle in the Peruvian Andes, at an elevation of nearly eight thousand feet, it is a complex of two hundred residences, temples, and support buildings, along with the Intihuatana—a sacred stone functioning as a clock and a calendar, believed to help hold the sun in the sky. The structures, connected by crisscrossing terraces, were sustained by stepped mountainside gardens and sophisticated irrigation/drainage systems.

Set in a cloud forest, Machu Picchu was probably designed as a retreat for the Inca emperor Pachacuti Inca Yupanqui. But for all the artistry and labor that went into its creation, this archeological marvel was inhabited only briefly, from around 1450 to 1532. No one, to this day, knows why it was abandoned.

We booked tickets and were especially looking forward to the scenic train ride from Cusco, Peru, through the lush Sacred Valley, dotted with ruins, into the Andes and up to the threshold of Machu Picchu. In December 2022, uprisings against the Peruvian government had blocked the rail tracks. Tourists stranded inside the complex had to be rescued via airlift. Despite that news, we kept our reservations even after Machu Picchu was closed, as a result of the political unrest, on January 22, 2023—"indefinitely," the announcement said. (It actually reopened a short time later.)

We monitored conditions till, literally, three days before our flight to Peru. At that point we figured that, even if Machu Picchu reopened, we risked walking into a firestorm, the way we had in Syria. So, with no debate or hand-wringing, we turned on a dime, canceled our plans, and booked a flight to Buenos Aires, Argentina.

We were flying blind in Argentina, with no idea of what to see and do there. We hadn't done a lick of research on the sights or the culture. We got a budget hotel close to the city center, feeling pretty confident that somehow we'd scare up an adventure.

We take pride in our ability to adapt—to stay positive and pivot as the situation warrants. As people get older, too many seem to get stuck in one groove. We see rolling with changes (and even punches) as exercising the wisdom of age—putting the resourcefulness and cunning gained over years of living to good use.

> **We take pride in our ability to adapt—to stay positive and pivot as the situation warrants. As**

people get older, too many seem to get stuck in one groove. We see rolling with changes (and even punches) as exercising the wisdom of age—putting the resourcefulness and cunning gained over years of living to good use.

Once we got settled in our hotel, we hit the streets. Much of the architecture on the major avenues dates from the nineteenth century and reflects a range of the grander, more ornamental European styles. One reason for the European character of Buenos Aires is that, from the nineteenth century on, millions of immigrants have settled there. The influx from Spain and Italy alone tripled the city's population between 1887 and 1915. But the porteños, as they're called, come from all over the world, making Buenos Aires one of the most diverse cities in the Americas.

Buenos Aires is known as the "Paris of South America" for its rich cultural life, especially live theater—every weekend, there are some three hundred productions staged, more than in any other city in the world. It also boasts an internationally renowned opera house, several symphony orchestras, and countless museums encompassing every aspect of the visual arts.

But we were interested in Argentinean, not European-style events. We found lots of options right on the street, where hawkers from tour groups stood holding up placards, all claiming to be "the best." One caught our eye because it promised a tango exhibition and a visit to Don Silvano's Gaucho Estancia. We couldn't guess what a dance show and a "cowboy ranch" had in common, but it seemed worth asking.

"Oh, you must see a tango show!" the young man told us—tango being so integral to Argentinean identity that it's included on the UNESCO Intangible Cultural Heritage List.

We followed him back to his tour group office, to see that he was legit, and bought tickets for that evening.

The show took place in a beautiful dinner-theater setting. We were served Argentinean steaks, which are famous throughout the world, since they come from cows grazed on the country's vast grasslands, called pampas. Argentineans consume more beef than people in any other country. Even by our exacting Texas standards, the steaks were delicious.

And the dancing! The tango is extremely romantic, performed by two people holding each other close (chest to chest, in traditional Argentinean style) while executing long, elegant swoops or complicated footwork. We were dazzled by the dancers' gracefulness and electric connection to each other. The sparks flying off them were dizzying.

We left feeling dreamy, picturing ourselves dipping and gliding around the floor in the embrace of smooth dancing partners. Whew!

The next day, we were driven out to the ranch through the pampas, which blanket almost three hundred thousand square miles of the country. Seeing the open plains of grasses four feet high rippling in the wind struck a nerve in Ellie, evoking the prairielands of Oklahoma. "Don Silvano's ranch reminded me so much of my family's farm," she says. "It felt like a homecoming, flooding me with memories."

We got an even closer look at the pampas on a horse-drawn carriage ride. We roamed the ranch and met the gauchos, cowboys in baggy pants, who have long been seen as iconic in Argentina. The gauchos treated us to a horse show, like a rodeo without the cattle, racing and performing such tricks as aiming a spear through a small ring while galloping past it.

Ellie couldn't pass up the chance to get on horseback herself. "My horse was not the kind the gauchos rode," she says. "He was more the tired, tourist kind, whose giddy-up-and-go had got up and gone. But it was fun."

Sandy also tried riding but quickly dismounted. "It was my usual problem, being short," she says. "My feet didn't reach the stirrups. But I do know how to ride. One year I even rode a horse in the downtown Fort Worth parade. That day at the ranch, it just didn't feel right—and what I did that night was even more brave."

That night, there was a dance show on a stage at the ranch with a phenomenal emcee. The audience was made up of tourists from around the world, and the emcee performed a popular song, in its original language, from each country. In between numbers, a pair of tango dancers demonstrated some amazing moves.

At the end, the male dancer came to the edge of the stage and announced that he was going to choose a tango partner from the audience. We were seated right up front, at a table of mostly Europeans in their twenties and thirties. But he didn't pick any of them. "He saw Sandy smiling and couldn't resist," Ellie says.

"Of course, I felt nervous and shy," Sandy says, "but I thought, 'Why not?' The dancer took my hand and guided me through simple steps and swoops. I kept laughing, partly from embarrassment but mostly because it was fun.

"In the part of Texas where I grew up, in the church where I worshipped, dancing was seen as sinful and forbidden. But when I vacationed with Don, who liked cruises, he enjoyed watching other couples dancing. Some of them were really good, almost like Fred Astaire and Ginger Rogers. 'Let's try that,' he urged me; so we took ballroom dance classes.

"Don proved to be an excellent dancer, but I was always rhythm-challenged. I also didn't like dancing with other men. But Don insisted, saying, 'Sandy, in order to learn, you have to dance with the instructor.'

"Some of those classes must have taken hold, because I found that I could follow the tango dancer. So, I guess I didn't make a complete fool of myself."

"You did better than that," Ellie insists. "During your first dance, the whole audience got up and started doing the tango. Men were lined up, waiting to cut in and dance with you, like that young Polish guy and the one from Monaco. I have a photo of a kid in basketball shorts whirling you around. It was so cute—you were the belle of the ball!"

"Pictures don't lie," Sandy says, "but my children still can't believe I ever did that!"

The final highlight of our stay in Buenos Aires was a visit to the beautiful Recoleta Cemetery, full of elaborate marble mausoleums in a range of styles from baroque and neo-Gothic to art deco and art nouveau.

One of the most famous people buried there is Eva Perón, or Evita, as she was popularly known. Born into poverty, she wound up marrying Juan Perón and, by mobilizing workers and the indigent, helped him become president of Argentina. Though accounts of her sanctity in popular culture (including the Andrew Lloyd Webber musical *Evita*) may be exaggerated, she was said to be fanatical about fighting inequality through her Eva Perón Foundation, which provided job training, education, health care, and direct financial subsidies to the poor. She helped women win the vote and founded Argentina's first female political party, with half a million members. Her husband dubbed her the Spiritual Leader of the Nation.

Evita died of cancer in 1952, at age thirty-three. Worshipful crowds thronged the streets to see her body as it lay in state, crushing eight people to death and sending two thousand others to the hospital. During the construction of her mausoleum, her husband was ousted in a military coup and fled into exile. The insurgents kidnapped Evita's body and hid it for sixteen years to keep it from becoming a symbol for the resistance.

Finally, in 1971, Perón recovered her corpse and kept it in his home in Spain until he could return to power. In the mid-1970s, Evita was finally buried beside him in Recoleta Cemetery in a simple tomb, not the grand monument Perón had planned. Even today, to pay their respects, people drape it with flowers.

We were so inspired by the story of a woman who came from nothing and became such a powerful advocate for the voiceless. It was one of the reasons that our last-minute pivot to Buenos Aires was so fulfilling and well worth it. As often as not, when you're driven off course, you land someplace better than you could have imagined. Machu Picchu, in all its glory, could wait for another trip.

> **As often as not, when you're driven off course, you land someplace better than you could have imagined.**

Lapland and the Arctic

The Arctic is not a continent but an ocean at the top of the world, surrounded by eight countries—Canada, Denmark (Greenland), Iceland, Finland, Sweden, Norway, Russia, and the United States (Alaska)—with regions that penetrate its "circle," an invisible line of latitude drawn below the North Pole, about three-quarters of the way up from the Equator. Of these, we picked Finland for our next adventure, which was the quest to witness a phenomenal natural wonder, the aurora borealis, or the northern lights.

"My whole life, I've yearned to see them," Sandy says. "They were always at the very top of my bucket list. Ellie had never seen them either, so we were both anticipating a magical experience."

From Buenos Aires, we had to fly to Madrid and then London

to catch a plane to Helsinki, Finland's capital. Landing at 11 p.m., we had an eight-hour layover before heading to our ultimate destination, Rovaniemi, Lapland.

We were tired and wanted nothing more than to sink into bed, but the airport hotels were very expensive. It didn't seem worth it to blow our budget on just a few hours' nap. Coincidentally, Ellie had read an article rating airports on their "sleepability," and Helsinki was ranked number one. Not only did it have top-notch security and spick-and-span cleanliness, it offered different perches for weary travelers, including free pods in some areas and designated multilevel sleeping platforms.

We couldn't find any pods nearby, so we decided to try a platform. The travelers who'd already staked it out—young backpacker types—had bedrolls, not an amenity we'd ever needed. Still, we stretched out, with our coats as blankets and sweaters as pillows. Above our heads was a video display of the northern lights.

After dozing for a while, Sandy awoke in pain. "I had to nudge Ellie to say, 'Sorry, this hard surface is crunching my bones.' My hip, especially, couldn't take it."

So, we gathered our few belongings and struck out in search of cushions. We spotted a café, closed at that hour, with a worker inside. Comfy-looking padded banquettes lined its walls.

"Could we sleep here?" we asked.

He didn't seem a bit surprised. "Of course," he told us. "No one will bother you. Just don't be alarmed when the cleaning crew arrives."

Talk about a sleep-friendly airport! Where else would a closed café allow two strangers to camp out? We found the banquettes very comfortable and fell into a deep sleep. If the cleaning crew came through and mopped around us, we never knew it.

THE NEXT MORNING, WE FLEW TO ROVANIEMI, WHERE WE WERE BOOKED into Guesthouse Borealis, a family-run bed-and-breakfast. The city was a snowy wonderland, wreathed in white. Surprisingly, it felt colder than in Antarctica, apart from the frigid winds. This was wintertime in the Arctic, where temperatures hovered around zero.

Our first night, we set off on a northern lights tour. "Sandy was giddy with excitement," Ellie says. Since we'd be standing outdoors to await the spectacle, the tour company outfitted us in what we called "moon suits"—puffy, insulated coveralls, paired with heavy boots and thick gloves. After dark, dressed in our gear, a group of us waddled onto a bus and rode to the spot where we'd wait and watch for the magic to begin.

We stood for hours in the snow, heads tilted back, peering at the night sky for any hint that the light show was beginning. The tour company had explicitly warned that there was no guarantee that the aurora borealis would appear on any given night. Still, we kept waiting and hoping—and freezing. Nothing. Finally, with collective sigh of grave frustration, we gave up.

The next morning, we mentioned our disappointment to the desk clerk. We must have sounded downright pitiful, saying that we'd come so far, that seeing the northern lights was a lifelong wish, that we'd probably never get another chance, etc. We were crushed.

"The company my boyfriend works for doesn't go out unless

they're confident that you'll see the northern lights," she told us. "Of course, they can't promise. You want me to call?"

"Please do!" we said.

It turned out that they had space for us, but at a price—double what we'd paid for the night before. That gave us pause. Paying a premium was one thing, but double the price? When it was no more likely that, if we tried again, we'd actually see the northern lights?

But we didn't agonize long. We wouldn't waste money on mere hours in a hotel, but this was an experience, one that we'd dreamed of forever and might never encounter again. If that didn't warrant a gamble, nothing did. In unison we said, "Let's do it!"

> **We wouldn't waste money on mere hours in a hotel, but this was an experience, one that we'd dreamed of forever and might never encounter again. If that didn't warrant a gamble, nothing did.**

We joined a group of five, led by Aki, known on social media as the Prince of Lapland. Born and raised there, he was a professional photographer with a true passion for the aurora borealis. He even had some kind of software to predict its action—that's how much of a devotee he was. He showed us the app on his phone that could detect the colors building about fifteen minutes before the first rays of light appeared. It was incredible—and, he assured us, it worked!

That night the moon rose full and white. Its beams, reflecting off the snow, illuminated the scene like a spotlight. "I hope it's not too bright to see the aurora borealis," Sandy said.

But the sky above, black and prickling with stars, seemed like a worthy canvas. We stood on a path in a snowy field, staring into the sky above the trees. Then, suddenly, the show began with a swelling horizontal band of emerald light. We all oohed and ahhed as it grew in size, then started emitting flares, vertical ribbons of electric color: purples, yellows, greens, and blues. "My camera captured an even broader spectrum of color than was visible to the naked eye," Ellie says. "I saw it later in the photos."

No one spoke. We were all mesmerized, lost in the rhythm of the dancing lights—magnificent, supernaturally beautiful. It was freezing cold, but the reverent awe surging through us blocked any sense of the subzero temperature. We were witnessing one of nature's most dazzling displays of might, hinting at mysteries beyond human grasp. It felt like a benediction to us—a sacred experience, a life milestone.

> **We were witnessing one of nature's most dazzling displays of might, hinting at mysteries beyond human grasp. It felt like**

> **a benediction to us—a sacred experience, a life milestone.**

NOTHING ELSE WE FOUND IN LAPLAND COULD COMPARE WITH THE sheer, humbling magic of the northern lights. But we did have fun.

As always, we asked Marti, our driver in Rovaniemi, what we should see. "How about a reindeer farm?" he offered.

"Great," we said, fully expecting some tourist place, with an entry fee, like a petting zoo. Along the way, we admired the countryside, a winterscape of white fields and snow-laden trees, dotted with red wooden barns. Finally, he turned onto a narrow road and announced that we'd arrived at what was clearly a working farm— his family's place, where he'd grown up.

When we arrived, his uncle Oula was feeding a herd of about forty reindeer, which looked like small beige deer, with pronged antlers. As we got out of the car, Marti warned us to be careful. "The frozen snow is slippery," he said, so we'd have to develop "ice legs," like sea legs, to keep our footing.

Uncle Oula explained that, while the reindeer were wild and unpenned, they were considered "his," since they came to the farm daily to be fed. The reindeer were not pets but were cultivated, like sheep and cattle elsewhere, for their meat. In Lapland, reindeer husbandry is a traditional skill handed down through the generations.

Marti and his uncle filled us in on some fun reindeer facts: unlike deer, both female and male reindeer have antlers; antlers are shed once a year then regrow at the rate of nearly an inch a day (faster than any other animal bone); and there are some two hundred thousand reindeer in Lapland, exceeding the number of humans.

Uncle Oula let us feed his reindeer some kind of hay and green branches. Then he went into his barn and came back to present each of us with a small rack of antlers.

Marti next suggested that we try a husky sleigh ride. Doubting that we'd get lucky twice, we again assumed that it would be touristy—maybe a painted sleigh with jingle bells and lap robes, traveling in a circle around a small track. But as we kept driving deeper into the countryside, we began to wonder what awaited us. No way could we have guessed!

The sleigh was, in fact, a real, working dogsled, maybe ten feet long, flat on the ground, without runners, like a toboggan. But in the front, where a toboggan would curve up, there was a sort of prow to which the huskies were tethered. The back had railings to lean against, in front of a platform where the musher, or driver, stood. Flimsy-looking railings running along the side were all that would keep us from tumbling out.

"This is amazing!" Ellie said.

We settled into the sled, with Sandy sitting in back and Ellie up front, camera ready. Then our musher, who was a young woman, took the reins attached to the dogs' harnesses, and told us, "Hang on tight!" Gripping the side rails, we heard the whish of her long whip slice the air—and then we were off, the huskies bolting for the forest.

Who would have dreamed that eight dogs could run that fast? We sped on a broad snow path through the trees, holding our breath as we careened around sharp curves. Ellie managed to snap shot after shot with one hand, while clinging to the railing with the other. The wind whipping our faces was cold but exhilarating. (Our backsides, jolting on the unpadded wood, did protest.)

We covered two or three miles at top speed before circling back to our starting point. The dogs were barely winded, but we were out of breath from laughing in excitement at our thrill ride.

Finnish people consider Rovaniemi to be the official hometown of Santa Claus. There's even a Santa Claus village close to town, with a post office where visitors can read Santa's letters and a "headquarters," where it's possible to chat with the man himself and pose for photos.

After our authentic experiences, meeting the fictional Santa seemed anticlimactic. But being right there, how could we skip it? So, we dropped in, during Santa's "office hours."

We don't know what Santa would have thought of our final meal in Finland. On the day we flew out, we stopped at a small Helsinki coffee shop. We both ordered lattes and the most exotic entrée on the menu, reindeer mushroom quiche. Yes, we did it—we ate Rudolph (or maybe Donner or Blitzen). We plead guilty, without remorse. Our quiche was delicious.

Rome and London

While in Lapland, we stopped at the arctic circle signpost for that obligatory photo showing how far we were from major cities. Roma, 2,985 KM, it read, or roughly 1,850 miles. Rome was our next stop, where we'd make a brief touchdown to see the Colosseum, before heading to London for the date with CBS News we'd arranged in Ushuaia.

When we landed, we needed transportation to our quaint pensione near the Colosseum. On this trip, we usually reserved airport taxis in advance, through a website, but the price it quoted seemed excessive. So, we decided to find a cab the old-fashioned way. Big mistake! For the very first time, our habit of befriending taxi drivers failed us.

We spotted a sweet-looking older man holding a sign reading Taxi. Since he was in the airport, he seemed legit; we'd encountered this before. We didn't even flinch when he led us past the taxi stand to the parking garage. At least it wasn't the restaurant kitchen we'd had to cut through in Melaka.

His car seemed unusually nice. "Yes, we're a specialty service," he told us. "We drive a lot of businessmen and VIPs."

Okay, we could buy that. He quoted us a price that was high-ish but still cheaper than the website's. So, we got in. With such a short stay in Rome, we didn't have time to fool around with public transportation.

We had a lovely conversation en route, hearing all about his family. When we reached the hotel, Ellie handed over her credit card to pay the fare. "I need to take your picture for verification," he said, which seemed reasonable. After Ellie signed the receipt, he told us, "Oh no, the card didn't go through," so we repeated the whole routine of photo and signature.

A few weeks passed before Ellie checked her statement and discovered that we'd been triple-charged—once, for the original fare, which had indeed gone through, and then again, but doubling the fare, for the second try. She challenged the charges with the credit card company, but since the driver had photos of her signing the slips, she lost out. Later, when Ellie told a friend about the charges, he said, "Oh, don't be embarrassed. Roman cabbies are notorious for being crooks."

So, now we know! There's a maxim, "Never step twice in the same river," which could be adapted: "Never run your credit card twice for the same charge." But one bad apple couldn't sour us on taxi drivers, who over the years have been our greatest travel resources.

> **There's a maxim, "Never step twice in the same river," which could be adapted: "Never run your credit card twice for the same charge."**

The Colosseum was as impressive as we imagined. It's an elliptical open-air theater in the center of Rome, built in the first century

AD, that originally seated as many as eighty thousand spectators. The events staged there included gladiator contests, wild animal hunts (featuring elephants, rhinos, and lions), re-creations of famous battles, and public executions (possibly of early Christian martyrs, though most were killed at the Circus Maximus). Now a ruin, damaged by earthquakes and scavengers, it is still, two millennia after its construction, the largest standing amphitheater on earth.

To make the most of our short visit, we grabbed a Hop-On, Hop-Off bus to see the magnificent artworks of the Vatican and the Sistine Chapel, among other marvels. After several hours of sightseeing, we paused at a charming sidewalk café graced by a mural of the 1950s movie *Roman Holiday*. "That made me laugh," Sandy says. "Everyone claimed that my grandfather looked just like Gregory Peck, the male lead. My little sister once resembled a young Audrey Hepburn, the female star. So, I snapped a picture of the mural and sent it to my sister with the question, 'When we were kids, why did you and Papa sneak off to Rome without me?'"

Of course, we couldn't leave the Eternal City without visiting the fantastically baroque Trevi Fountain. Legend holds that those who throw coins in the fountain are destined to return to Rome. Many try it—$1.5 million in coins are scooped from its waters each year and donated to people in need.

When throwing our coins, we also expressed a few personal wishes. Ellie wished for happiness, which, she says, "Luckily, I got."

Sandy says, "I don't remember my wish, but surely it came true. If it didn't, I'd still be wishing it."

~~~~~~~~

THEN WE WERE OFF TO LONDON FOR ANOTHER BRIEF VISIT. OUR flight was delayed, so we arrived too late for anything but dinner and bed. The next morning, CBS sent a gleaming black car to pick us up. We were wearing our T-shirts, ready for our interview.

To our surprise, the interview wasn't held in some sleek, modern newsroom but in the historic Victoria Pub. Built in the 1830s, around the time of Queen Victoria's coronation, the pub had a beautiful, solid mahogany bar, carved floor-to-ceiling wooden columns, ornate fireplaces, and etched and gilded mirrors on the main floor. Every free inch of wall space was covered with memorabilia from its famous patrons, including Charles Dickens, who supposedly wrote part of his final novel, *Our Mutual Friend*, there; Charlie Chaplin; Winston Churchill, who lived nearby; and others.

Its upstairs bar was bedecked with artifacts from the demolished Gaiety Theatre, where in the nineteenth century, British musicals and musical comedies were born. Another upstairs room was outfitted with the huge spotlights and video equipment that CBS would be using for our taping.

Not being drinkers, we had a Coke and a coffee in the main bar, then were escorted up to the studio. The female producer shepherding us seemed surprised that we could climb the stairs. "Wow, you two move well," she said.

She was actually genuinely impressed, not condescending. But we couldn't help bristling, thinking, "How decrepit do you think we are? We're traveling around the world! You think we can't manage a flight of steps?"

We used the banister not out of feebleness but "on Dr. Sandy's orders," Ellie says. "She always insists, 'No climbing stairs without holding the railing.'"

"Well, people who don't do it land in the emergency room," Sandy replies. "I'm just practicing preventive medicine."

Our interviewer, Ramy Inocencio, a celebrated journalist, welcomed us as warmly as he would some VIP, immediately putting us at ease. We'd done scores of presentations and workshops and, of course, the airport spot in Dallas, but this was our very first sitdown television interview.

We weren't scared, exactly, or overconfident. We instinctively knew that, in an up-close conversation, with the cameras rolling, all we could be was who we are. In a normal personal encounter, we'd never try to create a calculated impression, so we weren't about to do it on television. We just sat back and welcomed the questions, determined to have fun.

Ramy asked about our itinerary and our budget-travel principles. Sandy described her response when other women say, "Oh, I'd love to travel like y'all." "Right away, I look at their hands," she told him. "If they're well-manicured, with painted nails, I think, 'No, in fact you would *not* love to travel the way we do.'"

He laughed, saying, "Put out your hands."

"So, we did," Ellie says. "Mine are not only unmanicured but knobby and gnarled from arthritis. Sandy's are straight but pretty witchy."

"Yes, they are," Sandy says. "Once, when I was in my sixties, a patient's daughter asked my age because she said my face was young but my hands looked old. I said, 'That's because I wash them thirty times a day!'"

They got a big kick out of broadcasting that image of our overworked hands. It was a fun moment that helped us bond with Ramy and the crew.

The formal taping lasted about four hours. Ramy, with his good nature and stimulating questions, made it easy. Afterward, he said, "Well, I can see that this isn't your first rodeo"—meaning that we came across as comfortable and natural. Given our inexperience— it *was* our first rodeo—we were stunned. What a compliment from such an accomplished professional.

Then it was time for B-roll. We were filmed repeatedly getting in and out of a taxi. The taxi drove us to the Houses of Parliament, also known as the Palace of Westminster, which is home to the famous tower clock Big Ben. As we walked along, chatting, with the palace in the background, Ramy told us that he wished his mother was agile enough to travel. Sandy piped up, saying, "We have four artificial knees between the two of us. Still, we can do full squats"— and she demonstrated, right there in front of Parliament.

"When she went into her deep knee bends—dipping straight down, not holding on—I joined her," Ellie says. "They filmed the two of us, eighty-one years old, doing squats on the sidewalk!"

Aging doesn't have to mean inertia—we hope that's a positive message we can share. We're great believers in staying active. Ellie swims and walks a few miles a day, while Sandy does the same on her treadmill at home. Exercise has kept us limber enough for more exciting activities, like traveling. If there's a single secret to life, it's

"Keep On Moving," putting one foot in front of the other, until your baby steps become adventures.

> **Aging doesn't have to mean inertia . . . If there's a single secret to life, it's "Keep On Moving," putting one foot in front of the other, until your baby steps become adventures.**

We ourselves got a useful takeaway from that interview: the older you are, the more you can get away with. What would be interesting about the hands of a thirty-year-old or a youngster doing squats in a public place? But we had fun doing those segments, which were totally spontaneous, and others enjoyed them because of our age. That realization freed us to act silly on the spur of the moment, laughing at ourselves so others could laugh with us.

As we parted, Ramy urged us to keep him abreast of dramatic prospects in our travels so they could do follow-ups on the interview. Our story aired in three segments and got covered in the London newspapers, as well as—unbeknownst to us then—around the world. It wasn't long before the press became almost a third passenger—unexpected but not unwelcome—on our trip.

The same driver who'd picked us up that morning came to return us to the hotel. When he heard that we were leaving without doing any sightseeing, he insisted on showing us around. "CBS is paying for the car," he told us. "Why not take advantage of it?"

The tour was an idiosyncratic view of London, highlighting the driver's brushes with fame. "Here's Buckingham Place," he'd say casually, then focus on where he was parked when Princess Diana came out and he got to see her up close. He was so charming and enthusiastic about sharing his personal "hot" spots that he infected us with his joy. It was a sweet, lighthearted end to our intense though pleasurable day and our whirlwind visit to Europe.

Zanzibar

Sandy's lifelong dream had been to see the northern lights. Ellie's was to visit Zanzibar. "For thirty years, I'd talked about going," she says. "Everything about it enchanted me. Even its name is romantic, with its poetic rhythm and those two *z*'s. I love Africa, especially the bush terrain of mainland countries like Zambia. But Zanzibar's island landscape and culture are totally different. It's a side of Africa I'd never seen.

"I never got there because my family chose more far-flung places to visit when coming home from the medical mission. So, when Sandy and I planned our eighty-day trip, I was thrilled when she agreed to put Zanzibar on the list."

Zanzibar is actually the name of an archipelago, a string of islands near the coast of Tanzania. But in everyday usage, the word refers to Unguja, its main island, which has Zanzibar City as its capital.

We flew there from London through Nairobi, Kenya. For at least a millennium, Zanzibar was a trading post, where Swahili merchants brokered deals for East African goods like gold and ivory, as well as Indian cloth, among Persian, Arab, and Indian wholesalers. Then colonizers arrived—Portuguese in the fifteenth century, Muslim sultans from Oman from the seventeenth century on, and later German and British.

In the nineteenth century, the sultans ran one of the world's largest and most brutal slave-trading centers. As many as fifty thousand people a year were trafficked through Zanzibar City until the British abolished slavery in 1873. The biggest slave market was replaced by the Anglican Christ Church Cathedral, with its altar deliberately positioned where the whipping post once stood.

Today, Zanzibar's population is mostly ethnic Swahili, with an Arab minority and a small number of Persians, Somalis, and Indians. The dominant religion is Islam. But Zanzibar's culture is unique, a fusion of all its influences.

We knew we wanted to stay in Stone Town, the historic district, located on a spit of land jutting into the Indian Ocean. The area gets its name from the coral stone, or reef-coral-infused limestone, used to construct most of its buildings, giving its streets a faint pinkish glow. We found a great hotel, the Dhow Palace, built in 1559 as the home of a sheikh and expanded over the centuries into its current form: a three-story, thirty-room hotel with an atrium, complete with a fountain, a swimming pool, and a spectacular rooftop restaurant.

"Wow," Sandy said, when she saw our room. An archway with double doors led to our balcony, overlooking the pool, outfitted with a table and chairs. Dark wood moldings and ceiling beams, as well as our carved wooden beds, evoked the grandeur of the past. Above each bed, tethered to the headboard, was a cloudlike canopy that could be unfurled for privacy. But the most fabulous feature was the bathroom, with a shower stall containing a thronelike structure, constructed of ornate blue tile, that you could sit in while spraying yourself.

What glamour—and for just sixteen dollars each per night!

The next day, we set out on foot to explore the city, with a guide. Much of Stone Town is an intricate maze of twisting alleys too narrow for cars. Some of them were lined with open storefronts selling traditional men's kanzus, or long, white robes, and women's kangas, or bright, printed fabric to be draped around the body. Though we saw signs imploring Please Respect Our Culture—meaning no bare shoulders or plunging necklines—we did see some spaghetti strap Western-style sundresses for sale.

Most of the shops were run by women. Where were the men? Some strolled the streets, carefree, and we spotted a few in white kanzus sitting in a courtyard, down a little alleyway, playing dominos.

Our guide was essential because we could never have found our way through the labyrinth of streets, which was like an open-air version of the Aleppo souq. Many of the buildings looked dilapidated—coral stone is crumbly—but we could see in their architecture the cultures that shaped Stone Town: European, Arabic, Persian, Indian, and African. Along residential streets, the most fascinating features were the wooden doors: some studded with brass, Indian style; others carved with verses from the Qur'an or with motifs like flowers; still others inlaid with decorative designs. The doors were of two distinct shapes: Indian, with rounded tops; and Arabic, which were rectangular.

"I must have shot dozens of photos of doors," Ellie says. "I've often thought the doors of Zanzibar would make for a good exhibition or a poster."

We ducked into the Hamamni Persian Baths, a traditional facility built by a sultan in the 1870s. Open to the public (serving men and women at separate times), it was restricted to the wealthy because of steep admittance fees. Inside were rooms for cold and hot communal baths, with water supplied through underground aqueducts, along with shaving areas, and even a restaurant. The baths remained functioning until the 1920s and, now restored, are a tourist attraction.

"Too bad they're not working," Ellie said. "I could sure use a cooldown!" After walking for three solid hours in the ninety-degree heat, we were roasting. Just a week before, we'd been in the Arctic, freezing, in subzero temperatures. Our body thermometers were out of whack.

THE NEXT DAY, WE HIRED A CAR AND DRIVER TO SHOW US MORE OF the island. At the shoreline stood a row of historic cannons, pointing out to sea, making us think of the ships, friendly and predatory, flying under so many different flags, that had sailed within range of those weapons over the centuries.

We explored the Old Fort the seventeenth-century sultans built to defend Stone Town against European invaders. A heavy, square-shaped bastion with battlements at the corners, it is now a cultural center, with shops on its upper level, above amphitheater seating for the concerts staged there. The Old Fort is the site of the annual Zanzibar International Film Festival, which welcomes entries from Africa and the "Dhow" countries of Southeast Asia, the Arabian Peninsula, the Persian Gulf, India, and Pakistan.

Since cooking and gardening are great pleasures for both of us, we were eager to visit one of Zanzibar's famous spice farms. We learned, among other things, that cloves are dried, unopened buds of trees that reach as high as fifty feet; that our familiar cinnamon is actually tree bark; and that vanilla, a member of the orchid family, is hard to grow because its flowers must be individually hand-pollinated.

We couldn't even guess which spice came from the trees laden with fruit that looked like apricots. Then our host at the farm sliced open a piece of fruit to reveal its reddish seed covering, which becomes the spice mace, and inside it, the pit, which we know as nutmeg.

We also saw plants that yield black pepper (berries), cardamom (seeds), saffron (threads picked by hand from crocus flowers), ginger and turmeric (root stocks), lemongrass (stems that can grow nine feet tall), and many others.

We must have been judged prize pupils because, at the end of our tour, our hosts presented us with floral crowns, declaring us Queens of Spice Island. "What a relief to have my own coronation," Ellie says. "Now I felt on equal footing, more than a mere lady-in-waiting, to Sandy, Queen of Easter Island."

The most disturbing part of the day was glimpsing the cruelty of enslavement. All over Stone Town, there were vestiges of it, like signs for the Slave Market Memorial, which featured an open pit full of statues in neck chains, along with the preserved "slave cellar," fifteen low-ceilinged rooms where people were crammed, in suffocating heat, to await the auction block. We had decided to skip the memorial because it seemed voyeuristic and revolting to view such vivid evocations of human suffering. While slave trading went on all over the island, the Stone Town markets were said to be the most pitiless.

But after driving past sparkling white beaches dotted with palms and picturesque villages with thatched-roof homes, our driver mentioned that we were nearing some "slave caves." Did we want to see them? We took a deep breath and said yes, feeling that we should somehow bear witness to this dark side of paradise.

The caves were used to hide enslaved people who would be traded in defiance of the ban the British tried to enact as early as the 1840s. Thirty years later, it would take the threat of a total blockade, killing all commerce, to force the sultans to finally accept the prohibition on human trafficking.

Beyond their illegal use, the caves are important archeological sites where bones, stone tools, ceramics, and other artifacts have been found, suggesting that Zanzibar was inhabited as far back as ten thousand to twenty thousand years ago. There are at least 120 known caves on the island, created through erosion of the soft limestone by rainwater. In some, which are considered sacred, local villages have set up shrines.

The caves we entered, through a narrow passageway, seemed more forbidding than holy. In spots, stalactites hung from the ceiling and stalagmites thrust up from the floor. The dark air felt dank and unhealthy to breathe. Beneath our feet, the ground was craggy, making it difficult to walk. "Where could someone trapped here even sit, never mind lie down?" Sandy said.

We could only guess at the shell shock an abductee would have felt, torn from the familiar, every shred of personhood stripped away, jostling with others in this hellhole in the earth, terrorized by the inevitability of horror. "How could someone even stay sane?" Ellie said.

We couldn't bear to stay long but breathed fervent prayers for the souls of those who'd so grievously suffered.

By then it was late afternoon. Our driver, who seemed to anticipate our distress after the caves, asked, "Would you like to see some of our fishing fleet?"

"Oh yes," we said, grateful for the chance to get oceanside and shake off the claustrophobia of the underground.

He brought us to a place where men were clustered around dhows, or Arab-style, half-crescent-shaped boats. At anchor, their large, triangular sails were rolled shut to keep them from catching the wind. Some men were standing in the shallows, loading gear into their dhows, others were fooling with the rigging, while still others sat onshore, tending to their nets—all of them working with good cheer. Some boats were grounded, upside down, with men clambering over their hulls, making repairs. After dark, the driver told us, they'd sail out, returning in the wee hours with their catch.

We were struck by the beauty of the wooden dhows, all hand-made, and clearly objects of pride. But they seemed so small to brave the vastness of the ocean. The men, talking and laughing, buoyed by generations of tradition, didn't seem worried.

We wound up the day with a walk on the beach, enjoying the

salt air and the seabirds calling. "Was Zanzibar as great as you imagined?" Sandy asked.

"Oh yes," Ellie said. "I loved the confluence of history, so many cultures converging on one island. I loved the sense that I was walking the same ground as the ancients from ten thousand years back. Who were they? Paleolithic people? I loved the visuals, the pinkish buildings and the magnificent doors, and the scent of spices everywhere. I loved that farm, with all the mysteries of flavors. You have to think, how did humans discover those? I loved the people, who seemed so happy—and who wouldn't be, in this tropical wonderland?

"Yet 1 feel so haunted by the ruthless violence of enslavement. And I feel helpless, knowing that we haven't evolved and stripped such vicious evil from the human psyche."

"I know," Sandy said. "All we can do is sow kindness and joy when we get the chance."

> **"All we can do is sow kindness and joy when we get the chance."**

11

HOME FIRES CAN
SPARK RENEWAL

Zambia

It was now the midpoint of our trip. We'd decided to mark it with a breather on home ground. Zambia is a major touchstone for us, the place our friendship was born and where, individually, we'd blossomed, becoming self-determined women, committed to public service, and yearning for lives transcending the ordinary.

In Zambia, we could check off another of the Seven Natural Wonders of the World, the magnificent Victoria Falls . . . and we could get our clothes washed! Sink laundry—and dodging drying garments overhead—had definitely gotten old.

As codirector of the Zambia Medical Mission, Ellie has a home at the Namwianga Mission, about five hours outside the capital, Lusaka. When we landed in Lusaka, two of our nearest and dearest picked us up, Robby Banda and Patrick Kawinga. Former students at the mission, both Robby and Patrick are cherished family members, who greeted us with hugs and laughter. "We've been following you on Facebook," Robby said. "We're so glad you're finally here!"

What a joyous reunion with people we love! Our hearts were bursting.

Robby is not only beloved but essential to the mission's functions. He's our computer guru and general high-tech wizard. Right after high school, he broke a leg in a motorcycle accident and suffered a wound that developed tetanus. Tetanus is a cruel disease, causing muscle spasms that can be strong enough to fracture bones. Tetanus can stiffen the face—that's why it's called lockjaw—impair swallowing and breathing, and bow a patient backward into an excruciating, frozen arch. Even with treatment, many victims don't survive.

There was no available human serum to treat Robby, but miraculously, horse serum saved his life. Kelly nurtured him during his illness, forging a special bond that encompassed Ellie and later Sandy.

At the mission, we got a hearty welcome from Leonard Sichimwa, who oversees the house and all of our guest facilities. Leonard "adopted" Ellie and Kelly in 1983, when they first moved to Zambia to run the school and were lodged in the headmaster's residence. "I come with the house," Leonard announced when they walked into their new home, and ever since then, he has been Ellie's Rock of Gibraltar.

A tall, imposing man, Leonard not only manages the house compound but serves as its head chef, alongside Andrew, his brother, and Harold, his son. Ellie's grandchildren, who call him their uncle, nicknamed him "Yummy, Yummy Leonard" because of his skill at baking cookies. He has eleven children of his own, including two named Ellie and Kelly.

Leonard quickly pulled Ellie aside. "Madam, we just killed a black mamba near your front door," he said. "Do you want to see it?"

"Oh no," Ellie told him. "Don't breathe a word to Sandy. She'll drop dead on the spot."

Snakes, even more than bugs, are Sandy's kryptonite. And rightly so—the black mamba is one of the world's deadliest snakes, with a bite causing collapse in forty-five minutes and death in a matter of hours. They're also huge—typically seven or eight but up to fifteen feet long—and highly aggressive. "I was once riding in a Land Rover charged by a black mamba," Ellie says. "It struck my window—which, thank goodness, was rolled up—and got thrown off the car."

We make mission trips in July, the Zambian winter, when it's too cold for most snakes to flourish. But now it was February, the "green season," when rains turn the dry land to jungle. "I've had some crazy close encounters in green season," Ellie says. "Like a spitting cobra in my house. I photographed it before the staff killed it with spears. Then there was the time when Kelly and I were out walking and, suddenly, a king cobra reared up in front of us. Fully erect, with its hood spread, it stood taller than we were. 'Ooh, ooh,' Kelly said—he was deathly afraid of snakes—but we both knew better than to make sudden movements. We inched away very slowly, and the snake backed down.

"By now, I'm used to snakes and avoid their haunts. But Sandy, the city girl, can't abide them. Leonard and I kept our lips zipped about the mamba near the house until the day Sandy and I left Zambia."

~~~~~~~~~~~

LEONARD BAKED US A BEAUTIFUL "WELCOME HOME" CAKE. FOR DAYS, friends dropped by to visit: Martin, another beloved former student; the amazing Elizabeth, who single-handedly raised ten orphans and now manages the medical mission's Zambian volunteers; Leonard's family, who'd invited Ellie, after his mother's death, to accompany him to lay flowers on her grave; and so many others who heard we were back and wanted to see us. We were so uplifted by the outpouring of love.

How good it felt to come home!

Ellie's home has long been the social center for the mission. "It's the most convoluted house you've ever seen," she says. "When we moved back to the States, we gave up the headmaster's residence but built ourselves a one-room thatched guesthouse to stay in on mission visits. Over the years, that guesthouse mushroomed, with a couple bedrooms added here, another couple there, along with a bunch of bathrooms and five showers. Then, because we needed gathering space, we built a big front room with a fireplace that gets used a lot in July, Zambia's winter, since the house isn't heated.

"Of course, we needed a large kitchen, since we're always hosting groups of people. We created an outdoor one with four rooms— an office for Leonard, a room with two refrigerators and our propane and electric stoves, a room for handwashing clothes, and another for ironing. The kitchen even has its own bathroom, a flush toilet out in the yard.

"The final touch was a veranda, spanning the front of the house, that can accommodate fifty people. I almost didn't build it because

I had a beautiful, very fruitful avocado tree out front. After I sacrificed it for the veranda, I replaced it with four others—but, wouldn't you know it? None of them has yielded a single avocado. My other trees are more productive, especially my huge sycamore figs, an ancient species mentioned in the Bible.

"In the yard behind the house, there's a big firepit, where people tend to gather in the evenings. I don't have a TV at the house, but even if I did, the electricity is hit-and-miss. So, people gather around the firepit, sing, and tell stories, then we all turn in early. It's a different way of life than in the States.

"One of the classic tales we like to recount is the walkie-talkie story. On one medical mission bush trip, a female staffer went out to the pit latrine (called the chimbusi in the Tonga language) very early in the morning. Not quite awake, she fumbled when juggling her skirts and her walkie-talkie, which team members use to communicate. The walkie-talkie slipped from her grasp down into the hole—gone, beyond recovery. But, for days, until the batteries ran out, the hole kept squawking, 'Ellie to Ray' . . . 'Come in, Ray . . .' blaring team conversations like a radio.

"A more heartwarming story involved Jimmy, a young team member, who felt carsick on the bus returning from a bush trip. We stopped on the road to let him get a bit of fresh air. But when we got back to the mission, Jimmy realized that he'd lost his cell phone. We'd never be able to find our stopping place—if that's where he dropped it—so we all assumed that Jimmy's chances of ever recovering the phone were zero.

"But some villagers had found it and, unbeknownst to us, had already mobilized to return it. One person volunteered to walk for a few hours to get the advice of a wise chief, who recommended announcing the find on a local radio show. They called the station, and when a Zambian member of our team heard the broadcast, he dispatched a bicycle courier to retrieve the phone and bring it to the mission. Jimmy was thrilled to get his phone back and amazed by the 'miracle.' So were the rest of us, who, a bit more cynical, were stunned that no one kept the phone or tried to sell it. Instead, the villagers had launched a major effort, taking hours, to get the phone back to its rightful owner. Shame on all of us for our lack of faith in human goodness!"

"Don't forget the best, most incredible cell phone story," Sandy says. "It involves my grandson, Matthew, who was fourteen at the time, and Ellie's grandson, Caleb, who was twelve.

"The four of us were doing a mini-safari, riding elephants into the bush. Now, I must say I much prefer riding elephants to camels— not just because of the proper seat, instead of a blanket to straddle, but also because you don't have to climb onto them. You stand on a platform and just step off it onto the elephant's back. Which makes sense because they're huge—maybe thirteen feet high.

"Life has a different feeling in the bush: intense, enchanting. Even on a cellular level. Africa changed us, humbles us—and we've seen it do the same for so many others. We each climbed aboard the gentle giants near a magnificent baobab tree, and within minutes were caught up in that strange, hypnotic elephant cadence, and, feeling the shift, gave ourselves over to this otherworldly place and pace.

"We were rocking along, each on our own elephant, with a grandson each perched in front of us, when Caleb whisper-shouted, 'I dropped the phone!'

"He'd been clutching Ellie's cell phone and now it was somewhere underfoot, hidden down in deep grasses rustling with venomous snakes, poisonous insects, and even menacing animals. Here in Africa, things can kill you, from one-celled organisms to many things that swim, fly, slither, float, leap, and run. Hippos emerge out of the water at night to forage in the high grass on the banks; get in between one and the water and it will bite you clean in half.

"Our little procession stopped, but we all knew not to dismount.

"Then, suddenly, my elephant began to gently shift his weight. He moved his massive feet sideways as we clutched our seat railing. With his huge ears flapped back, he lowered his trunk—and brought it back up with Ellie's phone in its grip! We all gasped as he calmly handed the phone back to Caleb.

"How on earth could that elephant have understood our predicament? He deftly problem-solved what had left us humans frozen in place, uncertain about what to do."

WITH ROBBY AND MARTIN, WE SET OUT TO VISIT MOSI-OA-TUNYA National Park, about seventy miles from the mission. Robby, who was driving, stopped the car when he saw some men holding AK-47s. After chatting with the men in Tonga, he told us, "The rhinos are here! They're sleeping in the field. Do you want to go see them?"

White rhinos, which are actually gray, were hunted to near-extinction by poachers because their horns are highly prized in traditional Asian medicine. Today, Zambia's small population is protected by armed guards who follow the herd as it freely moves around grazing.

"Of course," Ellie said, grabbing her camera.

"No way!" Sandy countered.

"It'll be okay," the guard tried to assure Sandy, with Robby translating. "Just stay behind me as we walk toward them, and be quiet."

We followed the guard into the field, where we could see a huddle of rhinos in the near distance. "Shhh!" Sandy urged at every raised voice, begging us, "Don't wake them!"

Finally, we were close enough for Ellie to shoot photos through her zoom lens. But as she crept in, seeking new angles, Sandy's distress was mounting. The "Sandy look" appeared on her face, and Ellie knew it was time to turn around and go back to the vehicle.

"I couldn't blame her for being concerned," Ellie admits. "Her fear, after all, was my fault."

Sandy's concern was caused by Ellie's previous rhino encounter. A few years earlier, when Ellie was visiting Livingstone, Zambia, she decided to go see the rhinos at Mosi-oa-Tunya National Park. "It was the green season," she says, "and the animals can be hard to spot in the jungle foliage. For ten dollars, a guard agreed to help me find them, armed for safety with his AK-47.

"We drove into the park in my cherry-red Land Rover. A storm was brewing, darkening the horizon with blue-black clouds. After nosing around for an hour, we got lucky. There, in a clearing, were three white rhinos, peacefully grazing.

"As I shot photos from the car windows, the rhinos ignored us. They're enormous beasts—only elephants are larger—reaching thirteen feet long and six feet high at the shoulder and weighing four to five thousand pounds. With their humped necks and double-horned snouts, they look almost prehistoric. Despite their bulk, they're quick and agile, able to hit speeds of up to thirty miles an hour, but can only run straight, not swerve off on angles.

"Since the rhinos seemed relaxed, I asked the guard if we could approach on foot for better pictures. He agreed, positioning me behind him and his gun. We made sure to stay downwind because rhinos' dominant sense is smell, followed by hearing. They have poor sight and can't detect much more than motion from a distance.

"I got close enough to one rhino to zoom in for some excellent shots. Then, as the clouds shifted with the coming storm, I adjusted a few settings, and—*pow!*—my flash suddenly went off. The rhino recoiled for an instant, then charged!

"My heart pounded, as the guard yanked me behind him, out of its path. That final flash photo actually captured the rhino's foot in mid-charge!

"We stood off to the side, shaking, as the rhino barreled past us. Then it stopped, sniffing the air, honking, ears waggling, seeking the source of the maddening light. It whirled, and like a car bearing down on us, headed back, hitting the ground with a terrible rhythmic pounding.

"The guard and I raced for the car. I dove in, crash-landing on the seat. Beneath me was something hard, which I realized moments later was my phone. As the rhino stalked off, abandoning the attack, I checked it, only to find that I'd accidentally butt-dialed Sandy.

"Quickly, I punched the off button. It was 2 a.m. in Texas, and I hoped that Sandy had slept through the call. But just then, the phone rang back. It was Sandy, calling me to ask, 'Are you all right?'

"Panting, adrenaline still surging, I choked out the story of my narrow escape. I could barely breathe, never mind speak. The sheer terror was hard to shake off.

"'Oh, Ellie, how frightening,' Sandy said.

"Now, wouldn't you know, years later, I'd done it again—gone after rhinos, despite my close call, and this time, exposed Sandy to potential menace. There are two types of people in the world— risk-takers like me and those like Sandy, who, as she always says, 'practice preventive medicine.' It's striking a balance between our very different temperaments that makes our friendship thrive— spurring Sandy to adventure and, by curbing my gung ho impulsiveness, probably helping to keep me alive!"

> **There are two types of people in the world—risk-takers like me and those like Sandy, who, as she always says, "practice preventive medicine." It's striking a balance between our very different temperaments that makes our friendship thrive.**

WE BOTH ENJOYED VISITING VICTORIA FALLS, FOR WHICH THE PARK was named. "Mosi-ao-Tunya" in the tribal language Lozi means "The Smoke That Thunders." Located on the Zambezi River at the border of Zambia and Zimbabwe, it's not the tallest waterfall in the world (though it's twice as high as Niagara) but is considered the largest because its curtain of water is the greatest on our planet.

We'd both been there before, in the dry season. Now it was the green season, when the flow of water is vastly amplified and the spray—the "smoke that thunders" of the falls—rises 1,300 feet or more, higher than the Empire State Building. Though clad in rain gear, we got drenched to the bone by the water's furious pounding. Still, we were beaming, feeling that the falls had given us a special show of majestic and overwhelming might. It was like a baptism, ushering us into the next stage of our journey.

Soon, we'd leave Zambia for a very different region of Africa— Egypt—to experience World Wonders created by human hands.

12

TOLERANCE, INTERVENTION, INNOVATION, AND RITUAL

Egypt

In the fifth century BC, the Greek historian Herodotus compiled the first known list of humanity's greatest creations, the Seven Wonders of the World. Only one of those wonders—the oldest, as it happens—is still standing, the Pyramid of Khufu, also known as the Great Pyramid of Giza. The largest of the hundred-plus pyramids in Egypt, it dominates the Giza Necropolis complex that stands on the outskirts of Cairo. Sandy had never seen it. "I wanted to share the incredible experience with her," Ellie says. "Besides, how can you do a world tour without visiting the pyramids?"

We were lucky on this trip because Ellie's daughter, Sheryl, who has taught internationally, had a personal connection to Nick, the owner of a local travel outfit in Egypt. Nick and his wife were Europeans who'd fallen in love with and resettled in Cairo.

Not only was Nick delighted to help vet our plans for our time in Egypt, but he appreciated our off-the-beaten-path preferences as budget travelers. So much so that he offered to join us our very first day to show us some of his own favorite sights.

He arranged for a driver to pick us up from the Cairo airport and meet him at Bab al-Futuh, one of three remaining gates in the wall of the Old City. Built in 1067, it is an imposing archway seventy-two feet tall and seventy-three feet wide, with an over-hang, like an awning, supported by engraved stone brackets. Nick pointed out the historical significance of the decorations on the gate—carved patterns of rosettes and crosses, an eight-pointed star, rams' heads representing Mars in the zodiac, and more— explaining their symbolism and influences. He was so knowledge-able about the artistry and excited to explain why he found the gate so special. We were completely enthralled.

Then he led us down some fascinating streets in the Old City, describing the architectural history of important buildings. The narrow streets, lined with small shops, were jammed with pedestri-ans interweaving with motorcycles and cars, along with dogs, cam-els, and cows—not as many cows as we'd see in India, but enough to unnerve Sandy.

"Of course, I'm no stranger to cows," Sandy says. "But I'm used to seeing them behind fences, grazing. Not meandering willy-nilly beside you through the tight, narrow streets. So, I was relieved when Nick took my arm to guide me through the chaos."

After this quick glimpse of Cairo, we headed to our lodgings, transferring our bags from Nick's driver's car to a taxi. We'd done a lot of research on where to stay and finalized our plans after run-ning our top choices by Nick. He'd endorsed the Royal Pyramids Inn, just a five-minute walk from the Giza complex. "You won't believe the views," he said. We were sold! Incredibly, our stay, including breakfast, cost each of us only thirteen dollars per night—one of our proudest finds of the trip!—and we also took some pleasure in knowing that the high-priced, five-star hotels had views of the pyramids nowhere near as good as our budget gem's.

But we were admittedly worried at first when the driver dropped us off, with our luggage, at the mouth of an alley. "Why should we get out here?" Sandy asked. The driver explained that, to reach the hotel, we'd have to walk halfway down the alley to an iron gate. "Just rattle it," he told us, "and they'll let you in."

The alley was deserted and eerie, but we quickly spotted the gate, which bore a small sign with the name of the inn. To our relief, when we rattled the gate, a man appeared with a big smile and open arms. "Welcome," he said.

Whew!

The charming inn was a six-story home that, after their parents' death, four brothers had converted into a guesthouse. Family members still lived there, no doubt on the lower levels, since we were directed to the fifth floor. There was no lobby and no elevator—just a covered staircase running up the side of the building. With our hosts carrying the luggage, we climbed the five flights to find a tiny but clean, comfortable room, with two beds and a small, lovely balcony.

The inn's real claim to fame, though, lay a floor above us. Its rooftop afforded a truly jaw-dropping, million-dollar view of the pyramids—which is what made Nick recommend it. The peaks of two Giza pyramids rose just beyond the terrace balustrade, so close that we were almost in their shadow. Magnificent by day, they were breathtaking by dark, lit up and glowing. They were even more dramatic during the nightly Sound and Light shows, with shifting colors rivaling fireworks. We could see the magic unfold, without joining the tourist swarm or buying tickets, while enjoying a bed-time snack on our private rooftop.

THE ROOFTOP ALSO SERVED AS GENERAL GATHERING PLACE AND DIN-ing room, where we enjoyed a complimentary continental breakfast before heading out to explore each day. Nick set us up with a won-derful guide, Kyrllos, who lived and breathed Egyptology. He gave us a lively history of the pharaohs, who ruled Egypt for at least 2,500 years, as the intermediaries between mortals and the gods.

The three main pyramids at Giza were built as tombs for the Pharaoh Khufu, his son Khafre, and his grandson Menkaure be-tween 2600 and 2500 BC. They're surrounded by smaller satellites, called "queen's pyramids," temples, and tombs for lesser nobles. The complex is guarded by the Great Sphinx, an enormous statue—240 feet long, sixty-six feet high, and sixty-two feet wide—with the body of a lion and the head and headdress of a king, who is thought to be Khafre.

The four corners of the major pyramids point almost precisely to the four points of the compass. No one knows how the materials used to construct them were quarried and placed, using the rough hand tools of the time. Originally, the pyramids were encased in polished white limestone, much of which was stripped by scaven-gers, as were their tips, once probably sheathed in granite or ala-baster (or, some like to imagine, gold). The exteriors we see today are yellow limestone or possibly a form of concrete, joined with mortar. Inside, walls and floors were constructed of mud brick, lined with pink granite or pale alabaster.

As for their unique shape, there are myriad theories. To mention a few: pyramids are exceptionally sturdy, with their weight concentrated at their base; they may have been modeled after the primordial stone from which Egyptians believed the earth was created; or they may have been aimed at the sun to help the pharaoh's ka, or spirit, ascend to the heavens.

UP CLOSE, THE PYRAMIDS WERE AS AWE-INSPIRING AS ANY HUMAN creation we'd ever seen. The Great Pyramid, Khufu's tomb, is massive, rising some 450 feet above the ground, with a base length of 756 feet. For four thousand years, it was the tallest manmade structure in the world. But beyond its size, it radiates the majesty and gravitas of great age. Standing in the presence of something 4,600 years old—the span of 180 generations—not just viewing it from a distance, took our breath away. The experience was deeply moving and made us feel a part of the continuum of history. Though humbling, it's also tremendously inspiring to see such marvels of human invention and capability.

> **Standing in the presence of something 4,600 years old—the span of 180 generations—not just**

> viewing it from a distance, took our breath away. The experience was deeply moving and made us feel a part of the continuum of history. Though humbling, it's also tremendously inspiring to see such marvels of human invention and capability.

Kyrllos asked if we wanted to crawl into the interiors of some pyramids. When we said yes, he drove us to nearby Saqqara, site of the Pyramid of Djoser, known as the Step Pyramid. The Step Pyramid, a four-sided structure, with six layers of decreasing size, was the first ever built and anchors Egypt's oldest necropolis complex. After years of restoration, it had just reopened to visitors in 2020.

We'd agreed to crawl into the Step Pyramid without quite realizing what "crawling" meant. Kyrllos explained that we'd have to creep down steps in low-ceilinged shafts to reach the few open chambers deep inside the structure. The intended functions of various shafts in pyramid walls remains mysterious, especially since many are too narrow to admit humans. Were they exit hatches for workers in the internal chambers? Ventilation ducts? Were they left open in hope that the pharaoh's ka could rise through them?

At the entrance to the pyramid, the staff seemed a bit dubious about admitting us. "Do you really want to go down there?" someone asked.

"You bet!" Ellie said.

"Well, good for you," the staffer replied, as if patting us on the head for being brave old ladies.

Though mildly annoyed, we just smiled. As adventurous octogenarians, we're accustomed to being underestimated.

> ## As adventurous octogenarians, we're accustomed to being underestimated.

Sandy went first, following the guide into the cramped, hot passageway. "Even being shorter than Ellie, I had to duck," she says, "and at some points, actually bend over."

Ellie, much taller, was practically crouching. "But that didn't stop me from taking photos," she says. "Including a classic shot of Sandy's backside in the tunnel. That makes our families laugh, but I think she should be proud. It proves how intrepid she is."

Luckily, the passage was lighted, and neither one of us is claustrophobic. We crept down, down, down the steep, narrow stairs, finally winding up in an open chamber, where we could stand. That's where, suddenly, the mind-blowing artisanship of the pyramid struck us—all the walls were engraved with the picture language hieroglyphics.

"While the guide described what we were seeing, I photographed madly," Ellie says. "I wasn't paying much attention to Sandy. Then I caught sight of her peering at some alabaster carvings pinpointed by the guide's flashlight. Her hands were pressed to her cheeks, as she stared, dumbfounded."

"I was just amazed," Sandy says, "and so excited. I felt transported back to ancient biblical times."

The guide, an older Arab man in a long white robe and a headdress, broke into a huge grin at Sandy's delight. Then he reached out and engulfed her in a bear hug.

"It was totally spontaneous," Ellie says. "It's rare for an Arab man to express such affection for a strange woman. But her enthusiasm was so infectious that he couldn't help himself. In fact, the whole room was beaming."

"It was just a big old hug, as if I were his little girl," Sandy says. "And I felt like one, with that kind of childlike wonder."

WE CRAWLED DOWN A FEW MORE TUNNELS THAT DAY BEFORE RE-turning to Giza. Then Ellie said, "We have just enough time for a camel ride around the grounds. Don't forget that we need B-roll."

"No way," Sandy said. "I told you in Syria, no more camel riding for me. I'm not doing that again."

"But I promised Ramy footage of us on camels at the pyramids," Ellie begged. Sandy balked until Ellie pulled out the big gun, a solemn vow. "Sandy, I swear that if you get back on the camel just this once, I will *never, ever* ask you to do it again."

When Sandy reluctantly agreed, Ellie handed Kyrllos her phone to snap some photos and shoot video of us getting on the camels. Like many helpers, he shot video that was vertical (not ideal for TV), but we sent it, along with photos, to CBS and other media outlets who'd asked to be kept posted on our adventures. We only heard about the stories airing about us from friends and family, who were tickled to see us popping up on the news! "So, apparently vertical footage was better than nothing," Sandy said, noting her personal favorite that day was a photo of Ellie loping on a camel behind its wrangler. "She looked so happy, arms outstretched, in that 'Look, Ma, no hands' pose," Sandy said. "And I know that I can trust her to keep her vow never to subject me to another camel ride."

On the way back to our guesthouse, Kyrllos asked us, "Are you hungry?"

We were, so he showed us the Cairo version of a drive-in restaurant. He simply stopped the car dead in traffic in front of a café. A waiter came running out with a notebook as the cars behind us jerked to a halt, honking wildly. "Order whatever you like," we shouted to Kyrllos, over the din.

The waiter dashed back inside with his notes, then reemerged with sandwiches of falafel and chicken shawarma, thrusting them into our hands amid the cacophony of blaring horns. It was a fitting symphonic send-off from ancient Cairo, where cows and camels, cars and motorcycles choked the streets in an ever-shifting jumble of old and new.

WE THEN HEADED TO LUXOR, ONE OF THE WORLD'S LONGEST-inhabited cities, located in Upper Egypt, about ten hours from

Cairo by train. Having struggled so often with signage we couldn't read and announcements in languages we couldn't understand, we were very grateful when Kyrllos insisted on taking us not just to the railway station but inside, straight to our train platform.

As usual, we'd booked passage on our favorite mode of transportation, a second-class sleeper car. We were pleased to find that, once again, we had our own compartment, instead of bunks in a flimsy-curtained dorm.

In Luxor, we planned to emulate Phileas Fogg by riding in a hot-air balloon. There may be no greater sight from the air than "the world's greatest open-air museum," as it's been called—the ruins of the temple complexes of Karnak and Luxor and, across the Nile, the cliff tombs of the Valley of the Kings.

For approximately five hundred years, from 1539 to 1075 BC, pharaohs and nobles were buried in elaborate tombs carved into the limestone bluffs of the Valley of the Kings. So far, some sixty-five tombs have been unearthed, ranging from simple pits to the convoluted structure labeled KV5, featuring more than 120 chambers for the sons of Ramses II (aka Ramses the Great). The typical construction was a long corridor thrusting downward into the cliffside, sometimes jogging 90 degrees before passing through one or more hollowed-out chambers en route to the burial hall. The interiors of the tombs were lavishly decorated, often with images of the sun passing through the twelve "gates," or hours of night, symbolizing the passage of the dead to the afterlife.

We met for our balloon ride before dawn, when the sunrise would bathe the Valley of the Kings in dramatic light. The operator thoroughly coached us in the balloon's basket on ways to brace in case of turbulence. But as hot air entered the mouth of the balloon, wafting it into the air, we felt surprisingly peaceful and confident. "We rose like a feather," Sandy says. "You could barely detect any motion."

The pinkish dawn light and tranquil air lent an otherworldly atmosphere to the Valley of the Kings, with its rugged cliff walls, laced with secret tunnels and rooms, and the remains of pillared temples far below us. "We were flying over history," Ellie says. "You see it but, even more, feel it."

The Nile was a blue demarcation between timeless and contemporary—the barren, rock faces of the Valley on its west bank and, on its east, the modern buildings of present-day Luxor, a bustling metropolis of 1.3 million people. Nestled within its sprawl are the ancient Karnak and Luxor temple complexes. The juxtaposition of the glorious monuments of the past, resplendent even in ruins, against the buildings of our time was so striking.

All too soon, it was time for our balloon to touch down. It glided to a stop without so much as a tiny bump. What an awesome experience—the feeling of drifting so effortlessly through the air above a realm of such momentous human achievement. That balloon ride, which had originally seemed like a lark, a fun nod to Phileas Fogg, turned out to be one of the most rewarding adventures of our eighty-day trip.

Most of the tombs in the Valley of the Kings are closed to the public because of ongoing research and their delicate condition. But we were able to visit one that had a straightforward entryway—no crawling this time—to see the intricate decoration of its corridors and chambers. The walls and even the ceilings were carved with figures and symbols, which were then painted in vivid colors still visible today (whether preserved or restored).

"What an amazing sight!" Sandy says. "It was like being in a gorgeous cathedral underground."

We'd have loved to linger in Luxor, but another wonder awaited: the great temples of Abu Simbel in the Aswan district. Nick had arranged a driver for the five-hour trip and encouraged us to book a guesthouse, Nubian Dreams, that turned out to be one of our all-time favorites. Finding it, though, would be a challenge.

We arrived in Aswan and, as directed, took a ferry to Elephantine Island in the Nile. From the ferry landing, steep steps led up to street level (more accurately, building level, perforated by narrow passages). At the top, we wandered blindly, lugging our gear, until we spotted what looked like a restaurant at the back of a building. "Let's ask there," Ellie said.

It was then that we spotted the Nubian Dreams sign, and standing beside it, our host Mustafa, resplendent in his traditional attire, a flowing white robe and turban.

The accommodations he had for us were truly spectacular, a rooftop "suite" with sweeping views of the Nile. We had a bedroom, an open-air courtyard with a kitchen and seating, and beyond it, a second structure that held our bathroom, covered in vibrant Egyptian tile. There was a gate we could lock to bar trespassers from our private paradise. All for less than twenty dollars each per night! The place was a jewel.

Mustafa was a wonderful adviser on sightseeing, like our trip to the Aswan Dam and, even better, our ride in a felucca. Feluccas, or traditional wooden boats with triangular sails, ply the swift-flowing Nile alongside noisy, less picturesque modern motor craft. It was fun to breeze along imagining ourselves as Egyptian queens in a style of boat dating back to the pharaohs.

Then, around midnight, we set out for Abu Simbel, near the Sudanese border. Our car joined a caravan for security reasons, since unrest in the area made lone vehicles vulnerable to attack. "I didn't confess that to Sandy," Ellie says. "Nick thought that we'd be safe to go."

The two Abu Simbel temples, considered the nation's grandest, were built by Ramses II in an effort to "Egyptianize" Nubia, an important trading region that he controlled. Constructed over twenty years starting around 1264 BC, the temples were eventually abandoned and, by the sixth century BC, buried in sand. European explorers unearthed them in the early nineteenth century. In the 1950s, they were again threatened by the construction of the Aswan Dam to divert the floodwaters of the Nile, which rise annually, and create hydroelectric power. The reservoir for the flood runoff, named Lake Nasser, would have submerged them.

A worldwide fundraising campaign sprang up to save the temples. Finally, in 1964, under the aegis of UNESCO, an international team began a four-year rescue process that involved cutting the temples—which were not freestanding but carved into a mountain—into thirty-ton blocks, to be reassembled, like a puzzle, inside an artificial hill at a new site. The work is one of the greatest archeological engineering feats ever attempted.

Just one of the challenges of the reconstruction was maintaining the primary, or Great Temple's solar alignment. The original structure was oriented precisely to let the sun's rays penetrate its internal sanctuary twice a year, around February 22 and October 22, dates significant to Ramses II. When sunlight struck the statue of the pharaoh in the sanctuary, his spirit supposedly gained power. Even with modern technology, recapturing the exact alignment was problematic, especially since the tilt of the earth has changed over the past three millennia.

The solar alignment would also pose a challenge for us!

Our caravan arrived at Abu Simbel around 4:30 a.m. We were shocked to find literally thousands of people already there, corralled with ropes, waiting to be funneled into the Great Temple. "I read that a few hundred people visit here a day," Ellie said. "I wonder what's going on."

We soon learned that we'd happened to arrive on February 22, the day of the half-yearly solar alignment. Tourists from around the world had thronged to witness the sun's rays penetrate the two-hundred-foot corridor to the sanctuary and illuminate the Ramses statue. Through sheer luck, we'd stumbled into Abu Simbel at exactly the right time.

But the crowds! As dawn approached, they were growing restive, pushing and jostling to get close to the temple entrance. Tall Ellie could see over the heads of the tightly packed horde, but Sandy, smack in the middle of the crush, could hardly breathe. "People were getting shoved and stumbling," she says. "A couple were knocked off their feet. If the crowd surged, we'd surely be trampled.

"So, I planted my feet wide apart, with my fists on my hips, clearing a space around me with my elbows. I kept a smile on my face to avoid provoking those pushing. But I was determined—no one was going to squash me or shove me down."

"I was scared, but Sandy seemed fearless," Ellie says. "I could practically see steam rising off her. She looked just like a tiny bull bracing itself but ready to charge. I knew that she was steely beneath her smile, but I'd never seen her so ferocious."

"Well, an older woman doesn't get through med school and build a career as a doctor by being passive," Sandy says. "I learned to stand my ground by dealing with the big egos of certain male MDs."

Finally the pressure eased as people made it to the Great Temple, fronted by four sixty-foot-tall statues of Ramses II, with figures of his mother, Tuya; his chief wife, Nefertari; and some of his children at his feet. We passed through two imposing halls to reach the sanctuary where, during the solar alignment, light illuminated statues of Ramses II and the gods Amun-Ra and Ra-Horakhty. (The figure of Ptah, the other god in the group, who is linked to the realm of the dead, was exiled to the shadows beyond the sun's reach.) Though we were too late to see the very first rays penetrate the darkness, the effect of the sun spotlighting the statues was dazzling indeed.

Next to the Great Temple stands the so-called Small Temple dedicated to the goddess Hathor and Queen Nefertari. An important feature of its facade are statues of the queen and the pharaoh that are of equal size—thirty-three feet high—which is very unusual in Egyptian art. Nearly all side-by-side statues of Egyptian royal couples have the queen's statue much smaller—reaching no higher than the pharaoh's knees. That Nefertari must have been some consort—our kind of gal!

~~~~~~~

THE NEXT MORNING MARKED DAY 42, JUST OVER THE MIDPOINT OF our trip. We flew to Cairo to catch a plane to Delhi, India, our next stop. Nick met us to say goodbye, with a generous offer. Since his wife was away and he'd be out that afternoon, he said, "Why don't you use my place to relax before your flight?"

He brought us to his comfortable apartment in an expat enclave of the city. "Take a shower, wash clothes, whatever you need—just make yourselves at home," he told us. He showed us where to hide the keys on our way out, promising, "I'll have a driver pick you up here to take you to the airport."

How kind Nick was! Part of the reason, no doubt, was his connection to Sheryl, Ellie's daughter. But there's also a camaraderie that expats everywhere share—a spirit of community born of the love of new experiences and different cultures. We like to think that Nick recognized in us that same openness to novelty and adventure— the eagerness to immerse ourselves in and embrace, not just observe, the world.

India

From the moment your plane lands at Indira Gandhi Airport in Delhi, India, your senses spring into action. What they first detect is the smog, from car and industrial emissions, as well as smoke from "stubble burning," or torching fields after harvesting crops. The second is the noise, from relentless traffic in the world's second most populous city, with some 30 million people living in its metropolitan area. There's an adage: "To drive in Delhi, you need good brakes, good horns, and good luck." From personal experience, we say, "Amen!"

But these negatives are vastly outweighed by the magic of India—its rich mix of age-old cultures, the lavish glory of its architecture, the beauty to be glimpsed everywhere, even on a backdrop of poverty—and the tremendous warmth of its people. The slogan we kept hearing during our stay was Unity in Diversity, an expression of tolerance—actual or hoped-for—and pride in India's complex cultural tapestry. To our minds, Unity in Diversity should be the motto of every country on the globe, including ours.

> **The slogan we kept hearing during our stay was Unity in Diversity, an expression of tolerance—actual or hoped-for— and pride in India's complex cultural tapestry. To our minds, Unity in Diversity should be the motto of every country on the globe, including ours.**

In Delhi, we'd been invited to stay with the lovely Sushmaa Sethi (Pinku) and her family, whose parents had befriended Ellie and Kelly years before, in Zambia. We landed at 2:30 a.m. and took a taxi to their apartment—or tried to. Our driver kept squeezing his cab through the warren of narrow streets, choked with parked cars, but couldn't find the address. Even repeated phone calls to his dispatcher didn't help locate it. Finally, the driver decided to get out and search on foot. Eventually he returned triumphant, with a big smile, saying, "Found it!" That was our introduction to the idiosyncrasies of the Delhi street grid.

Despite the hour, Pinku greeted us happily and showed us to the room where we'd share a bed. As it turned out, the apartment was less a separate unit than a collection of rooms, spread over two stories, occupied by her family, with a hallway bathroom that seemed to be shared by the family inhabiting the rest of each floor.

It was fascinating to experience such semi-communal living, hard to imagine in our culture of deadbolts and video doorbells. Of course, we met all the neighbors, who treated us like honored guests, as did our wonderfully hospitable hosts.

We were also struck—and inspired—by the religious devotion we observed in India. Every morning Pinku's husband visited his Hindu temple, lit candles, and chanted prayers at a small altar in their home. We are both committed Christians who try to live by our values, and in our travels, we've often witnessed a kind of everyday holiness that reminds us not to be casual about our own spiritual practices.

> **We are both committed Christians who try to live by our values, and in our travels, we've often witnessed a kind of everyday holiness that reminds us not to be casual about our own spiritual practices.**

Our first day, we set out to explore Delhi on foot and by bicycle rickshaw—one guy pedaling hard enough to pull the two of us in a wheeled cart. Many streets in the old city seemed to be only one-rickshaw wide, making it hair-raising when another one approached us head-on. But somehow the cyclists knew just how to swerve to scrape past each other, so we came to relax and trust their navigation skills.

Walking was a bigger challenge because of the cows. In Egypt, there were plenty, but in India, they ruled the streets. Cows are revered by Hindus as the representation of the Mother Goddess, giving milk selflessly to provide nourishment, among other blessings. We had a guide who explained, "People in India take better care of their cows than their mothers."

"I laughed out loud at Sandy's expression," Ellie admits. "The pursed lips, the eyes staring over the glasses. She quite literally frowned on that sentiment."

"I clung to our guide for dear life," Sandy says, "trying to steer clear of those cows, goddesses or not."

But, walking or riding, what delighted us in Delhi was all the color—the jewel tones of saris on women in the streets and of fabrics hanging in shops, a vivid rainbow of silks and cottons, some glittering with gold thread. Everywhere we looked, there were bursts of brilliant hues. Even the fruit stands—with golden mangos, pebbled green jackfruits, and scarlet pomegranates, lychees, mangosteens—were feasts for the eyes.

We were also thrilled by the ubiquitous monkeys—mostly small rhesus macaques—congregating, chattering on walls, scurrying across rooftops, climbing buildings, and even clutching power lines, risking electrocution. Monkeys are sacred in Hinduism as symbols of the god Hanuman, half man, half ape, honored for rescuing the god Rama's wife from a demon. So, thousands of them are allowed to run wild through the city, sometimes disrupting traffic and even attacking humans. During a G20 Summit, the government set up cutouts of fiercer monkeys, silver langurs, with humans mimicking their cries, to scare off macaques who might harass the diplomats. But to us, they seemed playful and funny—"a lot cuter and less menacing than cows," Sandy says.

We were keen to see the major sights, starting with Qutab Minar, an impressive, fluted minaret constructed in the thirteenth century. Standing some 230 feet tall, it is the world's largest brick minaret and, with the mosque complex at its base, one of the oldest surviving Muslim outposts in India. Its style, however, is very different from religious architecture of the Middle East and represents a fusion of Hindu and Muslim traditions. Since 1981, Qutab Minar has been closed to the public, so we weren't even tempted to climb its 379 steps to the top.

Delhi's principal mosque, Jama Masjid, is much grander, the last great monument built by Shah Jahan, who commissioned the Taj Mahal. It is one of the city's most iconic structures, the anchor of the imperial capital and the symbol of Islamic power in India until the establishment of the British Raj. Muslims today represent about 15 percent of the population, the largest minority group in an over-whelmingly Hindu nation.

AS MUCH AS WE ENJOYED OUR STAY IN DELHI, WE SOON HAD TO MOVE on to see more of India's wonders. Since our time was limited, we decided to concentrate on the state of Rajasthan, about eight hours from Delhi, which is known for its magnificent forts, temples, and palaces. Ellie's daughter, Sheryl, who has lived in India, encouraged us to visit Udaipur to escape the hustle and bustle and experience the beauty of the countryside.

Udaipur, known as the City of Lakes, is surrounded by seven linked bodies of water. We chose a hotel, the Kankarwa Haveli, located on beautiful Lake Pichola. The term *haveli* refers to a traditional mansion in an Indian city. Ours had been built in 1820 as the home of the Kankarwa family, who restored it in the 1990s and continue to run it as a so-called historic Heritage Hotel.

We had a large, airy room that had a cozy cushioned window nook, enclosed in a scalloped frame, where we could lounge and enjoy the view of the lake. "That was my favorite spot," Ellie says. "But at night, the strangest thing happened. Attracted by the light in our room, gulls would attack the window and try to get in. I felt just like Tippi Hedren in *The Birds*."

Luckily, we escaped unpecked.

The next day, we rode two and a half hours into the Aravalli foothills to visit the Ranakpur Temple complex, an architectural marvel that's one of the most important places of worship for India's Jains. Like Hindus and Buddhists, Jains believe in reincarnation, based on karma, or the consequences of a person's actions. Their highest value is nonviolence, so they are strict vegetarians, who don't even eat root vegetables, to avoid killing plants. Instead of worshipping gods per se, they venerate twenty-four Tirthankaras, or spiritual leaders who have transcended the death-and-rebirth cycle though enlightenment. There are some five million Jains in India, making this ancient faith the smallest of the country's six major religions.

The Ranakpur complex of five temples is breathtaking, possibly the most extravagant construction we've ever seen. Built over a fifty-year period in the fifteenth century, it was inspired by a Jain merchant's vision of a celestial vehicle. He spent years finding an artist to sketch his dream and then managed to convince a king to execute it in white marble. From the outside, the complex, topped by towers, cupolas, and scores of red-spired turrets, looks something like an incredibly ornate medieval castle.

As we waited to enter, we were advised of the temple rules: visitors were required to wear full-length clothing, like pants or long skirts; women were to cover their heads; and leather goods, including belts and wallets, were prohibited, as were shoes, purses, and backpacks. Of course, we were happy to comply, as a matter of respect.

Ahead of us in line was an off-putting tourist, who, to our embarrassment, was American. When asked to leave her shoes and purse at the gate, she refused, insisting that someone might steal them. The guards very patiently explained that this was a holy site, and that their religion didn't make exceptions. They couldn't have been more gracious. Listening to her argue, we couldn't help but murmur to each other, "Kick her out."

Finally, Ellie had enough and, politely but firmly, said, "Just leave the stuff with your driver in the car."

"Oh no, I can't do that," she told us. "These are far too expensive."

At that, we nearly snorted in dismay. Who wears designer gear when traveling, anyway? We felt bad for the staff and appalled by the disrespect the woman was showing them and this holy place.

Finally, they pulled her aside to let the line progress. She was still arguing as, with apologetic smiles to the attendants, we made our way into the complex.

The forty-eight thousand square feet of its main temple, Chaturmukha, contains 1,444 exquisitely carved marble pillars—no two alike—spread over twenty-nine halls. There's one unfinished pillar from which, legend has it, any workmanship attempted by day vanishes overnight. We drifted through the halls, wearing headsets with a recording describing the symbolism and stories behind all the intricate designs: mythological scenes, elephants and other animals, flowers, and geometrical figures. The most famous carving, made of a single slab of marble, depicts Parshvanatha, the twenty-third Tirthankhara—believed to have lived around the eighth century BC—protected by the hood of a serpent against a backdrop of 1,008 tangled snake heads and bodies. Throughout the temple, the sculptural detail was magnificent.

Too soon, it was time to return to Udaipur and catch a train to our next destination, the Taj Mahal.

WHENEVER WE BOOKED A SECOND-CLASS SLEEPER, WE KNEW THAT WE might be in for an adventure. Our train out of Udaipur had separate compartments with four bunks but no doors—just a blue curtain screening them from the main corridor. Anyone heading for the bathroom could just pop into our compartment. When we heard children's voices, we peeked out and saw a young family, so at least we weren't the only women in the car, which was, as usual, filling up with men.

We'd reserved the two bottom bunks, facing each other, and stowed our luggage underneath them. Given the lack of security, Sandy decided to sleep with her backpack in the bunk. "Of course, I understood," Ellie says. "But one time, Kelly and I stayed at a hostel in Switzerland, which had separate dorms for men and women. Alone on the women's side, I was worried about my cash and passport so decided to sleep with them tucked under my pillow. Imagine my embarrassment the next morning, when I awoke from a restless sleep to find my valuables strewn all over the floor, there for anyone to steal. They would have been much safer stowed in my luggage under the bed. That's why I'm no longer supercautious when I travel."

We had tea and dinner—rice and some kind of curry, served

from a rolling cart, reminding Ellie that India's president, Narendra Modi, was once a train-station tea porter. We were settling into our bunks when, suddenly, the curtains parted, and two twenty-something men pushed into our compartment. At the sight of us—two older women, lounging on the lower bunks—they stopped dead and gawked for a moment. We almost laughed. But, without a word, they heaved up their bags and climbed to the upper bunks. It was a very silent night.

In the morning, we stopped at Bharatpur, about an hour outside Agra, for a lavish breakfast of northern Indian specialties at a former palace. It was a far cry from our curry-and-rice meal on the train. In Bharatpur, we connected with Twinkle, the daughter of K.D. Singh, the Delhi travel agent who'd booked all our guides and drivers. Twinkle had boarded the train with us at Udaipur but ridden in a different car.

A medical student, Twinkle was going to visit her husband's family and had no doubt promised her father that she'd keep an eye on his two grandmotherly customers. We were fascinated by the chance to talk to a young Indian woman one-on-one. She and Sandy enjoyed comparing notes on their medical studies. It gave us a new perspective on India to see that young women, from at least some of its cultures, could travel freely and enjoy such a degree of self-determination.

TWINKLE ACCOMPANIED US TO AGRA, THE SITE OF THE TAJ MAHAL, which is one of the most delicately beautiful and romantic mausoleums in the world. At age fifteen, Khurram, the young prince who

would become the emperor Shah Jahan, became engaged to Arjumand Banu Begum, the daughter of a Persian nobleman in his family's court. The couple had to wait for an astrologically auspicious
date to marry, which finally came in 1612, when Khurram was
twenty. In the interim, he would take other wives, but Arjumand
was his true love, accorded the title Mumtaz Mahal, or "Exalted
One of the Palace."

A poet fluent in Persian and Arabic, Mumtaz Mahal was celebrated for her beauty and compassion. She accompanied her husband on military campaigns, became his most trusted adviser, and
wielded great political power, including control of the imperial seal,
validating decrees. She was said to be a champion of the poor and a
patron of art and scholarship.

She died at age thirty-eight, while giving birth to her fourteenth
child (only seven of whom survived to adulthood). The emperor
was so distraught at her death that he went into seclusion for a year,
emerging with his hair snow white. Renowned for monuments said
to have launched a "golden age" of architecture, including Delhi's
Jama Masjid, Shah Jahan spent twenty years developing his greatest work, the Taj Mahal, as a tomb for his beloved wife.

Constructed of ivory marble inlaid with semiprecious stones,
the building and its surrounding gardens are perfectly symmetri-
cal. It's octagonal, with four long and four short beveled corner
walls, each lined with two stories of archways. It's topped by an
onion-shaped dome seventy-five feet high, with a thirty-one-foot
gilded finial ending in a crescent moon with horns aimed at the
sky. Smaller replica domes with open arches to let in light rise

above each of its four beveled corners. Its graceful design feels almost ethereal, too finely wrought to be made of stone.

Inside, the Taj Mahal is equally impressive. The upper-tier windows in the two-story archways are filled with glassed-in jali, or stone-lattice screens. Many of the interior surfaces are decorated with bas-reliefs, calligraphy, and intricate inlays of semiprecious stones.

At the very center of the main chamber stands the cenotaph of Mumtaz Mahal and, off to one side, that of Shah Jahan, who died thirty-five years later. The cenotaphs, bordered by an elaborate jali with jewel inlays, are ceremonial, with the real sarcophagi of the emperor and queen hidden on the basement level.

Naturally, Ellie was eager to photograph the Taj Mahal at sunrise, sunset, and in between. Its delicate marble seems to change colors at different times of day. Mr. Singh had set us up with a wonderful guide, Anil, who seemed to know every angle to get the best shots of the majestic monument. "I took more than two hundred pictures," Ellie says. "I shot color, black-and-white, photos of birds flying over it at sunset, the tomb framed by a decorative archway in the complex, close-ups of the magnificent interior detail—you name it. I've exhibited a number of those photos."

Funnily, we ourselves became the subject of lots of photos. At the Taj Mahal, we wore our T-shirts and got swarmed by other tourists, mostly young people—single visitors, couples, even whole families, from England, Denmark, Poland, and farther-flung places—who wanted to know all about our trip. Over and over, we heard, "You are such an inspiration." Invariably, they asked us to pose with them for selfies, as if we were visiting rock stars. It's wild to imagine them looking through those pictures years from now and asking, "Whatever became of those two traveling women?"

But our favorite photo is a novelty shot that Anil set up for us. We were standing along one side of the Taj Mahal when he asked Ellie, "Will you give me your water bottle?"

He took it and poured out a circle of water, about a foot in diameter, on the pavement. Then he had us pose, looking up, against the backdrop of the monument. He set Ellie's cell phone on its side at the edge of the circle of water and—*click!*—created an image of the Taj Mahal as if it were rising from the sea with the two of us reflected on its placid surface.

It was so clever and so evocative of what we stand for—the search for mystery and wonder. We loved the shot so much that we made it our business card.

Nepal

The border between Nepal and Tibet runs straight across the summit of Everest, the highest and most mythic mountain in the world. Its Tibetan name, Qomolangma, means "Holy Mother," and in Nepali/Sanskrit, it's called Sagarmatha, or "Goddess of the Sky." Rising 29,031 feet, 8.5 inches above sea level—a height finally established in 2020, after a century of international debate—it is the jewel of the Himalayas, the mountain range spanning five Asian countries, with peaks sacred to the region's religions: Buddhists, Hindus, Jains, Sikhs, and Muslims.

Everest itself has been irresistible to Westerners since the mid-nineteenth century, when British surveyors found it to be the world's tallest peak. Early expeditions to its pinnacle—notably George Mallory's in 1924—were met with failure or tragedy. The challenges for climbers are intense: blizzards, avalanches, and winds that can reach two hundred miles per hour; falls and other injuries; exhaustion; and altitude sickness, from low oxygen and air pressure. It was not until 1953 that New Zealander Edmund Hillary and Nepali Tenzing Norgay managed to beat the odds and become the first documented adventurers to reach the summit of Mount Everest.

Though summiting Everest remains a life-threatening adventure, today many more climbers succeed thanks to improved weather forecasting, cold-weather gear, and oxygen-delivery systems. But Everest's base camps—tent cities where aspiring summiteers pause to adjust to the altitude—are far more accessible and so are visited by some forty thousand trekkers each year. Reaching a base camp, unlike summiting, requires little in the way of special skills or training. The ascent to base camp is gradual, so the prerequisites are mainly good health and physical fitness.

"I'm positive we could do it!" Ellie said. Though we know our limits, we more than met the stated guidelines, being able to climb hills and to walk six or seven hours a day.

But there was a catch. Time. Due to the altitude, the relatively short forty-mile trek can take average hikers up to ten days. Coming back down is much quicker, but all told, we figured we'd need to block out roughly two weeks for the trek.

No way we could build two weeks into our eighty-day schedule.

Still, we were determined to experience Everest up close and, again thanks to Sheryl, we found a way. She connected us to Mani, a Nepali travel guide, who told us about a charter flight, leaving at sunrise, that circled close to the summit. "Weather permitting," he stressed. "It's a small plane so everyone has a window."

Incredibly, the Everest flight cost less than the forty-five-minute hop from Abilene to Dallas, Texas. "Let's do it!" we told him. "Let's book it for our first morning in Nepal." That way, if weather scuttled our flight, we'd have time to try it another day.

When we landed at Tribhuvan Airport in Kathmandu, Mani met us bearing fragrant leis and our tickets for the Everest plane. We wore our leis to check in to the charming Kasthamandap Boutique Hotel, where all the guest rooms have murals painted by local artists. After a wonderful dinner there, we turned in early. Mani's driver would pick us up in time to reach the airfield by 4:30 a.m. "No sooner," Mani warned, "because the ticket counter won't be open."

As we joined the group at the Buddha Air counter, we were bubbling over with excitement. "I wonder about the visibility," Sandy said. "Will we just see snow and clouds or a whole stretch of the Himalayas?"

Ellie, of course, was eager for sunrise shots over the Goddess of the Sky. So was Ramy at CBS News, who asked us, if possible, to send a photo. "He said they were getting ready to run a feature on us and would love to include a shot of Everest," Ellie recalls.

The counter opened shortly before the flight. When we presented our tickets, beaming, ready to board, a dismayed look came over the agent's face. "I'm sorry, but these tickets are for yesterday," he said.

"What? How can that be? What can we do?" We were shocked. Ellie tried to call Mani, but the phone kept ringing. It was, after all, not yet 5 a.m.

The agent pulled us out of line to plead our case to another official. Instinctively—and without a word spoken between us—we both went into "conciliation" mode. Pitching a fit never helps matters, especially when you're in the wrong. We were wearing our T-shirts, along with our most grandmotherly, disarming smiles, which we hoped might inspire mercy from the agents of Buddha Air.

> **Instinctively—and without a word spoken between us—we both went into "conciliation" mode. Pitching a fit never helps matters, especially when you're in the wrong.**

Luckily, we didn't have to rely on charm alone to make the flight. Ellie finally got through to Mani, who spoke briefly to the agent. Then, with a whir, the agent's machine spat out two new tickets, and with moments to spare, we boarded our little prop plane.

The flight was glorious beyond our highest expectations. We

took off just as the sun's rays came peeping over Langtang Lirung, the Himalayan peak closest to Kathmandu. We could chart the mountains we passed on a map, provided by Buddha Air, as our plane rose higher in the light of dawn. Below us were sharp, snowy peaks; icy ribbons of rivers; deep, dark lakes; and frozen glacial masses. Then the plane thrust into a cottony mist, and we were soon looking down on the white whorls and billows of the so-called Valley of the Clouds.

Suddenly, Everest, the Holy Mother, was beside us. We had desperately wanted to see Everest up close, and this was even better—to our minds—than if we had trekked to a base camp. We were able to circle and commune with the mountainside, face-to-face. Peering at its magnificent crags, we were awed, mesmerized by our proximity to the very zenith of the world. Everest's beauty is breathtakingly raw and wild.

Then our plane began its descent through the hazy white cloud bank, and the panorama of a segment of the Himalayas stretched before us: a stark and jagged assertion of nature's power. None of us could tear our eyes from the windows.

When we finally returned to the airfield, everyone on the plane seemed to exhale, as if awakening from a magic spell. We were all presented with certificates, reading, "We touched Mount Everest with our hearts." And indeed, we had.

KATHMANDU, NEPAL'S CAPITAL, IS ALSO ITS SPIRITUAL AND CULTURAL center. Until 2008, when Nepal became a democratic republic, it was the seat of its monarchs and a century's worth of hereditary "prime ministers." A major stop on the trade route between India and Tibet, the Kathmandu Valley developed a welter of palaces and temples reflecting the influence of both cultures.

We visited the principal temples, some Buddhist, some Hindu, echoing the dominant groups in the region. One of the most famous is the Swayambhunath complex, a sacred pilgrimage site. Its centerpiece is a Buddhist stupa, or place of meditation, which is a huge dome, representing the world, topped by a cube with the eyes and eyebrows of Buddha (representing wisdom and compassion) painted on each side. Above each of them is a third eye, said to emit the cosmic rays of Buddha's teachings. Below the eyes is a question mark–shaped squiggle that is the Nepali numeral one, representing the unity or "oneness" of all things in the world as the only path to enlightenment. A spire above the cube is ringed with thirteen tiers representing the spiritual stages to enlightenment through which all beings must pass.

Buddhist mythology accounts for the complex's huge population of holy monkeys, which roam freely and explain its popular name, the Monkey Temple.

We were fascinated by the stupa, festooned with strings of colorful prayer flags. We climbed the 365 steps and were rewarded with a spectacular view of the city. At the top, we encountered a young woman who noticed our T-shirts and asked us, "Are you two sisters?"

"No," we told her, describing our eighty-day mission. "Well, these are all my sisters," she said, introducing us to four other young women, as well as their mother, all beautifully dressed in colorful Nepalese kurtas, or tunics, balloon-legged pants, and contrasting scarves.

"My goodness," Sandy said. "My grandmother also had five daughters."

"So, your grandmother is like our mother," she said. "That makes you like one of our sisters."

They all clamored to embrace Sandy, their honorary sister, and asked her to join the six of them in a group photo. Then the mother of the clan wrapped Sandy in a heartfelt bear hug. "Today I'm your stand-in grandmother," she told Sandy.

The most sacred place we visited was the Pashupatinath Temple, which is revered as one of the abodes of the Hindu god Shiva. Only South Asian Hindus, Nepali and Tibetan Buddhists, and Indian Sikhs and Jains are permitted entry to the temple and its courtyard. All other visitors, including Hindus from the West, are limited to the satellite buildings and must view the main temple from the opposite bank of the Bagmati River.

Because Pashupatinath Temple and the Bagmati River are considered especially holy, many Hindus want to be cremated there when they die. Hinduism is the only religion that requires cremation of bodies, to be performed within twenty-four hours of death. Cremation returns the body to its original five elements—for Hindus, these are air, water, earth, fire, and space—and quickly liberates the soul to resume the cycle of reincarnation.

Standing across the river from the temple, we were able to observe the ritual, one of the most sacred in the Hindu religion. Such a public process of cremation was unlike anything we had experienced, and it was a bit jarring at first. But we also realized that they were celebrating the release of the spirit of their loved one. And that we understood. Indeed, something our faith shares with Hindus and many other religions is the belief that the spirit lives on once the physical body is gone. That idea is one of the comforts that faith can offer.

Beyond the experience of the cremation, what struck us about the Pashupatinath Temple was the fact that it admitted Buddhists, Sikhs, and Jains, as well as South Asian Hindus. In Nepal, we encountered many places of worship where multiple faiths seemed to unite in an expression of respect for the mystical—of a holy realm beyond everyday understanding. We were again reminded of the transcendent, uplifting power of spirituality and the importance of upholding it in our own lives.

We were again reminded of the transcendent, uplifting power of spirituality and the importance of upholding it in our own lives.

WE LOVED KATHMANDU BUT ALSO WANTED THE CHANCE TO SEE THE countryside. Mani suggested that we visit the town of Nagarkot, nestled in the mountains about an hour outside the city. The summer retreat of the Nepali royals in centuries past, it is now a collection of about a thousand houses perched in the nooks and crannies of slopes at an elevation of 7,200 feet. Nagarkot's claim to fame is its views of no less than eight ranges of the Himalayas, as well as the sunrise over Mount Everest.

Of course, just the prospect of sunrise photos was enough to pique Ellie's interest.

The drive into the mountains was scenic. We could tell we were climbing, but the sensation of height was mitigated by the constant sight of terraced rice fields—beautiful and green—cut into the hillsides. We passed through quaint little villages, where we marveled at the sight of inhabitants at work, trudging up the road with large, unwieldy loads strapped to their backs. What strength! And, as in India, the colors were dazzling—both men and women, even in rural areas, deck themselves out in traditional garments in vivid hues.

Mani recommended that we stay at the Hotel Country Villa, also known as the Hotel at the End of the Universe. Set into the mountainside, it offers sweeping views of the entire Kathmandu Valley and the Himalayas. We got an amazing top-floor room with a balcony, perfect for observing the landscape—if only the Valley hadn't been shrouded in thick clouds.

But we could hardly complain, having experienced the whole panorama of the mountains on Buddha Air—and besides, the chilly, enveloping fog had its own mysterious power.

We enjoyed a delicious dinner in the hotel restaurant, then walked out into the courtyard, where some young men were playing table tennis under the lights. They were obviously experienced players, slapping the ball fast and hard. Then one of them spotted us and handed a paddle to Ellie. "Would you like to play me?" he asked.

Never one to resist a challenge, Ellie grabbed the paddle. "I hope I can return the ball just once," she murmured to Sandy.

Sandy laughed and started filming with her phone, as Ellie and the guy began volleying, with the other men watching from the sidelines. They were kind enough to cheer whenever Ellie hit a strong return against her obviously superior opponent, who was less than half her age. "He did try to make me feel good," Ellie admits. "He wasn't out to clobber me."

Still, she lost. Undaunted, she accepted a challenge from another player. "He was really good, too," she says. "I don't want to use the altitude as an excuse—7,200 feet is a lot higher than Texas—but it didn't help. I didn't embarrass myself, though. I did okay."

Another defeat—but who's counting? Ellie remains proud. "After all, I held my own in a game I hadn't played in years against two young guys who never thought that I'd offer a lick of resistance. Those games proved to be more of a contest than they—or certainly I—ever expected. So, win or lose—score two for the grannies!"

On the day we departed for our next destination, Japan, we saw a sign reading: Nepal: Never Ending Peace And Love. While Nepal's history (even in recent times) is no less battle-scarred than any other country's, the slogan seemed to evoke perfectly the expansive, mystic consciousness we encountered in this land dominated by the Goddess of the Sky.

13

SMALL MOMENTS CAN LEAD
TO MONUMENTAL SHIFTS
IN PERSPECTIVE

Japan

Entering Japan, on the heels of Egypt, India, and Nepal, was like landing on another planet. Our first jolt of culture shock was the gleaming clean of it all—everywhere—the airport, the streets, the buildings, inside and out. We doubt that a white-gloved finger, run over any surface, would pick up so much as a speck of dust. We'd come from wondrous lands steeped in history—and sand, which we'd grown accustomed to shaking out of our gear at day's end and long afterward. We hadn't really thought much about the sand until we landed in pristine Japan. The people, too, were perfectly turned out—well-dressed, with barely a hair out of place.

Our second jolt of culture shock was the sheer newness. Still under the spell of the ancient pyramids, the Taj Mahal, and the sacred temples of India and Nepal—our heads still swimming with mythology, history, and mysticism—we found the modernity hard to process. Emerging from the storied past into the frenzy of

Tokyo—Skyscrapers! Neon! Millions of people on the move!—was downright dizzying.

Japan, of course, has a richly complex history, dating back as far as 3600 BC. But Tokyo, its capital, is ultramodern, rebuilt twice, after a devastating earthquake in 1923 and again following World War II. Our visit to Japan would be too brief to let us venture much beyond it, but we planned to see the iconic, sacred Mount Fuji. We'd wanted to touch down in Japan because it was a stop on the eighty-day journey of our fictional inspiration, Phileas Fogg.

The greatest challenge for us about Tokyo's newness was its technological sophistication. Billed as the world's most futuristic city, it seems to have automated every function. It boasts hotels where the front desks are manned by robots, as well as cafés with robot servers. Vending machines, present on every street corner, sell anything from soft drinks and fresh-squeezed orange juice to ramen noodles, books, and clothing. "Don't even get us started on the toilets," Sandy says. "They offer so many options, including wash and dry features, that we could barely figure out how to flush them!"

We were excited to see Mount Fuji, but getting there meant running the gauntlet of Tokyo's Shinjuku Station. It's the world's busiest, serving more than 3.4 million passengers a day. Five different rail lines pass through it, including the local subway, as well as bus lines, each with separate concourses and platforms. "The place is a maze," Ellie says. "We pride ourselves on being resourceful travelers, but, honestly, the labyrinth had us completely perplexed.

We appreciated learning later that even some Tokyoites find it bewildering."

None of our usual go-tos for directions were any help. The signage was almost exclusively in Japanese, and our efforts to seek assistance from agents and officials were met with blank stares. Even the ticket kiosks, beacons of hope, were useless because all their prompts were in Japanese, too.

We are nothing if not persistent. Still, standing in the swirl of humanity, hoping to flag an English-speaking passerby, we grew daunted. People seemed willing to help us, but often their directions defied understanding. One thing we *could* read were the digital clocks, which showed us how much time was passing. Surely, we were missing trains—and, possibly, blowing our chance to see the famous peak.

We began to feel defeated. Then, suddenly, we heard a voice. "I know you!" said a young man in glasses.

"What? You do?"

"I'm Ziggy," the young man told us. "I'm from Slovenia, but I read about you last week in the *Daily Mail*. Aren't you the two ladies who are traveling around the world in eighty days?"

It struck us then that we were wearing our T-shirts. T-shirts to the rescue!

Ziggy went on to say how much he admired our ambitious trip. "Isn't it amazing that I was just reading about you, and now I run into you here in Japan?"

To us, it was more than amazing—it was providential. Especially since he added, "I could see that you were having some kind of trouble. Can I help?"

We explained that we were trying—and failing—to reach Mount Fuji. "Tell you what," Ziggy said. "I was rushing to make a train, but my plans really aren't that important. Let me figure out how to get you to Mount Fuji, as my small contribution to your trip."

We thanked him, over and over, as he worked his way through the system and discovered that a bus, rather than a train, would be best for our purposes. He helped us buy tickets and steered us to the right bus bay. "Oh, Ziggy, you're our hero!" we gushed, meaning every word.

The kindness of strangers—how lucky we felt!

> # The kindness of strangers—how lucky we felt!

The kindness of strangers—how lucky we felt!

MOUNT FUJI, AN ACTIVE VOLCANO, LAST ERUPTED IN THE EIGHTEENTH century, so it remains a popular site for tourism and mountaineering. It is a not part of a range but a solitary, almost perfectly cone-shaped, snow-capped mountain, rising some 12,500 feet into the sky.

Because of its serene symmetry, Mount Fuji has inspired centuries of poetry and art. In the nineteenth century, the woodblock prints of Katsushika Hokusai, notably the series "Thirty-Six Views of Mount Fuji," dazzled the West and established the image of Mount Fuji as the symbol of Japan.

Sadly, our epic inefficiency in the train station meant that, by the time we reached Mount Fuji, it was late in the day. We had little time to explore. Since the weather was hazy, our sight of the graceful peak was less than perfect. Still, we got a sense of the peace and awe that it has instilled in so many generations of viewers.

By seeing Mount Fuji—thanks to Ziggy's generosity—we felt that we'd been able to maximize our brief stop in Japan. Now we were on to Bali!

Bali

Bali has been called the Island of the Gods, and we can hardly even imagine a place more heavenly: black and white sand beaches, glorious tropical foliage, wonderful preserves for animals and exotic birds, a central mountain range with terraced slopes of emerald-green rice paddies, beautifully ornate temples, a vibrant culture emphasizing the performing arts, and a warm, welcoming, deeply spiritual populace, to name just a few reasons for its allure.

As we entered the homestretch—the final weeks of our trip— Bali was the perfect place to alight for a few days of pure enjoyment. We've never been the kind of travelers who want to lie on the beach, doing nothing. Bali offered the ideal combination of relaxation in natural beauty and the chance to pursue our love of discovery.

We stayed at the Ananda Ubud Resort, a traditional Balinese compound nestled in the rice fields. Once an extended family's home, graced with beamed roofs and carved wooden appointments, it had an open-air restaurant and a welcome desk, connecting via planted walkways to charming bungalows for guests. Ours had a private garden with a fountain and waterfalls, as well as a luxurious bathroom with a giant soaking tub. At twenty-eight dollars each per night, it was an incredible bargain, especially since, each day, fresh flowers were strewn on our beds. There was even a laundry man, who came each morning to collect our clothes, returning them in the evening in perfectly folded stacks.

We were fascinated to see that there was a Hindu temple on the grounds, likely established by the resort's original family owners. Bali is the one Hindu region in the Indonesian archipelago, an expanse of islands constituting the world's most populous Muslim nation. We would learn that, while there were lots of public Balinese Hindu temples, private ones, where daily rituals were performed, were essential features of many family compounds.

One reason we love staying in local lodgings, versus Western hotels, is the eagerness of the staff to share insider tips on what to see and do. Through the staff, we met Ketut, the wonderful driver/guide who would introduce us to Mount Batur and the Happy Swing, among other adventures. He even managed to get Ellie's eyeglasses fixed late one evening. A great, knowledgeable resource, he was also a fun companion, one whom we came to consider a friend.

It was also through the resort that we found a cooking school. We like to say that cultural immersion begins in the kitchen. So, we were delighted to spend a day learning to prepare delicious Balinese cuisine. Bob, who ran the school with his wife, Eta, picked us up in the morning. On the drive to the cooking school, he told us the story of its founding.

> ## We like to say that cultural immersion begins in the kitchen.

Originally, he and Eta had owned a business called Bike Around Bali, which grew very successful renting bicycles to vacationers. Then came COVID, which shut down tourism. Over time, to make ends meet, Bob and Eta sold off their bicycle stock to the locals, which left them without a business—or a way to make a living— once the country reopened.

"The answer struck me one night at dinner," Bob told us, "when I realized that I was married to the best cook in Bali. So, we opened our school, which really took off."

We loved that story because it confirmed that we'd experience real Balinese home cooking, as opposed to dishes designed specifically for tourists. We took a detour through the market—not to shop, but so that Bob could show us how typical meal prep would begin. Then we headed to the school, which was held in Bob's family compound, where he and Eta lived alongside his father, brother, and other relatives. We were very eager to see a multigenerational, middle-class Balinese home.

It was a fenced-in collection of buildings—houses for the different families—connected by walkways, like a less fancy version of our hotel. Climbing the steps to the front gate, we could see that, off to one side, stood the ornate family temple, fronted by a courtyard with benches. As we entered, Eta met us with outstretched arms and wrapped us in warm hugs, as if we were long-lost friends. She'd brought along a basket of flowers, which, she explained, we would use to prepare an offering for the temple gods.

The offering, called a canang sari, is a small basket made of palm or banana leaves containing items representing the Trimurti—the three major gods Shiva, Vishnu, and Brahma—topped with flowers. Bob and Eta showed us how to create the baskets and position the flowers just so, to appeal to specific gods. Traditionally, white flowers point to the east to honor Ishvara, red to the south (Brahma), yellow to the west (Mahadeva, or Shiva), and blue or green to the north (Vishnu). Each day, these baskets were presented to the gods, Bob and Eta told us, as thanks for peace in the world and to bring the household prosperity and health.

We were so touched by their willingness to welcome us into their culture. The devotion of practicing Hindus—and how entwined faith is in their lives—had long impressed us. But this was the first time that we'd ever shared in a Hindu ritual. Of course, Bob and Eta weren't expecting us to join them in worship. They didn't invite us into their private temple, and we didn't ask. They were simply giving us firsthand experience of the rhythm of their days, which, in Balinese Hinduism, began with creating offerings to their gods.

We gave Eta our somewhat lopsided canang sari to deliver to the temple (provided that she thought the gods would accept our sincere, if amateurish, efforts). Then we followed her through her house and out the back to her kitchen, which occupied a large veranda, for cooking class.

That day, we were the only students. Eta explained that we'd be making a traditional Balinese meal of soup, fresh tuna, chicken, and vegetables, then enjoying the fruits of our labor for lunch. "She handed me a heavy pole, like a giant wooden pestle," Ellie says, "which I was to use to grind seeds and nuts into paste against a hollowed stone."

"Meanwhile, I was chopping herbs," Sandy says. "And crushing smaller spices. Boy, traditional cooking takes a lot of muscle."

When we finished those jobs, Eta had us grating coconut, slicing tuna, chopping chicken and vegetables to thread onto skewers, and more. We must have spent four hours just on the prep work. But it was fun. Eta pretended to boss Bob around, making him wash dishes, while he fake-resisted, groaning, grumbling, and making faces. "They were so cute," Sandy says. "All of us were laughing."

Finally, it was time to assemble our meal. Putting our soup—a mixture of rice, vegetables, and herbs—on to simmer, we transferred our chicken skewers to the grill. Then we scooped some of Ellie's paste, a sprinkling of herbs and spices, and the tuna onto banana leaves, folding and tying them into packets. To cook the packets, we lowered them into a pot of boiling, herb- and spice-perfumed water. The smells were enticing!

When the food was ready, Bob chopped a few coconuts off a tree. Then he sliced off the tops so we could drink the milk out of the shell, though straws. What a fine elixir it was, a perfect accompaniment to our array of dishes—all delicious—served on banana leaves. "We were so proud of our incredible lunch," Ellie says. "That experience was a highlight of our stay."

THANKS TO KETUT, WE HAD MANY OTHER MEMORABLE EXPERIENCES in Bali. Of course, the Happy Swing on Mount Batur was a great one. Afterward, we dined overlooking the volcano from the balcony of a lovely restaurant perched on a neighboring mountain. True to form, we struck up a conversation with the owner, who told us that the place actually began as a small café on Mount Batur but was destroyed by an eruption in the 1970s. He then reopened on a different mountain and did a great business with trekkers and sightseers.

After hearing about our trip, he pointed out his mother, who was poking around the restaurant. At age eighty-seven, she still worked full-time, managing the gift shop, overseeing the buffet, and generally keeping tabs on the staff. "You two remind me of her," he said. "She loves working, to see people and stay active."

His mother greeted us warmly. But unlike so many people who seem astonished by our travels and adventures, she didn't seem overly surprised. Her attitude was more like, "Of course, you're traveling in your eighties, just like I'm doing work I love. Age is no obstacle for women like us."

Age is no obstacle for women like us.

We proudly posed with her for a picture and took several of her alone, with her worn, smiling face. "I hope that's us in a few years," Sandy said. "God willing that we'll be going strong at eighty-seven."

"Sure we will," Ellie said. "In fact, I'm counting on it."

On the way down the mountain, we passed through a charming village with decorative stone walls and thatched-roofed houses. Along the road, we saw women in colorful sarongs walking with what looked like huge, tiered goblets balanced on their heads.

"What's going on?" we asked Ketut.

He explained that this was a day of celebration at their local temple. The "goblets" that the women carried were in fact baskets of offerings—tiers of whole fruits, flowers, fanciful elements, and even canned goods—which must have weighed ten to twenty pounds. Yet they carried them gracefully and seemingly effortlessly, never missing a step.

Each woman had designed her own offering, Ketut said, making her best effort to please the gods. "The whole village will go to the temple, including the men, all dressed up, carrying their knives."

"Their creations are so beautiful," we told him.

He agreed. "Days of worship are very special for us." He said that he'd never leave Bali for more than a few days for fear of missing out on these celebrations, which were constant. They were the guiding rituals of their lives. Again, we felt wistful, comparing his connection to the sacred to our more secular lives in the West.

KETUT STOPPED THE CAR AT ONE POINT SO WE COULD WALK THROUGH a rice paddy on a dirt path traversing the flooded fields of green shoots. He took us to a water temple, which was a small, ornate structure on a little island in the middle of a pond. Thousands traveled there to bathe in the spring-fed waters of the pond, which are considered sacred, and to take some holy water home.

We enjoyed visiting a plantation to taste different coffees. Among the specialties offered were beans that had been eaten by elephants, pooped out, and cleaned, yielding a highly prized brew. We both tried it and found it enjoyable, but in Ellie's words, "not good enough to justify its sky-high price."

At Ketut's urging, we also visited a preserve sheltering twenty-seven endangered Sumatran elephants. Though smaller than our familiar African variety—standing only six to ten feet high—they were no less formidable. A cranky one slapped Ellie with his ear and nearly knocked her down. Other wonderful stops Ketut suggested included a bird preserve, full of huge vividly colored parrots that were brave enough to perch on us; and a butterfly park, where some of the fluttering beauties had wingspans as broad as ten inches.

The Monkey Forest proved to be one of our favorite places. We'd originally thought of skipping it because we'd seen monkeys throughout our trip. But the forest is not just a preserve but a spiritual center, with three temples, dedicated to the Hindu principle of Tri Hita Karana, or promotion of harmony among humans, between humans and nature, and between humans and the divine. Because monkeys hold a special place in Hindu mythology, the center is also a free-range sanctuary for some 1,200 Balinese long-tailed macaques.

Since the moneys have lost their fear of people, we could see them up close, fighting, grooming one another, and caring for their young. We'd been told that they'd ignore us unless they thought we had food, in which case they might grab our bags or even try to pick our pockets. A staff member sat us down and placed a monkey in our laps. It was about the size and weight of a four-year-old child, and so darned cute—it ate food right out of Sandy's hand. "Of course, we got photos to impress my kids," Sandy says.

In the photo we like best, the monkey is leaning on Ellie and reaching to the camera (actually, food in the staffer's hand) as if it were snapping a selfie. That picture still makes us laugh.

There was so much to see and do—traditional Balinese theater with elaborate costumes and a show with a firewalker, unscathed by standing on hot coals; snorkeling in the coral reefs that ring Bali (Ellie) and drinking coconut milk in a beach chair (Sandy). "We loved every minute in Bali," Ellie says. "Even when it rained."

The place that had special resonance for Sandy was the Bali Orchid Garden, a serene, beautifully landscaped expanse with thousands of tropical plants. We've made it a point to visit botanical gardens on most of our trips. But something about the Bali Orchid Garden awakened childhood memories in Sandy.

"Living in working-class Fort Worth, we didn't see all that much greenery," she says. "The city was more about oil, longhorn cattle, and natural gas wells."

The main oasis was the Fort Worth Botanic Garden, the oldest in Texas, with woodlands, a tropical-plant conservatory featuring orchids, rose and begonia gardens, and plants native to Texas, among others, amid natural springs, rock formations, and elevated walkways and bridges.

"So, it became our tradition, whenever my extended family

gathered, to spend the day together at the Botanic Gardens," she says. "We'd wander its paths, admiring the flowers, and take lots of group photos against the backdrop of its beautiful scenery.

"In Bali, I flashed back to that Fort Worth garden. Maybe the reason was that, with our trip winding down—just two weeks to go—I was struck by how far I'd come. We'd traveled a great distance on our round-the-world journey. But I'd traveled even farther from my Fort Worth childhood—through marriage, motherhood, medical school, and devastating loss into a new light: the miracle of friendship, the joy of service, and now, the thrill of adventure. Being in the Bali Orchid Garden felt like a culmination, as if I'd reached a plateau of serenity and beauty where I could simply rest and enjoy.

"Wanting to share that peace, but without getting heavy, I sent pictures to my son, Larry, with a joking caption, 'Do you think my garden could ever look like this?'

"He shot back, 'Not a chance! Not in West Texas. How about if you get a place in Bali, and we all come visit?'"

If only we could have stayed! But Australia beckoned.

14

MAKE A DIFFERENCE

Australia and Tasmania

Australia was beckoning us, literally. We were about to catch an overnight flight from Bali to Sydney when we got a surprising call from an Australian TV network. The moment we landed, they wanted to whisk us to their studio to appear live on a top morning talk show.

We were stunned, to the point that we thought it was a mistake. It was surreal enough to us that local Texas media would feature our story. It was even more startling when that led to other—national and global!—news networks chronicling our travels, like CBS interviewing us in London. Back then, we were a novelty, a feel-good item to add to a broadcast, followed by a brief flurry of coverage in the daily papers. Since then, though we'd been dutifully forwarding our B-roll to CBS and to the other outlets that had requested it, surely interest in our around-the-world adventures had faded—or so we thought.

Yet, unbeknownst to us, public interest had not waned. No sooner had we hung up from one network inviting us to appear than another talk show called also wanting to book us—and then a third. All three were competing to have us on first. Talk about surreal!

"What's happening?" we asked each other. "And what should we do?"

We weren't sure that we wanted to invest the last precious days of our eighty-day journey doing media, as opposed to having adventures. But in talking it over, we decided that appearing live on TV—in front of an audience, not as part of a canned, edited feature—might be exciting, an unexpected adventure (the best kind). Invoking our motto, Just Say Yes, we accepted the first network's offer, though we would ultimately appear on all three talk shows on competing Australian stations.

We touched down in Sydney at 6:30 a.m. and were immediately shuttled, luggage and all, to the studio. There, a kindly staffer took us to a nearby café for a quick breakfast. We'd changed into our best Around the World T-shirts on the plane. When the café owner saw them, realizing who we were, he made a point of serving us himself and even brought us lattes with our faces etched in the foam! We were charmed, though Ellie whispered, "Is my nose really that long?"

Back at the studio, we asked to freshen up and were placed in the hands of a professional makeup artist. Rather than glamorize us— as we hoped!—she merely daubed us with face powder and pronounced us "Ready!" Then we were led onto the set and introduced to Tristan, our host.

We felt a strong rapport with Tristan from the moment he welcomed us onstage. We embraced the show like any other discovery, with curiosity and delight. The live audience was amazing. We loved them! After the show, the producers showered us with praise that left us blushing. "We could hardly believe it," Sandy says.

After promising to send the network updates on our time "down under," as Australia is termed, as well as any future adventures, we were ushered into a car and taken to our hotel. We hadn't even checked in, but after a few hours in Australia—being warmly welcomed by the network staff and the friendly audience—we already felt at home.

At that point, we were beat from having been up all night on a red-eye flight. The adrenaline high of doing the TV show also took a toll. Neither of us is a napper—one reason why we're so travel-compatible—because we love activities too much to waste the day sleeping. But when we saw those two comfortable beds, we decided to postpone touring Sydney until we'd closed our eyes for a quick power nap.

Fully committing to the novel decision to nap, Sandy put on her usual pajamas—her navy-blue scrubs—and Ellie changed into a nightgown. We both fell fast asleep the minute our heads hit our pillows. Then, suddenly, we were jolted by a blaring siren and an announcement, looping over and over, "Fire! Fire! Evacuate now!"

We sprang up, confused and groggy, but snapped awake at the sight and smell of smoke. Clearly, this was no false alarm. We've always had the habit of stowing essentials, like money and passports, in our backpacks, which we grabbed then raced, barefoot, to the stairs.

Outside, we sat on our backpacks on the hotel lawn, watching firemen in full regalia stream into the building. Because it was mid-day, most of the guests were out exploring, so we felt a bit sheepish sitting there with the sprinkling of stragglers, shoeless and in our nightclothes. That meant we were stuck. It would be hours before we got the "all clear" and could return to our room.

On the way, a sixtyish woman, a member of the cleaning staff, stopped us. "I was looking for you," she said. "I believe you dropped this on the stairs."

In her hand was a sheaf of bills, about three hundred Australian dollars. "Oh, my goodness," Ellie said, checking her backpack. The money pocket was half unzipped, and in the haste of our retreat, the cash had fallen out.

Amazed by her honesty, we thanked her profusely. "Please let me express my gratitude with a reward," Ellie said. But the woman adamantly refused to accept a cent, saying only, "I'm just relieved that I could find you and give it back."

What luck! Or more accurately, what a blessing it was to encounter such kindness. We're always deeply moved by such affirmations—and we've seen plenty—of the goodness of humanity.

> **We're always deeply moved by such affirmations—and we've seen plenty—of the goodness of humanity.**

Whatever had triggered the fire alarm had left our room still smoky. Besides, we were done with naps! We quickly pulled on our clothes, eager to head out and explore the city. We took the train down to its famous harbor, the site of the Sydney Opera House, a masterwork of twentieth-century architecture. The outside of the Opera House is fourteen curved concrete "shells" or "sails," divided into two groupings, said to be inspired by clouds or whales breaching. The shells are covered in more than a million V-shaped glossy white and matte cream tiles, designed to reflect light differently throughout the day. Interestingly, because the tiles are curved, they're scoured by the wind and rain, so they never need cleaning. What a spectacular sight!

Beyond the Opera House stands another Sydney landmark, the Harbour Bridge, topped by its distinctive arch. We loved poking around the harbor and enjoyed a terrific hamburger at a sidewalk café. Funny thing about Australian food—it's very much like our familiar West Texas cuisine. After so many exotic meals, it tasted great.

Finally, it was late enough for us to hit our cozy beds for a sorely needed good night's sleep. "Thank goodness," Ellie said. "That nap was a bust. Nothing but trouble and bad luck."

Sandy agreed, laughing. "No naps, ever again," we pledged.

OUR NEXT STOP WAS CAIRNS, THE FAMED PORTAL TO ONE OF THE Seven Natural Wonders of the World, the Great Barrier Reef. One of the few living structures visible from space, it's a vast ecosystem of 2,900 individual reefs and nine hundred islands spread over some

133,000 square miles. Culturally and spiritually important to Australia's Aboriginal peoples, the Great Barrier Reef supports an incredible diversity of life forms: whales and dolphins, sharks and stingrays, seventeen species of sea snakes, five thousand species of mollusks, and an incalculable number of fish, many brilliantly colored and patterned, as well as crocodiles, some 1.5 million birds, and more than two thousand plant species.

Cairns is a vibrant city, with a lively marina, lots of restaurants, a seaside esplanade with interesting sculptures and a "lagoon"—a huge saltwater swimming pool—and a "night market," with live entertainment and stalls selling everything from handicrafts to street food. We enjoyed exploring it, although the weather was very warm. When we started wilting in the heat, we spotted an aquarium. "Let's pop in there and cool off," Sandy said.

We wound up feeling glad we did because the aquarium specialized in sea life and animals native to Queensland, Australia, the Great Barrier Reef, and the Cairns Wet Tropics rainforest preserve, featuring more than sixteen thousand creatures, grouped by habitat, over nine ecosystems. We loved seeing fascinating species like emerald tree monitors—slim, green, three-foot lizards that looked like dinosaurs, with tails twice as long as their bodies. We saw a strange, T-shaped hammerhead shark, with an eye at each end of its flat, rectangular head, the better to scan the ocean for food and to detect the magnetic fields of nearby fish. Sadly, these marvels of creation are now endangered. Another curiosity was the ribboned pipefish, or ribboned sea dragon, which looks just like a branch when floating in the water.

These natural wonders piqued our eagerness to see the Great Barrier Reef.

ELLIE HAD SNORKELED IN THE GREAT BARRIER REEF DECADES BEFORE and was determined to reprise the indelible experience. This time, though, she anticipated the possibility of some pushback on account of her age—that our operators might consider her a legal liability. When we boarded the white tour boat, headed to the reef, we noted that we were by far the oldest passengers. "I'll have to convince them," Ellie told Sandy. "I can't miss the chance to snorkel the reef again."

About two hours from shore, the boat dropped anchor. The crew announced that, at that point, everyone could snorkel close to the boat. But a professional guide would lead a group—strictly limited to experienced snorkelers and strong swimmers—farther out to explore the reef itself. Ellie sprang to her feet and went straight to the pro guide to plead her case. "I'm a long-distance swimmer and former water-safety instructor, proficient in lifesaving and water rescue," she told him. "I've snorkeled all over the world, including here. I'm not only fully capable, but I'm also very eager to join your group. I'll sign any releases you need."

They stood toe-to-toe for a minute or two, locking eyes, until the guide gave Ellie the go-ahead to join. Ecstatic, she ditched her life vest and pulled on a full-body wet suit, complete with hood, mask, and fins. "Wet suits help you stay buoyant and glide through the water," Ellie says. "I didn't need one in Bali, for paddling around and casual snorkeling. But for serious snorkeling, a wet suit is a must. The Great Barrier Reef is really the ultimate for snorkelers."

"Of course, I was glad to relax on deck," Sandy says. "Given the choice, I don't go into water that's any deeper than a bathtub. I worried a little about Ellie, though she knows her ability and capacity. Still, it was comforting to see all those snorkels periodically poking up out of the waves."

After an hour, the snorkelers were summoned back by a horn blast. Ellie emerged from the sea in a state of bliss. "Eels and turtles swam right past me!" she told Sandy. "I saw a reef shark, which spooked me, because one almost charged me the last time. Luckily, this one ignored us. But what I saw beneath the surface was pure magic—beautiful, waving fans and ferns; fascinating coral formations in different shades; vividly colored fish—yellows and oranges, dotted and striped, with neon accents—some of them just gigantic. And the faces—some of the fish look placid, others puckered and whiskered. It's like a whole hidden parallel universe down there."

"Was it just as awesome as your first time?" Sandy asked.

"Absolutely!" Ellie said. "I'd go back again tomorrow if we had time. It's ever-changing and a mind-boggling adventure."

MEANWHILE, OUR PHONES STARTED BLOWING UP. THE SHOW WE did with Tristan had opened the floodgates, and suddenly, media requests—broadcast and print—were streaming in from Australia, the UK, the big US networks; in fact, from all over the world!

Although our trip remained the priority, we decided to say yes to these interviews, for a reason: wherever we went in Australia, people recognized us. When they did, without fail, they thanked us for inspiring them, as if our story was striking a chord.

We'd had our share of such encounters throughout the trip, but before Australia, they'd seemed like isolated—fleeting and flattering—incidents. Now, they were becoming much more of a steady drumbeat. Clearly, something had shifted. We had to ask ourselves why.

We'd seen ourselves mainly as a fluke—two older ladies circling the globe, capturing the media's fancy. But could our eighty-day trip, celebrating our milestone birthday and our decades-long friendship, have a larger purpose than we ever contemplated? Might it be that our example and our positive message were aspirational to a broad cross section of people, young and old? Did we have something to offer—a capacity to uplift others and to inspire them to look to new horizons?

> **Did we have something to offer—a capacity to uplift others and to inspire them to look to new horizons?**

We're both committed to public service—Sandy as a doctor and medical volunteer, Ellie as a medical mission director—but it now seemed that an unexpected chance to make a difference lay right under our noses. It seemed necessary—almost a responsibility—to embrace it. So, from then on, when media opportunities arose, we no longer viewed them as larks, but as a chance to perform what we'd come to see as a new kind of service. We accepted as many as we could, often squeezing in interviews late at night or very early in the morning, so they didn't disrupt our adventuring.

THE NEXT DAY, WE WERE HEADED TO AUSTRALIA'S TOP END, THE TIP of the continent closest to Asia. In Darwin, the territory's capital, we planned to indulge our love of trains by riding the legendary Ghan, which spans the country from its northern to southern shores. When we discovered that the full, 1,800-plus-mile journey would cost thousands of dollars, we decided to take the train to its midpoint, Alice Springs, in the heart of the Australian outback, at a fraction of the cost.

Darwin is mostly a modern city, rebuilt after devastating cyclones and Japanese bombing during World War II. Visiting its museum, we were surprised to learn that greater tonnage was dropped on Darwin than on Pearl Harbor. At the nearby Royal Flying Doctor Service Facility, we got our first glimpse of the outback and the pioneering medical teams who over the years have provided lifesaving care to its remote areas.

The Ghan train's logo is a camel, recalling the ones the British imported in the nineteenth century to work the arid regions of Australia. Today their descendants run wild, constituting the world's largest feral camel population, which at its peak may have numbered more than a million animals.

The Ghan was unlike any overnight train we've ever ridden. For

one thing, it has no second-class service, so even the cheaper accommodations we chose felt like a five-star hotel. Rather than share
a cabin—never mind a "dorm" car with blue curtains—we got private compartments across the aisle from each other. Instead of trolley carts in the aisles with pots of mystery food, there was a gracious
dining car with fine silverware and crisp white table linens. The
chef-prepared cuisine, using local ingredients, was delicious. At
night, we didn't have to chase down an attendant for sheets because
the helpful staff made up our beds. It was the height of luxury for us.

Outside Darwin, the landscape was lush and green, a tropical
rainforest that quickly gave way to rugged sandstone bluffs. We
passed vineyards and old gold-mining towns. Near Katherine, the
train paused for an excursion (included in the fare), a dramatic boat
trip through the red-sandstone Nitmiluk Gorge. The thirteen
gorges in Nitmiluk National Park are culturally significant to its
indigenous "traditional owners," the Jawoyn people, and are the site
of many aboriginal rock paintings, some a thousand years old.

Katherine is known as the town "where the tropics meet the
outback," and the scenery begins to shift to drier, scrubbier plains.
This region is the largest intact savanna (or grassy woodland) on
earth. We like to describe it as "the Sahara without the sand."
Though we didn't see many unusual animals, like kangaroos and
wallabies, along the route, we were happy to spot at least a few.

That night, before we settled into our posh, private compartments, Sandy said, "Isn't it strange being on a train full of tourists?"
Ellie agreed. "Yes, it's so staid, compared to the second-class cars!"

So, while we enjoyed the Ghan's comforts, we couldn't help missing the freewheeling spirit of second class, with children roaming

the halls and locals eager for conversation. Some of those trains were like parties on wheels—in fact, socializing seemed as central to the travel experience as covering miles. We even felt nostalgic for the hilarity of having strange men bunking overhead and dodging legs sticking out of berths on night trips to the bathroom. On the Ghan, the well-behaved fellow travelers kept to themselves. When our paths crossed, we of course exchanged niceties, but there were no lengthy, getting-to-know-you, bonding dialogues with other travelers. We made no new friends—unusual and disappointing for us—the entire ride.

After a day and a half, we pulled into Alice Springs. As teenagers, we'd both read *A Town Like Alice*, a novel about a young woman, a war refugee, who wants to make her bleak outback settlement thrive like Alice Springs, her husband's hometown. So, naturally, we couldn't wait to see it.

Alice Springs is located in the so-called Red Centre of Australia, a desert area named for its rust-colored soil. A town of some twenty-nine thousand people, it is about 20 percent Arrernte, the Aboriginal traditional owners who have inhabited the area for millennia. This cultural mix is reflected in its art galleries and craft centers, many of which showcase Indigenous people's work. Despite its small size, it's a major tourist hub and service area for the region, with some large hotels, a convention center, and plenty of interesting attractions.

We'd booked a room at a bed-and-breakfast, Kathy's Place, run by a friendly couple from New Zealand, who'd fallen in love with Alice Springs in the early 1970s. Kathy herself picked us up from the train station. We'd been warned that Alice Springs was "one of the most dangerous towns in the world," but Kathy quickly dispelled such fears. "You might get robbed if you're out late at night," she told us. "But otherwise, you don't have to worry." That was a relief because there was so much we hoped to see.

After breakfast, served by Kathy and her husband, Karl, we set out walking. That wasn't the best idea because the heat was oppressive. Fortunately, we soon came upon a cluster of interesting galleries and museums, all of which had the benefit of great air conditioning.

One of our favorites was the Women's Museum of Australia, located on the grounds of the historic town jail. One of its slogans really spoke to us: Ordinary Women, Extraordinary Lives. The exhibits featured women historical and current, Aboriginal and nonindigenous, who made a difference in every walk of life—medicine, law, journalism, education, the arts, and more. There was a fourteen-foot tapestry celebrating women pilots, a risky but critical job in the vastness of the outback, and a quilt signed by more than three hundred women who were the first in their fields.

A display that we especially loved was called "Adventurers—Women Refusing to Stay Home," which included female explorers, Indigenous women, and outback pioneers. All of them defied convention to lead lives of daring. The theme of adventure inspired us so much that we read every single story. Of course, we had to take our photo under the "Refusing to Stay Home" headline.

We also popped into the Alice Springs Reptile Centre, billed as home to "things that hiss and slither, which are rare, impossible, or undesirable to come across in the wild."

"'Undesirable' applies to just about all of them," Sandy says, laughing.

We caught the tail end of a show featuring live crocodiles, which were being walked offstage as the audience, including a group of schoolchildren, applauded. Then the female ranger/emcee asked for a volunteer. Ellie's hand immediately shot up.

By the time Ellie reached the stage, the ranger had wrapped herself in a huge python. As its head undulated, testing the environment, the children shrieked a little in nervous delight, clutching one another. Standing next to Ellie, the ranger indicated that she would ease the snake over so it could twine itself around Ellie's body.

"Ellie half-smiled and nodded," Sandy says. "I wanted to cover my eyes!"

The snake was an olive python, one of Australia's largest species, reaching about thirteen feet long and weighing up to forty-four pounds. It encircled Ellie's stomach, then with the ranger steering, climbed her chest and wrapped its upper body around her neck.

"That snake was heavy!" Ellie says. "It was hard to hold it up, but I didn't want to jerk and spook it."

The children were out of their seats, babbling excitedly, as their teacher shushed them. "The snake started squeezing my stomach, and I went *Ooohhh*," Ellie recalls. "Then the kids really freaked out. I didn't dare look at Sandy."

Fortunately, that's when the ranger coaxed the snake back onto her own body. Ellie stepped free, with a triumphant smile, as the audience went wild, clapping.

"Just another traveling-with-Ellie-Hamby adventure!" Sandy says.

~~~~~~~~

THE NEXT DAY, WE AWOKE BEFORE DAWN TO CATCH A BUS TO ULURU (once known as Ayers Rock), a huge sandstone monolith sacred to Aboriginal people throughout Australia and especially to its local traditional owners, the Anangu. Legend holds that it was formed in the Dreamtime, their cultural prehistory; geologists place its age at around five hundred million years. It has a perimeter of six miles, rises more than 1,100 feet above the ground, and extends a mile and half deep into the earth. Beyond its sheer mass, it's famed for changing color with the movement of the sun, from red to orange to purple and back again.

As we awaited the bus on the dark street corner, Ellie checked her phone and said, "Strange—I have three calls from the same New York number."

Trying it, she reached ABC *World News Tonight.* David Muir wanted to interview us for the *America Strong* series, to air that very evening. "Thank you, but we'll be out of commission for eighteen hours because we're heading deep into the outback," Ellie told him. They quickly suggested building our trip into the show by shooting a video of ourselves in front of Uluru while delivering a message to viewers. We agreed, shaking our heads in amazement that calls from major media outlets were becoming our "new normal."

Uluru was a magnificent sight. We found it mesmerizing, despite the savage hundred-degree heat and an assault by hundreds of flies. Ellie carefully staked out a position so she could best capture the sunset and, luckily, got some spectacular shots of the rock's fiery orange glow before the clouds swooped in and obscured it. Before then, we stood in front of this ancient natural wonder and recorded a video, which ABC spliced onto a montage of stills and B-roll of previous stops in our journey. The segment wrapped up with our call to action: "Get up off the couch, get out of your comfort zone—whatever your age—make some plans, and *LIVE!*"

AFTER ULURU, WE WERE OFF TO TASMANIA, WHERE WE HAD THE benefit of a close personal connection. Michael Dor, a Ukrainian dentist, had volunteered at the Zambia mission while living in South Africa and had since relocated to Hobart, Tasmania, with his family. When he picked us up the airport, the first thing he said was, "I had no idea that you two were such celebrities."

"What on earth do you mean?" we asked.

He explained that we were all over Australian TV, which aired in Tasmania. Being on the road, we ourselves had not seen the actual segments. "Believe me, we're shocked that people care about two old ladies traveling," Ellie told him. "But now that it's happening, we feel ordained to use this media not for our own glory but to motivate and inspire. It seems that our message of uplift, friendship, and living joyfully is touching hearts. We've come to feel that sharing it is almost our assigned calling."

Michael kindly took time away from his busy dental practice to show us the beauty of his remote island, Australia's least populous state. "What's that?" we asked, about a sign reading Tessellated Pavement. It proved to be a large, flat expanse of siltstone rock at the water's edge that had fractured in neat lines, so it looked like a patio of manmade tiles. The fracturing occurred because of the movement of the earth, a process called jointing. Crystallizing saltwater keeps etching the jointing pattern. The tessellated pavement at Eaglehawk Neck in Tasmania is the world's finest example of this rare natural phenomenon.

Though part of Australia, Tasmania has a different feeling—less tropical and desert-like than the areas we'd seen. It's an island 150 miles from the mainland, cut off from it an estimated twelve thousand years ago by rising seas. In climate and appearance, it resembles the Pacific Northwest, and is Australia's most densely forested area. Its terrain is rugged and mountainous, with unusual, often column-like rock formations created by molten magma two hundred million years ago. In the southwest, the mountains formed from harder quartzite, so they are more sharp-edged and jagged. Because of their quartzite peaks, some of them look snowcapped year-round.

Aboriginal people inhabited Tasmania for at least forty-five thousand years. At the time the British colonized the island in 1803, the indigenous population was thought to number some seven thousand. By 1830, British purges had reduced that number to mere hundreds, most of whom then succumbed to imported diseases.

From the beginning, British settlements in Tasmania centered on convicts. After the Revolutionary War, the British could no longer dump the overflow from their crowded prisons in America. So, Australia became the site of new penal colonies, which from 1788 to 1868 housed more than one hundred sixty-two thousand convicts. Australian prison rebels and repeat offenders were sentenced to the harsher penal facilities in Tasmania, which also got their own shipments of convicts from Britain. Some seventy-five thousand "transported" convicts would serve time in Tasmania, among them about twelve thousand women.

Port Arthur, active from 1833 to 1877, was a high-security prison. Set on the Tasman Peninsula and surrounded by (supposedly) shark-infested waters, it was said to be impossible to escape. Though housing the most incorrigible convicts, it was considered an "enlightened" prison, replacing corporal punishments like whippings with psychological ones like solitary confinement or sensory deprivation by being hooded. Of course, these treatments could be just as brutal.

A separate division of the colony was reserved for children—the second juvenile prison in the British Empire. Like the adults, the young people served their sentences by doing hard labor but with the "enlightened" additions of basic education and skills training.

We took a boat to visit the Port Arthur complex. In the late nineteenth century, it was left to decay, in an effort to bury the prison's grim past. Fires and an earthquake claimed some of the buildings, but what remains are the ruins of the penitentiary—supposedly haunted—and the restored guard tower and church, among others. Today, to attract visitors, they're encompassed by a lush, green park, with beautiful gardens. "I couldn't get over the contrast," Ellie says, "between the gorgeous landscaping and the abject misery the place commemorated."

"It was heartbreaking to read all the tragic stories," Sandy says. "Especially the children's. Can you imagine the terror of an eight- or nine-year-old, thousands of miles from anything familiar? It's sickening to realize that most of the kids' crimes were minor, like stealing. Their suffering was so profoundly disproportionate."

We toured the Isle of the Dead, where people who died at Port Arthur were buried. Fewer than 10 percent of the graves are marked, leaving more than a thousand lives unrecognized. Many of the convicts who survived until release built new lives in Tasmania. Today, 20 percent of Australians are descendants of convicts, but in Tasmania the figure is much greater—some say as high as 75 percent—giving its people a uniquely resilient identity.

AFTER THE SADNESS OF PORT ARTHUR, IT WAS A DELIGHT TO VISIT Mount Field National Park, Tasmania's oldest nature preserve. It boasts a range of fascinating landscapes, from a eucalyptus rainforest at lower altitudes to alpine vegetation closer to the summit of its five-thousand-foot mountain. Shaped by glaciers, it's laced with crystalline tarns, or small lakes, and glorious waterfalls.

We were awed by the magnificence of the giant ferns and massive eucalyptus trees—some three hundred feet tall—that we saw in the hushed, green forest en route to Russell Falls, a three-tier cascade that is a Tasmanian landmark. A sudden downpour—this was a rainforest, after all—didn't dampen our spirits one bit. Pushing up our umbrellas, we burst into a chorus of "Singin' in the Rain." We had Gene Kelly's exuberance, if not his footwork.

We'd hoped to see lots of exotic fauna on our walk, like wombats and platypuses and, especially, dog-sized, bushy-tailed Tasmanian devils. They're marsupials, gestating their young in a pouch, and, though they look cuddly, they have a bite that can reportedly cut through metal traps. No such luck, though—the devils are nocturnal and timid around humans. We had to be content with the sight of scampering wallabies, which look like mini-kangaroos.

MICHAEL INVITED US TO DINNER TO MEET HIS WIFE, LILA, AND HIS mother, Liydmyla, who had recently fled the war in Ukraine. Her home had been destroyed in the bombing and, speaking no English, she had been isolated and sad in her new environs. We met at their favorite restaurant, the Ball & Chain, where we feasted on great Tasmanian steaks.

Sandy made a point of sitting next to Liydmyla. "My specialty is geriatrics," she says. "I just love older people, and my heart went out to this woman—close to our age—whose whole world had just collapsed."

Sandy took out her phone and set its translation program to "English and Russian," which was close enough to Ukrainian that Liydmyla could understand. "I started typing in questions about her life and children, then passed the phone over to Liydmyla to respond. As we went back and forth, I expressed my sorrow about her homeland."

"She just lit up at being able to communicate," Ellie says. "It was so wonderful to see her come alive."

Michael mentioned that the one thing his mother really wanted was a large-print Bible. "After my mission work in Russia and Romania, I had contacts who could supply that," Sandy says.

She sent out some emails, and by the end of the evening, thanks to a friend, a large-print Russian Bible was on its way to Tasmania. "It was such a small effort on my part for such a big payoff in comfort," Sandy says. "So often, it doesn't take much to make a huge difference to someone else."

> So often, it doesn't take much to make a huge difference to someone else.

The Grand Canyon

Day 80 of our journey was approaching. It was hard to imagine resuming everyday life, though we missed our families and the work we love. "We'd been like kids in a candy shop," Ellie says, "waking up each day wondering what adventures it would hold. It's like we'd grown a little addicted to anticipation."

Sandy agrees. "Yes, and not just to anticipation but to the constant stimulation: coping with unfamiliar challenges, meeting new and interesting people, and especially, living in a state of surprise and awe. Experiences like these make your brain churn out new chemicals. They're the very best kind of workout for your mental muscles."

We did have one more adventure ahead of us: visiting America's great Wonder of the Natural World, the Grand Canyon. The mile-deep canyon, carved by the Colorado River in Arizona, exposes layers of rock from more than a billion years of our continent's history. At 277 miles long and ten to eighteen miles wide, it's not the world's biggest or deepest canyon, but it's one of the most beautiful, with its vividly colored walls, and most varied in its landscapes, encompassing several ecosystems.

We'd both visited the Grand Canyon before. But from the moment we spun the globe, planning our trip, we knew we had to include it—to give it the honor it deserves among the world's great marvels.

Our flight from Australia would land in Los Angeles on March 30. From there, we'd fly to Phoenix, Arizona, where LaDonna Armstrong, our dear friend from the Zambia Medical Mission, lives with her husband Bill. LaDonna would join us for our round-the-world trip's Grand Canyon finale.

A LITTLE PUNCHY FROM THE LONG FLIGHT, WE GOT OFF THE PLANE IN LA and made our way through customs into the Arrivals Hall. Back in the USA! The terminal was a bright, cheery expanse of stores and cafés, with people darting everywhere. Suddenly, a young woman detached from the fray and ran up to us. "You're the TikTok Traveling Grannies!" she said. "I follow you! I can't believe it."

We were wearing our T-shirts, as usual. While we were often recognized by then, we'd never heard that term. Throughout our trip, we'd entertained our families, friends, and whoever else with postings on Instagram and Facebook. A week or two before the end, urged by younger people in our lives, we'd looped in TikTok, with little knowledge of how it worked or its amazing reach.

All we could do was smile at our excited friend, who hugged us and asked to snap a selfie. "You inspire us so much!" she said. "Me and my friends. We all want to see the world the way you do."

No sooner had we said goodbye than another woman stopped in her tracks, asking, "TikTok grannies?" then told us how much our travels thrilled her. And then still another person popped up, exclaiming, "The TikTok Traveling Grannies! You're best friends, right? Do you even know how incredible you seem?"

By the time we reached the gate for our Phoenix flight, having taken selfie after selfie with strangers, we had to acknowledge that we'd been officially christened the TikTok Traveling Grannies. "Our whole world has changed," Sandy said.

In the beginning, we'd been approached one-on-one by people curious about our T-shirts. Local then national press had brought us bursts of recognition. Meanwhile, momentum had been building to a crescendo in Australia, when it seemed that we'd suddenly become international media darlings. Traditional media, that is— newspapers and TV. The LA airport was where we first grasped the immense power and influence of social media, beaming into every cell phone in every purse and pocket in the country—and even the world. And now, here we were, illuminated in its penetrating spotlight. The realization was deeply humbling.

WE SPENT A LOVELY EVENING WITH LaDONNA AND HER HUSBAND, then drove with her to the Grand Canyon. From a scenic overlook, we peered down into the vast chasm of exquisitely sculpted cliffs. "It's so fitting that our trip began and ended not with manmade glories," Ellie said, "but with natural ones—the magnificence of Antarctica and now, the Grand Canyon. These places just bowl you over with the artistry and genius of Creation."

We'd come to refer to these feelings of wonder and amazement as "awes." We'd experienced so many of them throughout our journey. Underlying the awes was gratitude for beauty so far beyond our expectations that just witnessing it felt almost like a form of worship.

We had to shake off the canyon's spell to do a video interview with *USA Today*, which we'd promised after landing in LA. It wasn't easy to find a spot deserted and quiet enough for the video, but we managed—only to be photobombed by a large, curious elk. We must have encroached on his territory, but he left us alone. Since we've never seen the broadcast, we don't know if his cameo made it on air.

Since we were doing the interview, we wore our Around-the-World T-shirts. That got the attention of many of our fellow tourists, all of whom wanted photos with the TikTok Traveling Grannies. Most of them, being TikTok followers, were our grandchildren's age. We spent a long time talking to a few, including a young man from the UK who stunned us by asking, "Where can I buy that T-shirt?"

"Really?" Ellie said. "You'd wear a T-shirt with a picture of a globe and two old ladies?"

"I'd wear it in a heartbeat," he assured us.

We've never been cool before. Was it possible that we were now?

In our conversations, it emerged that, while our travels excited people, the young ones were most enthralled by our friendship.

Two women with a decades-long bond, close enough to travel together—sharing hotel rooms and experiences, effortlessly and happily, even over a period as long as eighty days—seemed to many to be enviably connected. Young people, especially, seem haunted by loneliness, perhaps worsened by the pandemic. We were struck by the yearning in their voices as they asked about how we get along, how we decide where to travel, and above all, how we became so attuned to each other.

It's true that deep friendships like ours don't come along every day. But the truth is—happily—bonding with others isn't that hard. All over the world, we managed to "click" with people we'd just met, even without a shared language to let us communicate in words.

Virtually all of us not only have the innate capacity but the drive to connect with one another. What it takes is the willingness to shift focus from yourself—your self-consciousness and self-preoccupation—to the common ground that you might share with someone else. For our fleeting connections on the road, that common ground was shared circumstances, like traveling together or describing our lives, based on genuine mutual interest.

> **Virtually all of us not only have the innate capacity but the drive to connect with one another. What it takes is the willingness**

> to shift focus from yourself—
> your self-consciousness and self-
> preoccupation—to the common
> ground that you might share
> with someone else.

In our more profound, sustaining friendship, the common ground was the sense of purpose we recognized in each other through sharing mission work in Zambia. From there, our mutual admiration grew, as we saw each other in action, coping with challenges and pursuing joys. Generous acceptance—which includes laughing at our differences—is the bedrock of our bond.

> Generous acceptance—which
> includes laughing at our
> differences—is the bedrock
> of our bond.

All friendships have to start someplace. The first step in forging one is simply to open your heart and reach out to someone else. Put down your phone, we urge people, and try communicating one-on-

one, in real life. Conversations—as opposed to short blasts of information—nearly always offer unexpected bridges to connection.

Conversations—as opposed to short blasts of information—nearly always offer unexpected bridges to connection.

ON APRIL 1, EXACTLY EIGHTY DAYS AFTER WE HEADED TO ANTARCtica, our first destination, we touched down in Dallas, our home turf. Our families were there, buoyant, welcoming us with bouquets of flowers and, probably, at least a few sighs of relief. Fortunately, though, after all our years of traveling together, our kids know that we'll never fit the confines of the stereotypical stay-at-home grandmother.

And why should we? We have work we long to do, amazing places left to see, "awes" left to experience, joys left to discover. That's why our current motto is Eighty-Two and We're Not Through.

We're going strong—and we can't wait to see where life takes us next!

EPILOGUE

By the Grace of God

People often ask how much our eighty-day around-the-world trip cost. The answer, since we're strict budget travelers, is less than a cheap compact car. But even that sum troubled Sandy when we first began to plan. "I can more than justify spending money to do mission work," she says. "But spending it on pure fun just seemed so self-indulgent."

Sandy prayed for guidance about being so seemingly frivolous, asking that God close doors if our travels were against His will. Not only did doors stay open for us, but our trip also seemed blessed— no real mishaps, no injuries, not even any lost luggage. The same guardian angels who'd overseen us in the past were with us, enabling us to experience the magnificence of divine creation and human invention.

So, we give thanks for those supernatural guardians as well as the many human angels, known and unknown, who eased our passage. We've named many of them in this book—like Ziggy, our kindly rescuer in Shinjuku station—but our hearts also go out to the strangers: the cabbies who've proudly shown us their cities; the Argentine dancers who taught us to tango; the café workers who graced us with a good night's rest in the Helsinki airport; the wonderful Arab guide who embraced Sandy in Egypt; the Nepali mother and five daughters who made Sandy an honorary sixth sister; the inspiring eighty-seven-year-old working mother in the mountain café in Bali; the housekeeper in Australia who returned Ellie's lost money; and all the others whose vibrant humanity brightened our days.

As we always say, our joy lies less in the journey than in the people we encounter along the way. Over the years, we've been blessed by the warm acceptance of so many. What makes these flashes of friendship so fulfilling is that they're unexpected, like stumbled-upon treasure. Striking them up requires no special skills, experience, or familiarity with other cultures. All it takes is an open spirit and a humble willingness to engage with others. The reward is profound: an appreciation of the heart-and-soul connection of all human beings.

We also owe a debt of gratitude to the countless strangers who've approached us, claiming that both our adventures as octogenarians and, even more, our friendship have inspired them. In fact, it's the other way around—they've inspired us to share our experience by cheering us on with a passion greater than we ever could have imagined. We hope our story shows that the thrill of joy awaits if we summon the courage—and energy!—to fully inhabit all the seasons of our lives.

Joy awaits if we summon the courage—and energy!—to fully inhabit all the seasons of our lives.

ACKNOWLEDGMENTS

We always say: "We don't travel, we adventure." What we mean is regardless of how far we venture, we try to keep our minds and hearts open to enjoy the wonderful world all around us. Wherever we are.

Writing this book has been an adventure and we owe a great many people many thanks.

First, we thank Jules Verne, whose novel *Around the World in Eighty Days* inspired us to embark on our own fantastic world adventure, circumnavigating the globe in eighty days, at age eighty-one.

Ellie:

I want to express my deepest gratitude and love to my daughter, Sheryl, who encouraged me throughout the development of this book and who read every draft, providing valuable feedback. And to my son Moon, and his wife, Sharon, for cheering me on throughout. I must also acknowledge my son Kel, who passed away before he could contribute to the book. But Kel would have been beside me through it all; he loved books! To my brother, Cliff, thanks for being the best brother and for confirming that my recollections of our childhood were "spot-on." And a big thank-you to my grandchildren, Ruth, Luke (my fellow writer), Caleb, Callie, Danica, Cameron, Symone, Rob, Klenisa, and Montel, who listened to Nana's stories and whose positivity encouraged me throughout this long journey. Finally, to my great-grandchildren, Arie, Charlotte, CJ, Caydence, London, Serenity, and Racey, thank you for bringing such joy into my life.

I am boundlessly grateful to my entire Zambia Medical Mission team, including Linda, Courtney, Charles, James, Ray, Richard, and Klay, for your unwavering support. Your willingness to step in and assist when my book obligations conflicted with my Zambian work was a testament to our dedication and teamwork. Thank you!

A big thanks to my dear friends Drs. Odies and Kathi Wright. Thank you for your unwavering belief in me, for your support while I was working on this book, and for your example of living a life of service to others. You are a true testament to Christian living. Kathi, your understanding of us and your editorial insights made a tremendous impact on the book.

Many special friends waded into the weeds with me on this book, listening to passages and engaging in thoughtful discussions. Sheri Sears, a lifetime missionary in Zambia, was an insightful draft reader and offered invaluable feedback. And thank you to Jay and Shelli Starkey, who listened to me read the entire draft while we traveled over those bumpy bush roads deep in the heart of Africa.

Last but not least, a very special thanks to my best friend, Sandy.

Ever since our paths crossed, my life is fuller and more meaningful, and I am having a blast!

Sandy:

I want to express my heartfelt appreciation to my three children, Barbara, Larry, and Dawn, who have followed their father's example in being my biggest and most enthusiastic cheerleaders in all my endeavors. They, of course, were the first ones I told about the plans for this book, and from the very first moment, they have given continuous positive affirmations that the world needs to hear this story of joy and adventure and friendship. My seven grandchildren, Matthew, Paul, James, Lucy, Lily, Sam, and Jack, are all terribly biased regarding their Nana; they have ALWAYS thought the whole world knows and loves me, and that the world has been waiting too long for a book in order to know and love me more. Even my three granddaughters by marriage, Bradi, Jessi, and Carli, are excited and supportive about the book. Then, of course, since I am eighty-three, I also have great-grandchildren cheering me on, Katelynn, Abbey, Sawyer, Violet, Gracie, and Jensen, who bring great joy into MY life. I would be remiss if I failed to acknowledge my children's spouses and my grandchildren's spouses (and near spouses): Mark, Michele, Rob, Sabrina, Kat, Morgan, Cameron, Nate, and Jessica, who are all very supportive of this book. Finally, my younger siblings, twins Ron and Connie, who say that I have been a storyteller from their earliest childhood memories, so this book comes as no surprise to them. I wish also to acknowledge their spouses, Linda and Ron (yes, Connie's twin and her husband are both named Ron), who have been such encouragers to me. Thank you all.

ACKNOWLEDGMENTS

I am very grateful to all of my coworkers at Hospice of the Big Country, who are amazing supporters to me. I want to thank Dana and Burrell McKelvain and all of my many other friends and my patients who have also been supportive of me for so many years. Thank you all. Without your love and support, this book of joy and adventure and friendship would not be a reality in my life.

Last but not least, to my best friend Ellie, without your fearless spirit and boundless appetite for adventure—not to mention your amazing ability to plan and organize—our wonderful experience traversing the globe would not have been what it was. Most importantly, without your friendship, my life would not be what it is.

Sandy and Ellie:

To our church families, Daughtery Street Church of Christ and Hillcrest Church of Christ, we thank you for being there and for encouraging us in our walk of faith.

We are grateful to the Zambia Medical Mission team. Over the last thirty years, thank you for being a part of our story and encouraging us to serve others. We also want to acknowledge the part each of you played in the Zambian stories in this book.

We thank Helen Donalson for that fateful invitation she extended to us to speak at Wesley Court about our imminent around-the-world adventure and for inviting Noah McKinney with KTAB News. Noah, you were the first member of the media to learn about our story, and we appreciate your belief that it was something the world should hear.

Our social media presence would not be what it is today without Brandi Huddleston, who helped elevate our social media to a higher level.

ACKNOWLEDGMENTS

It is difficult to express how indebted we are to our agent, Laurie Bernstein. She believed in us and our uplifting message. She understood us so well that when she shared her vision for the book it made everything "click" for us while we were still searching to put it into words. Her determination and encouragement helped us through difficult times and her countless hours and unwavering support helped make this book a reality.

We feel lucky to have our wonderful editor, Laura Tisdel, who "got us" from the start. Her vision, brilliance, and collaborative spirit lovingly shepherded the project; we are forever grateful. Thanks also to the brilliance of the entire team at Viking, including publisher Brian Tart, publicity director Rebecca Marsh, publicists Carolyn Coleburn and Yuleza Negron, editorial assistant extraordinaire Carlos Zayas-Pons, marketers Mary Stone and Chantal Canales, production editor Brianna Lopez, and managing editor Tricia Conley. Bountiful thanks also to Elisa Petrini, our writer, who helped us take decades of stories and adventures and distill it all onto the page with her magic touch.

Finally, for those who crossed our paths on our adventures and became good friends, thank you for your kindness and for changing the trajectory of our journey: Noah, Aki, Ramy, Martin, Robby, Patrick, Leonard, Nick, KD, Twinkle, Pinku and family, Mani, Ziggy, Ketut, Michael and family, Israel, and Mohammed. This book would not have been possible without you.

Historical Note

The United Nations Educational, Scientific and Cultural Organization (UNESCO) World Heritage sites are protected cultural monuments, natural wonders, and intangible practices located around the world. The purpose of this designation is twofold: preservation and celebration. The UN works with nations around the world to preserve these globally recognized locations and customs for future generations to enjoy and to celebrate humanity's heritage across cultures, languages, and nations.

And, while not an official site due to its transient and occasional nature, the authors want to note the aurora borealis—or the northern lights—as another natural wonder.

Below is a list of all the UNESCO sites Ellie and Sandy visit in this book:

- Natural World Heritage Sites
    - Grand Canyon National Park—Arizona, USA
    - Great Barrier Reef—Australia
    - Lake Baikal—Russian Federation

- Sagarmatha National Park (Mount Everest)—Nepal

- Tasmanian Wilderness (Mount Field National Park)—
  Tasmania, Australia*

- Victoria Falls—Zambia and Zimbabwe

- Wet Tropics of Queensland—Australia

- Cultural World Heritage Sites

  - Abu Simbel Complex—Egypt

  - Angkor Wat—Cambodia

  - Australian Convict Sites (Port Arthur Historic Site)—
    Tasmania, Australia

  - Colosseum—Rome, Italy

  - Easter Island Moai—Easter Island, Chile

  - Historic Quarter of the Seaport City of Valparaíso—
    Chile

  - Kathmandu Valley—Nepal

  - Melaka and Georgetown, Historic Cities of the Straits
    of Melaka—Malaysia

  - Mount Fuji—Japan

  - Qutb (or Qutab) Minar and its Monuments—Delhi,
    India

  - Palmyra—Syrian Arab Republic†

  - Petra—Jordan

---

* Also considered a Cultural World Heritage Site.
† Inscribed on the list of World Heritage Sites in Danger

- Pyramids of Giza—Egypt

- Singapore Botanic Gardens—Singapore

- Stone Town of Zanzibar—Tanzania

- Sydney Opera House—Australia

- Taj Mahal—India

- Intangible Heritage

- Tango—Argentina

100 YEARS of PUBLISHING

———— ◇ ————

Harold K. Guinzburg and George S. Oppenheimer founded Viking in 1925 with the intention of publishing books "with some claim to permanent importance rather than ephemeral popular interest." After merging with B. W. Huebsch, a small publisher with a distinguished catalog, Viking enjoyed almost fifty years of literary and commercial success before merging with Penguin Books in 1975.

Now an imprint of Penguin Random House, Viking specializes in bringing extraordinary works of fiction and nonfiction to a vast readership. In 2025, we celebrate one hundred years of excellence in publishing. Our centennial colophon features the original logo for Viking, created by the renowned American illustrator Rockwell Kent: a Viking ship that evokes enterprise, adventure, and exploration, ideas that inspired the imprint's name at its founding and continue to inspire us.

———— ◇ ————

For more information on Viking's history, authors, and books, please visit penguin.com/viking.